AMERICAN WAR POETRY

AMERICAN WAR POETRY

An Anthology

EDITED BY

Lorrie Goldensohn

COLUMBIA UNIVERSITY PRESS   NEW YORK

Columbia University Press
Publishers Since 1893
New York   Chichester, West Sussex

Copyright © 2006 Columbia University Press

Permissions for the poems used in this anthology are found on pages 405–13.

Library of Congress Cataloging-in-Publication Data
American War poetry : an anthology / edited by Lorrie Goldensohn
p. cm.
Includes bibliographical references.
ISBN 0–231–13310–3 (cloth : alk. paper)
1. War poetry, American. 2. United States—History, Military—Poetry.
I. Goldensohn, Lorrie.

PS595.W36A46 2006
811.008′0358—dc22
2005054762

Columbia University Press books are printed on permanent and durable acid-free paper.
Printed in the United States of America

c 10 9 8 7 6 5 4 3 2 1

CONTENTS

EL SALVADOR, BOSNIA, KOSOVO, AFGHANISTAN, AND THE PERSIAN GULF 335

PREFACE

This anthology shapes a compact portrait of Americans at war, from the early days of their history up to the present time. Many other anthologies of war poetry focus on European poets or solely on English and American war poetry, or on the poems of a particular American war. This book stretches from 1746 to 2004, beginning with a poem about a skirmish with Indians in a colonial meadow and ending with poems about the desert wars in Iraq. Within each war, I have arranged the poems in chronological order by the poet's birth date, thus throwing into relief the long arc of a war's impact. Besides offering insight into what might be an American way of going to war, the poetry also gives a sense of how nearly four centuries of warfare continue to affect the human beings of a multiethnic society—the soldier and civilian, the old and young, male and female—as they find themselves in the age-old grip of collective violence.

It could not be easy to identify the best work on such an enormous topic. Many fine poems were also out of reach for this anthology, being too long or too expensive to reprint. I tried to limit the selection to those poems showing literary merit as well as a social, historical, or military relevance. And yet these qualities do not always readily combine: one poem or another would offer a kind of compelling interest that would tip the balance toward inclusion, as the urgency, originality, or historic texture of its observation sometimes outran the poem's performance as a literary object. In order to give the subject of war its natural amplitude, I found myself committed to an ever-widening definition of style. This meant giving the nod to less as well as more familiar writers: those writers drawn to write well about war were not always those who dominate the literature elsewhere. Occasionally, I have selected poems whose familiarity, rather than excellence, would appear to have earned their place in an anthology like this one; yet it seems to me that an affection for something we mem-orized early in life is something we should not give up easily. It may be that reading—instead of singing—the familiar stanzas of Francis Scott Key's "Defence of Fort McHenry," better known as "The Star Spangled Banner," or even taking on "The Battle Hymn of the Republic" in the context of other poems of its era will restore fresh and unexpected meanings.

Still, I took fewer poems from periods in which a strong canon of more than antiquarian interest was not yet formed. There were more poems of higher quality covering the larger engagements like the Civil War, World War II, and Vietnam. While World War I sent an army of two million American soldiers abroad, the greater volume of significant poems about that war can be found in the work of English poets like Wilfred Owen and Siegfried Sassoon: the preeminence of their poetry marks a literary period just converging with the general onset and rise of American modernism. A chronologically loose but large group of poems by and about Indians deals with the long, persistent war to subjugate the native peoples of a continent. This work runs like a subcutaneous layer through the whole of the national narrative, so it seemed right that a hefty section of poems should be allotted to these struggles. Poems by or about Indians in the colonial wars or wars of the twentieth century are under those headings.

The Civil War, our first industrial war, brought on proportionately and absolutely the heaviest casualties in one war, and this war remains to the present a cause for national mourning and avid analysis. World War II meant a lengthy and truly global mobilization against fascism, and nick-named "The Good War," it became the war about whose necessity most Americans agree. In contrast, the Vietnam War offered defeat, stalemate, and divided allegiance on the home front; even today, the issues of this war are returned to and refought with each successive show of American military force. These three wars have taken a prolonged measure of our national consciousness, stimulating a poetry that increasingly occurs in a breadth of styles and that voices sharply different perspectives. Yet every war, big or little, long or short, is charged with its own peculiar mix of social and geopolitical realities, visible in some way in the poetry of that time, or in retrospect. The present outpouring of work in response to the Persian Gulf wars is yet so diffuse and so immediately upon us as to defy adequate evaluation. And yet the attentive anthologist, like someone removing a finger from a hole in the dike, must make some attempt to catch or contain the spill.

Each war has brought poems that show how Americans have thought about soldiers, and the relation of soldiers to a democratic republic whose founders frequently expressed an aversion to standing armies and the militarist ambitions of rulers. Yet poetry from Joel Barlow on reveals the pressure to dominate the continent and to thwart the imperial expansion of foreign powers, or to contest the holdings of the indigenous native. From the first guerilla engagements using badly fed, thinly clad, and ill-armed farmers, to the latest glittering deployments of men and machines, American warfare has both changed and stayed the same. A spread of poems over more than three centuries cannot help but show this, as well as show how the resistance to war, placed against an equally loyal support for it, has come to frame a permanent tension in the war poem. In addition, as the thirteen colonies moved from the defensive posture of an agricultural society to become an aggressive and industrial America, and as the capabilities of modern warfare continue to extend the killing range and arena of devastation over time, distance, and population, our thinking about war as a legitimate means to political ends has necessarily altered. Any poetry of worth will reflect how these changes have stunned and galvanized the people who have endured our wars.

The American war poem, beginning with a national identity yet to be defined, and rooted in the starvation, hardship, and dogged will of revolutionary independence, often evinces an unabashed and optimistic patriotism and a deep love of country. Yet even in the early poems holding to such feelings, the moral conflicts that trouble the unequivocal acceptance of war are evident. Passages here and there point to the hot debates that have always smoldered beneath the fabric of a war, about who in a democracy should fight, and when and why, and at what cost. The first poems in this anthology sketch the coming of those questions and the testing of our national goals—goals that were set even before the Civil War and that climax in the elegiac reflections of Walt Whitman, who even while grieving remained a scribe of the spectacular and sensual aspects of war.

The record of battlefield advance and retreat, the daring and courage of leaders and men, as well as the despoliation of territory, the experience of prison camp and the making of refugees, the annihilation and wounding of human flesh, the grieving aftermath—all have wrung from the poets of war a wide response, a response that has also varied with the circumstances of a given war. While a longing for and celebration of heroic courage and a willingness to give "the last full measure" have remained constant, these older attitudes are increasingly accompanied by a sense of helpless, saddened vulnerability and by a more detailed recognition of war's underside of pitiless death and destruction. More than half of the poems chosen here result from direct witness of war. Many other poems bring in the memory of war's lingering aftermath, adding the thinking of those who are still assaulted in their own lives by the spreading injury that particular conflicts have imposed. While it is mostly young men who go to war, we see that war's effects are felt by everyone.

ACKNOWLEDGMENTS

Several anonymous readers at Columbia University Press helped this project greatly; even the crankiest among them gave excellent suggestions, which I did my best to follow. In stages early and late, Raymond Oliver, Anne Barrows, Paul Nelson, Howard Norman, and Frank Bergon were wonderfully generous and knowledgeable readers and editors to whom I owe substantial debts. Above all, however, I owe thanks to W. D. Ehrhart, without whose close, shrewd reading and multiple doses of sage, timely, and candid advice, the book could not have been completed. Whatever errors or undone tasks remain are my responsibility and not the doing of those who helped me.

Again, as with my previous book, Jennifer Crewe as overall editor and shepherd, Rob Fellman as copy editor, and Michael Haskell as the meticulous and informed production editor provided invaluable assistance and support from Columbia. I was lucky to have all three. I also must thank Tessa Kale for early exchanges of thoughts on the direction for this anthology, and Fred Courtwright for the labor of securing permissions. I thank Barry Goldensohn for supplying footnotes. In the initial stages of this project, Terry Diggory, Joseph T. Cox, and Jay Rogoff pointed out many war poems of the twentieth century unknown to me, and Kelly Sullivan and Justin Rogers-Cooper helped with the endless photocopying. Many libraries were important, including Skidmore College, the Library of Congress, the New York Public Library, the Harry Ransom Research Center at the University of Texas, as well as the libraries at the University of Vermont, George Washington University, and the Doe and Bancroft Libraries at the University of California in Berkeley. Thanks also to Rino Pizzi for aid in Texas, and to Robert Hass in Berkeley, who provided library introductions and whose well-stocked personal bookshelves I gladly picked clean. I am also especially grateful to four previous editors of war poetry. W. D. Ehrhart's *Carrying the Darkness* first set the standard for Vietnam War poetry, followed by his subsequent and unmatched collection of Korean War poetry in *Retrieving Bones,* a volume of Korean War literature that he coedited with Philip K. Jason. Cary Nelson's collection of Spanish Civil War poetry in *The Wound and the Dream* was unique and indispensable, as was Harvey Shapiro's *Poets of World War II* and Richard Marius's *The Columbia Book of Civil War Poetry.* Additionally, volumes 1 and 2 of *The New Anthology of American Poetry,* edited by Steven Gould Axelrod, Camille Roman, and Thomas Travisano were invaluable.

From start to finish, my patient husband, Barry Goldensohn, provided the friendly challenge and the loving support that were indispensable.

AMERICAN WAR POETRY

THE COLONIAL WARS

1746–1763

The General [Edward Braddock] received the wound of which he died; but previous to it, had several horses killed and disabled under him. Captains Orme and Morris his two Aids de Camp having received wounds which rendered them unable to attend, G. W. [Washington] remained the sole aid throughout the day, to the General; he also had one horse killed, and two wounded under him—A ball through his hat—and several through his clothes, but escaped unhurt. . . .

The shocking Scenes which presented themselves in this Nights March are not to be described—The dead—the dying—the groans—lamentations—and crys along the Road of the wounded for help (for those under the latter descriptions endeavoured from the first commencement of the action—or rather confusion—to escape to the second division) were enough to pierce a heart of adamant, the gloom and horror of which was not a little increased by the impervious darkness which in places rendered it impossible for the two guides which attended to know whether they were in, or out of the track but by groping on the ground with their hands.

—George Washington, on General Edward Braddock's defeat by combined French and Indian forces in 1755, from *Washington on Washington*, edited by Paul M. Zall

That they could fight as well as European regulars, or that they could be gathered up into an army at all—these were the issues facing the colonial militias of each Crown colony. Yet in these early battles, American soldiers were mustered and learned to fight effectively. Taking their cues from their Native American friends and foes, they adapted their strategies and tactics to accommodate the terrain on which they found themselves. War in early America was not fought on level ground cleared for the frontal engagements familiar to European soldiers, allowing for a tight discipline of firing and close battle formations, but rather was fought over mountainous, swampy, or heavily forested and unmapped ground, without roads to enable the passage of heavy artillery. From the beginning, American soldiers were citizen soldiers, and the command patterns and relations between men and officers were more informal, and lacked the organization of either long regimental tradition or hired mercenaries.

Indian tribes fought on all sides: with the British colonists, or with the French or the Spanish vying for continental possession and domination, the tribes themselves attempting to cling tenaciously to their ancestral ground, playing off one enemy against the other, and themselves being played. Throughout the eighteenth century, American literature follows the home culture, aping the English forms of either high or low literary pedigree. The anonymous "Song of Braddock's Men," describing Braddock's mission to Fort Duquesne in 1755, is particularly interesting. The ballad turns into a victory what was in fact a bloody and terrifying defeat, where panicked British regulars presented a clumped target against their free-ranging enemies, and in the dim wilderness fired mostly at one another. Joel Barlow presents the same material in formal terms, registers the defeat as defeat, but turns Washington, without much historical justification, into the savior of the day.

Lucy Terry, the ex-slave whose bare-bones account of a skirmish in a Massachusetts settlement functions as an exemplar of all these early battles for land, also sets in motion other issues that continue to haunt America's literature of war. First, the encounter between white and red man foreshadows the way that ethnicity and then race will try the national balance, as the poem points to what will be a major flashpoint throughout something like the next hundred and fifty years of the new nation's life: the displacement of native dwellers by European settlers. In "Bars Fight," her homely and radical use of direct speech contrasts sharply with the greater formality of the printed language of a veteran soldier and journalist like Philip Freneau, or with the ambitions of Joel Barlow's epic versification. A vernacular kin to Lucy Terry's will show up again more consciously in James Russell Lowell, giving color and stylistic opportunities to the poetry that will open a way for the distinctive and egalitarian American sound audible in both the free and metered verse of later centuries.

LUCY TERRY [PRINCE] (1730–1821)

BARS[1] FIGHT

August, 'twas the twenty-fifth,
Seventeen hundred forty-six;
The Indians did in ambush lay,
Some very valiant men to slay,
The names of whom I'll not leave out.
Samuel Allen like a hero fout.
And though he was so brave and bold,
His face no more shall we behold.

Eleazar Hawks was killed outright,
Before he had time to fight,—
Before he did the Indians see,
Was shot and killed immediately.
Oliver Amsden he was slain,
Which caused his friends much grief and pain.
Simeon Amsden they found dead,

Not many rods distant from his head.
Adonijah Gillett, we do hear,
Did lose his life which was so dear.
John Sadler fled across the water,
And thus escaped the dreadful slaughter.
Eunice Allen see the Indians coming,
And hopes to save herself by running,

And had not her petticoats stopped her,
The awful creatures had not catched her,
Nor tommy hawked her on the head,
And left her on the ground for dead.
Young Samuel Allen, Oh lackaday!
Was taken and carried to Canada.

---

[1] A colonial term for a meadow.

ANONYMOUS

The Song of Braddock's Men

Fort DuQuesue Expedition, 1755

To arms, to arms! my jolly grenadiers!
   Hark how the drums do roll it along!
To horse, to horse, with valiant good cheer;
   We'll meet our proud foe before it is long.
        Let not your courage fail you;
        Be valiant, stout, and bold;
        And it will soon avail you,
        My loyal hearts of gold.
Huzzah, my valiant countrymen!—again I say huzzah!
'Tis nobly done,—the day's our own—huzzah, huzzah!

March on, march on, brave Braddock leads the foremost;
   The battle is begun as you may fairly see.
Stand firm, be bold, and it will soon be over;
   We'll soon gain the field from our proud enemy.
        A squadron now appears, my boys;
        If that they do but stand!
        Boys, never fear, be sure you mind
        The word of command!
Huzzah, my valiant countrymen!—again I say huzzah!
'Tis nobly done,—the day's our own—huzzah, huzzah!

See how, see how, they break and fly before us!
   See how they are scattered all over the plain!
Now, now—now, now, our country will adore us!
   In peace and in triumph, boys, when we return again!
        Then laurels shall our glory crown
        For all our actions told:
        The hills shall echo all around,
        My loyal hearts of gold.
Huzzah, my valiant countrymen!—again I say huzzah!
'Tis nobly done,—the day's our own—huzzah, huzzah!

JOEL BARLOW (1754–1812)

"PROGRESS OF THE COLONIES. TROUBLES WITH THE NATIVES."

FROM *THE COLUMBIAD*, BOOK 5

Between the gulfs, where Laurence drains the world
And where Floridia's farthest floods are curl'd,
Where midlands broad their swelling mountains heave
And slope their champaigns to the Atlantic wave,
The sandy streambank and the woodgreen plain
Raise into sight the new made seats of man.
The placid ports that break the seaborn gales,
Rear their tall masts and stretch aloft their sails;
Full harvests wave, the groves with fruitage bend,
Gay villas smile, defensive towers ascend;
All the rich works of art their charms display
To court the planter and his cares repay:
Till war invades; when soon the dales disclose
Their meadows path'd with files of savage foes;
High tufted quills their painted foreheads press,
Dark spoils of beasts their shaggy shoulders dress,
The bow bent forward for the combat strung,
The ax, the quiver on the girdle hung;
The deep discordant yells convulse the air,
And earth resounds the war whoop's hideous blare.
   The patriarch lookt; and every darken'd height,
Pours down the swarthy nations to the fight.
Where Kennebec's high source forsakes the sky,
Where long Champlain's yet unkeel'd waters lie,
Where Hudson crowds his hill-dissundering tide,
Where Kaatskill heights the starry vault divide,
Where the dim Alleganies range sublime
And give their streams to every neighboring clime,
The swarms descended like an evening shade,
And wolves and vultures follow'd where they spread.
Thus when a storm on eastern pinions driven

Meets the firm Andes in the midst of heaven,
The clouds convulse, the torrents pour amain
And the black waters sweep the subject plain.
    Thro harvest fields the bloody myriads tread,
Sack the lone village, strow the streets with dead;
The flames in spiry volumes round them rise,
And shrieks and shouts redoubling rend the skies.
Fair babes and matrons in their domes expire
Or bursting frantic thro the folding fire
They scream, fly, fall; promiscuous rave along
The yelling victors and the driven throng;
The streams run purple; all the peopled shore
Is wrapt in flames and trod with steps of gore.
Till colons,[2] gathering from the shorelands far,
Stretch their new standards and oppose the war,
With muskets match the many-shafted bow,
With loud artillery stun the astonisht foe.
When like a broken wave the barbarous train
Lead back the flight and scatter from the plain,
Slay their weak captives, drop their shafts in haste,
Forget their spoils and scour the trackless waste;
From wood to wood in wild confusion hurl'd
They hurry o'er the hills far thro the savage world.
    Now move secure the cheerful works of peace,
New temples rise and fruitful fields increase.

"Hostilities between France and England
extended to America. Braddock's defeat."

From The Columbiad, book 5, continued

Too soon the mother states with jealous fear
Transport their feuds and homebred quarrels here.
Now Gallia's war-built barks ascend in sight,
White flags unfold and armies robed in white,
On all the frontier streams their forts prepare

---

[2] Colonists.

And coop our cantons with surrounding war.
Quebec, as proud she rears her rocky seat,
Feeds their full camp and shades their anchor'd fleet;
Oswego's rampart frowns athwart his flood,
And wild Ontario swells beneath his load.
    And now an equal host from Albion's strand
Arrives to aid her young colonial band.
They join their force and tow'rd the falling day
Impetuous Braddock leads their hasty way;
O'er Allegany heights, like streams of fire,
The red flags wave and glittering arms aspire
To meet the savage hordes, who there advance
Their skulking files to join the arms of France.
    Where, old as earth, yet still unstain'd with blood,
Monongahela roll'd his careless flood,
Flankt with his mantling groves the fountful hills,
Drain'd the vast region thro his thousand rills.
Lured o'er his lawns the buffle herds, and spread
For all his fowls his piscatory glade;
But now perceives, with hostile flag unfurl'd,
A Gallic fortress awe the western world;
There Braddock bends his march; the troops within
Behold their danger and the fire begin.
Forth bursting from the gates they rush amain,
Front, flank and charge the fast approaching train;
The batteries blaze, the leaden vollies pour,
The vales, the streams, the solid mountains roar;
Clouds of convolving smoke the welkin spread,
The champaign shrouding in sulphureous shade.
Lost in the rocking thunder's loud career,
No shouts nor groans invade the Patriarch's ear,
Nor valorous feats are seen nor flight nor fall,
But one broad burst of darkness buries all.
Till chased by rising winds the smoke withdrew,
And the wide slaughter open'd on his view.
He saw the British leader borne afar
In dust and gore beyond the wings of war;
And while delirious panic seized his host,

Their flags, their arms in wild confusion tost,
Bold in the midst a youthful warrior[3] strode
And tower'd undaunted o'er the field of blood;
He checks the shameful rout, with vengeance burns,
And the pale Britons brighten where he turns.
So when thick vapors veil the nightly sky
The starry hosts in half seen lustre fly
Till phosphor rises o'er the twinkling crowd
And gives new splendor thro his parting cloud.
    Swift on a fiery steed the stripling rose,
Form'd the light files to pierce the line of foes;
Then waved his gleamy sword that flasht the day
And thro the Gallic legions hew'd his way:
His troops press forward like a loose-broke flood,
Sweep ranks away and smear their paths in blood;
The hovering foes pursue the combat far
And shower their balls along the flying war;
When the new leader turns his single force,
Points the flight forward, speeds his backward course;
The French recoiling half their victory yield,
And the glad Britons quit the fatal field.

---

[3] George Washington.

THE REVOLUTIONARY WAR

1776–1783

> The army was now not only starved but naked. The greatest part were not only shirtless and barefoot, but destitute of all other clothing, especially blankets. I procured a small piece of raw cowhide and made myself a pair of moccasins, which kept my feet (while they lasted) from the frozen ground, although, as I well remember, the hard edges so galled my ankles, while on a march, that it was with much difficulty and pain that I could wear them afterward; but the only alternative I had was to endure this inconvenience or go barefoot, as hundreds of my companions had to, till they might be tracked by their blood upon the rough frozen ground.
>
> —Joseph Plumb Martin, 1777, from Joseph T. Cox, *The Written Wars*

When the thirteen colonies began their war for independence from Great Britain, there were no other republican commonwealths in existence. Filled with the sense of the new possibilities inherent in their revolutionary action, Thomas Paine could declare: "We have it in our power to begin the world over again. . . . The birthday of a new world is at hand." For poets like Joel Barlow and Philip Freneau, this meant an odd combination of a liberating conceptual freedom held in bondage to a highly conventional literary practice. The radical politics coursing through the new republic were turned awkwardly into the borrowed shape of earlier English poets like Pope and Dryden, who were themselves following generations of classical models. Joel Barlow's idea was to overwhelm and improve the classics, despite his own limited talent. He deplored the politics of the Iliad, and its lessons teaching "both prince and people that military plunder was the most honorable mode of acquiring property." In his new world, Barlow wanted "true and useful ideas of glory" implanted in the minds of men, taking the place of "the false and destructive ones that have degraded the species in other countries." Surely a noble desire: yet the sounds, acts, and names of the new world often roll with unintentionally comic—if delicious—effect through the grandly Homeric design of Barlow's *Columbiad*.

The first American war poems were needed to fix in place a national identity that would justify, to themselves and to others, the aims of the group fighting. The poems tell the how and where of fighting, mark potential patriotic shrines, and give recognizable and lasting symbols of the ongoing struggle. In each successive war, flag, country, and democratic mission strive to be reaffirmed within the amassing cultural tradition.

Henry Wadsworth Longfellow's poem "Paul Revere's Ride" uses historical detail freely to sketch a patriotic icon of American watchfulness. Much later, Ralph Waldo Emerson sets a pivotal battle monument firmly in place as a kind of secular altar. John Pierpont, in retelling a story from a time before his birth, reflects an urgency of command: how to make an army of citizen soldiers, rather than one of professionals and mercenaries, stand and fight. Philip Freneau treats sacrifice and loyalty as national virtues, and sanctifies the suffering soldier; his old soldier shows the army of the Revolutionary War not as an armed citizenry of all ages and conditions, but as a specific band of soldiers. The poem counters the contemporary prejudice against standing armies, which were widely believed to rely on the corruption of place and privilege. While detailing in one poem the shabby use made of foreign mercenaries in the enemy force, in another poem Freneau focuses on an image of the destitute and pension-deserving American warrior, upon whose loyal patriotism the larger population depends, and in so doing, he elevates the professional soldier to new respect.

THOMAS PAINE (1737–1809)

LIBERTY TREE

In a chariot of light from the regions of day,
    The Goddess of Liberty came;
Ten thousand celestials directed the way,
    And hither conducted the dame.
A fair budding branch from the gardens above,
    Where millions with millions agree,
She brought in her hand as a pledge of her love,
    And the plant she named *Liberty Tree.*

The celestial exotic struck deep in the ground,
    Like a native it flourished and bore;
The fame of its fruit drew the nations around,
    To seek out this peaceable shore.
Unmindful of names or distinction they came,
    For freemen like brothers agree;
With one spirit endued, they one friendship pursued,
    And their temple was *Liberty Tree.*

Beneath this fair tree, like the patriarchs of old,
    Their bread in contentment they ate,
Unvexed with the troubles of silver and gold,
    The cares of the grand and the great.
With timber and tar they Old England supplied,
    And supported her power on the sea;
Her battles they fought, without getting a groat,
    For the honor of *Liberty Tree.*

But hear, O ye swains, 'tis a tale most profane,
    How all the tyrannical powers,
Kings, Commons, and Lords, are uniting amain,
    To cut down this guardian of ours;
From the east to the west blow the trumpet to arms,
    Through the land let the sound of it flee,
Let the far and the near, all unite with a cheer,
    In defence of our *Liberty Tree.*

PHILIP FRENEAU (1752–1832)

The American Soldier

A Picture from the Life

> *To serve with love,*
> *And shed your blood,*
> *Approved may be above,*
> *But here below*
> *(Example shew,)*
> *'Tis dangerous to be good.*
>
> —Lord Oxford

Deep in a vale, a stranger now to arms,
Too poor to shine in courts, too proud to beg,
He, who once warred on *Saratoga's* plains,
Sits musing o'er his scars, and wooden leg.

Remembering still the toil of former days,
To *other* hands he sees his earnings paid;—
They share the due reward—*he* feeds on praise.
Lost in the abyss of want, misfortune's shade.

Far, far from domes where splendid tapers glare,
'Tis his from dear bought *peace* no wealth to win,
Removed alike from courtly cringing 'squires,
The great-man's *Levee*, and the proud man's grin.

Sold are those arms which once on Britons blazed,
When, flushed with conquest, to the charge they came;
That power repelled, and *Freedom's* fabrick raised,
She leaves her soldier—*famine* and a *name*!

Jeffery, or, The Soldier's Progress

Lured by some corporal's smooth address,
His scarlet coat and roguish face,
One half a joe[1] on drum head laid,

[1] Probably an American variant of half a guinea, or twenty-one shillings.

A tavern treat—and reckoning paid;
See yonder simple lad consigned
To slavery of the meanest kind.

   With only skill to drive a plough
A musquet he must handle now;
Must twirl it here and twirl it there,
Now on the ground, now in the air:
Its every motion by some rule
Of practice, taught in *Frederick's* school,[2]
Must be directed—nicely true—
Or he be beaten black—and blue.

   A sergeant, raised from cleaning shoes,
May now this country lad abuse :—
On meagre fare grown poor and lean,
He treats him like a mere machine,
Directs his look, directs his step,
And kicks him into decent shape,
From aukward habit frees the clown,
Erects his head—or knocks him down.

   Last Friday week to *Battery-Green*
The sergeant came with this MACHINE—
One motion of the firelock missed——
The TUTOR thumped him with his fist:
I saw him lift his hickory cane,
I heard poor *Jeffery's* head complain!——
Yet this——and more——he's forced to bear:
And thus goes on from year to year,
'Till desperate grown, at such a lot,
He drinks—deserts—and so is shot!

[2] The Prussian manual exercise.

A New York Tory, to His Friend in Philadelphia

Dear Sir, I'm so anxious to hear of your health,
I beg you would send me a letter by stealth:
I hope a few months will quite alter the case,
When the wars are concluded, we'll meet and embrace.

For I'm led to believe from our brilliant success,
And, what is as clear, your amazing distress,
That the cause of rebellion has met with a check
That will bring all its patrons to hang by the neck.

Cornwallis has manag'd so well in the South,
Those rebels want victuals to put in their mouth;
And Arnold has stript them, we hear, to the buff—
Has burnt their tobacco, and left them—the snuff.

Dear Thomas, I wish you would move from that town
Where meet all the rebels of fame and renown;
When our armies, victorious, shall clear that vile nest
You may chance, though a Tory, to swing with the rest.

But again—on reflection—I beg you would stay—
You may serve us yet better than if mov'd away—
Give advice to Sir HARRY of all that is passing,[3]
What vessels are building, what cargoes amassing;

Inform, to a day, when those vessels will sail,
That our cruisers may capture them all, without fail—
By proceedings, like these, your peace shall be made,
The rebellious shall swing, but be you ne'er afraid.

I cannot conceive how you do to subsist—
The rebels are starving, except those who 'list;

[3] Sir Henry Clinton, commander of British forces in America.

And as you reside in the land of Gomorrah,
You must fare as the rest do, I think, to your sorrow.

Poor souls! if ye knew what a doom is decreed,
(I mean not for you, but for rebels indeed)
You would tremble to think of the vengeance in store,
The halters and gibbets—I mention no more.

The rebels must surely conclude they're undone,
Their navy is ruin'd, their armies have run;
It is time they should now from delusion awaken—
The rebellion is done—for the TRUMBULL is taken!

ANONYMOUS

BURROWING YANKEES

Ye Yankees who, mole-like, still throw up the earth,
And like them, to your follies, are blind from your birth;
Attempt not to hold British troops at defiance,
True Britons, with whom you pretend an alliance.

Mistake not; such blood ne'er run in your veins,
Tis no more than the dregs, the lees, or the drains;
Ye affect to talk big of your hourly attacks;
Come on! And I'll warrant, we'll soon see your backs.

Such threats of bravadoes serve only to warm
The true British hearts, you ne'er can alarm;
The Lion, once rous'd, will strike such a terror,
Shall show you, poor fools, your presumption and error.

And the time will soon come when your whole rebel race
Will be drove from the lands, nor dare show your face;
Here's a health to great George, may he fully determine,
To root from the earth all such insolent vermin.

PHILLIS WHEATLEY (1753–1784)

To His Excellency General Washington

Celestial choir! enthron'd in realms of light,
Columbia's[4] scenes of glorious toils I write.
While freedom's cause her anxious breast alarms,
She flashes dreadful in refulgent arms.
See mother earth her offspring's fate bemoan,
And nations gaze at scenes before unknown!
See the bright beams of heaven's revolving light
Involved in sorrows and veil of night!
The goddess comes, she moves divinely fair,
Olive and laurel bind her golden hair:
Wherever shines this native of the skies,
Unnumber'd charms and recent graces rise.

Muse! bow propitious while my pen relates
How pour her armies through a thousand gates,
As when Eolus heaven's fair face deforms,
Enwrapp'd in tempest and a night of storms;
Astonish'd ocean feels the wild uproar,
The refluent surges beat the sounding shore;
Or thick as leaves in Autumn's golden reign,
Such, and so many, moves the warrior's train.
In bright array they seek the work of war,
Where high unfurl'd the ensign waves in air.
Shall I to Washington their praise recite?
Enough thou know'st them in the fields of fight.
Thee, first in peace and honours,—we demand
The grace and glory of thy martial band.
Fam'd for thy valour, for thy virtues more,
Hear every tongue thy guardian aid implore!

One century scarce perform'd its destined round,
When Gallic powers Columbia's fury found;

---

[4] This is the first use in print of this term for America.

And so may you, whoever dares disgrace
The land of freedom's heaven-defended race!
Fix'd are the eyes of nations on the scales,
For in their hopes Columbia's arm prevails.
Anon Britannia droops the pensive head,
While round increase the rising hills of dead.
Ah! cruel blindness to Columbia's state!
Lament thy thirst of boundless power too late.

Proceed, great chief, with virtue on thy side,
Thy ev'ry action let the goddess guide.
A crown, a mansion, and a throne that shine,
With gold unfading, WASHINGTON! be thine.

JOHN PIERPONT (1785–1866)

WARREN'S ADDRESS TO THE AMERICAN SOLDIERS

Stand! the ground's your own, my braves!
Will ye give it up to slaves?
Will ye look for greener graves?
    Hope ye mercy still?
What's the mercy despots feel?
Hear it in that battle-peal!
Read it on yon bristling steel!
    Ask it,—ye who will.

Fear ye foes who kill for hire?
Will ye to your homes retire?
Look behind you! they're a-fire!
    And, before you, see
Who have done it!—From the vale
On they come!—And will ye quail?—
Leaden rain and iron hail
    Let their welcome be!

In the God of battles trust!
Die we may,—and die we must;
But, O, where can dust to dust
   Be consigned so well,
As where Heaven its dews shall shed
On the martyred patriot's bed,
And the rocks shall raise their head,
   Of his deeds to tell!

RALPH WALDO EMERSON (1803–1882)

CONCORD HYMN

SUNG AT THE COMPLETION OF THE BATTLE MONUMENT,
JULY 4, 1837

By the rude bridge that arched the flood,
   Their flag to April's breeze unfurled,
Here once the embattled farmers stood
   And fired the shot heard round the world.

The foe long since in silence slept;
   Alike the conqueror silent sleeps;
And Time the ruined bridge has swept
   Down the dark stream which seaward creeps.

On this green bank, by this soft stream,
   We set to-day a votive stone;
That memory may their deed redeem,
   When, like our sires, our sons are gone.

Spirit, that made those heroes dare
   To die, and leave their children free,
Bid Time and Nature gently spare
   The shaft we raise to them and thee.

THE REVOLUTIONARY WAR   19

HENRY WADSWORTH LONGFELLOW (1807–1882)

PAUL REVERE'S RIDE

Listen, my children, and you shall hear
Of the midnight ride of Paul Revere,
On the eighteenth of April, in Seventy-five;
Hardly a man is now alive
Who remembers that famous day and year.

He said to his friend, "If the British march
By land or sea from the town to-night,
Hang a lantern aloft in the belfry arch
Of the North Church tower as a signal light,—
One, if by land, and two, if by sea;
And I on the opposite shore will be,
Ready to ride and spread the alarm
Through every Middlesex village and farm,
For the country folk to be up and to arm."
Then he said, "Good night!" and with muffled oar
Silently rowed to the Charlestown shore,
Just as the moon rose over the bay,
Where swinging wide at her moorings lay
The Somerset, British man-of-war;
A phantom ship, with each mast and spar
Across the moon like a prison bar,
And a huge black hulk, that was magnified
By its own reflection in the tide.

Meanwhile, his friend, through alley and street,
Wanders and watches with eager ears,
Till in the silence around him he hears
The muster of men at the barrack door,
The sound of arms, and the tramp of feet,
And the measured tread of the grenadiers,
Marching down to their boats on the shore.

Then he climbed the tower of the Old North Church,
By the wooden stairs, with stealthy tread,
To the belfry-chamber overhead,
And startled the pigeons from their perch
On the sombre rafters, that round him made
Masses and moving shapes of shade,—
By the trembling ladder, steep and tall,
To the highest window in the wall,
Where he paused to listen and look down.
A moment on the roofs of the town,
And the moonlight flowing over all.
Beneath, in the churchyard, lay the dead,
In their night-encampment on the hill,
Wrapped in silence so deep and still
That he could hear, like a sentinel's tread,
The watchful night-wind, as it went
Creeping along from tent to tent,
And seeming to whisper, "All is well!"
A moment only he feels the spell
Of the place and the hour, and the secret dread
Of the lonely belfry and the dead;
For suddenly all his thoughts are bent
On a shadowy something far away,
Where the river widens to meet the bay,—
A line of black that bends and floats
On the rising tide, like a bridge of boats.

Meanwhile, impatient to mount and ride,
Booted and spurred, with a heavy stride
On the opposite shore walked Paul Revere.
Now he patted his horse's side,
Now gazed at the landscape far and near,
Then, impetuous, stamped the earth,
And turned and tightened his saddle girth;
But mostly he watched with eager search
The belfry-tower of the Old North Church,
As it rose above the graves on the hill,
Lonely and spectral and sombre and still.

And lo! as he looks, on the belfry's height
A glimmer, and then a gleam of light!
He springs to the saddle, the bridle he turns,
But lingers and gazes, till full on his sight
A second lamp in the belfry burns!

A hurry of hoofs in a village street,
A shape in the moonlight, a bulk in the dark,
And beneath, from the pebbles, in passing, a spark
Struck out by a steed flying fearless and fleet:
That was all! And yet, through the gloom and the light,
The fate of a nation was riding that night;
And the spark struck out by that steed, in his flight,
Kindled the land into flame with its heat.
He has left the village and mounted the steep,
And beneath him, tranquil and broad and deep,
Is the Mystic, meeting the ocean tides;
And under the alders, that skirt its edge,
Now soft on the sand, now loud on the ledge,
Is heard the tramp of his steed as he rides.

It was twelve by the village clock,
When he crossed the bridge into Medford town.
He heard the crowing of the cock,
And the barking of the farmer's dog,
And felt the damp of the river fog,
That rises after the sun goes down.
It was one by the village clock,
When he galloped into Lexington.
He saw the gilded weathercock
Swim in the moonlight as he passed,
And the meeting-house windows, blank and bare,
Gaze at him with a spectral glare,
As if they already stood aghast
At the bloody work they would look upon.

It was two by the village clock,
When he came to the bridge in Concord town.

He heard the bleating of the flock,
And the twitter of birds among the trees,
And felt the breath of the morning breeze
Blowing over the meadows brown.
And one was safe and asleep in his bed
Who at the bridge would be first to fall,
Who that day would be lying dead,
Pierced by a British musket-ball.

You know the rest. In the books you have read,
How the British Regulars fired and fled,—
How the farmers gave them ball for ball,
From behind each fence and farm-yard wall,
Chasing the red-coats down the lane,
Then crossing the fields to emerge again
Under the trees at the turn of the road,
And only pausing to fire and load.

So through the night rode Paul Revere;
And so through the night went his cry of alarm
To every Middlesex village and farm,—
A cry of defiance and not of fear,
A voice in the darkness, a knock at the door,
And a word that shall echo forevermore!
For, borne on the night-wind of the Past,
Through all our history, to the last,
In the hour of darkness and peril and need,
The people will waken and listen to hear
The hurrying hoof-beats of that steed,
And the midnight message of Paul Revere.

PAUL LAURENCE DUNBAR (1872–1906)

BLACK SAMSON OF BRANDYWINE

> "In the fight at Brandywine, Black Samson, a giant negro armed
> with a scythe, sweeps his way through the red ranks. . . ."
>
> —C. M. Skinner's *Myths and Legends of Our Own Land*

Gray are the pages of record,
  Dim are the volumes of eld;
Else had old Delaware told us
  More that her history held.
Told us with pride in the story,
  Honest and noble and fine,
More of the tale of my hero,
  Black Samson of Brandywine.

Sing of your chiefs and your nobles,
  Saxon and Celt and Gaul,
Breath of mine ever shall join you,
  Highly I honor them all.
Give to them all of their glory,
  But for this noble of mine,
Lend him a tithe of your tribute,
  Black Samson of Brandywine.

There in the heat of the battle,
  There in the stir of the fight,
Loomed he, an ebony giant,
  Black as the pinions of night.
Swinging his scythe like a mower
  Over a field of grain,
Needless the care of the gleaners,
  Where he had passed amain.

Straight through the human harvest,
  Cutting a bloody swath,
Woe to you, soldier of Briton!
  Death is abroad in his path.

Flee from the scythe of the reaper,
    Flee while the moment is thine,
None may with safety withstand him,
    Black Samson of Brandywine.

Was he a freeman or bondman?
    Was he a man or a thing?
What does it matter? His brav'ry
    Renders him royal—a king.
If he was only a chattel,
    Honor the ransom may pay
Of the royal, the loyal black giant
    Who fought for his country that day.

Noble and bright is the story,
    Worthy the touch of the lyre,
Sculptor or poet should find it
    Full of the stuff to inspire.
Beat it in brass and in copper,
    Tell it in storied line,
So that the world may remember
    Black Samson of Brandywine.

THE WAR OF 1812

A fierce battle ensued. Fort McHenry opened the full force of all her batteries upon them [the British] as they repassed, and the fleet responding with entire broadsides made an explosion so terrific that it seemed as though mother earth had opened and was vomiting shot and shell in a sheet of fire and brimstone.

—Francis Scott Key, 1812

Francis Scott Key, a grim prisoner of war watching a crucial American fort burn, but still exulting in his country's indestructible flag, provides the image of an unshakeable national will fluttering and rippling yet over banks, cemeteries, and ballgames. As Philip Freneau rewrites Caesar's *veni vidi vici* in "On the Conflagrations at Washington," he offers his shock and indignation at the sight of the smoldering new capitol: "They came—they saw—they burnt—and fled."

The primary issues of the War of 1812 turned on American maritime rights and indignation over the forced impressment of American seamen by the British; yet the largest group supporting the War of 1812 came from the southern and western parts of the country, which were less affected by the crises in domestic shipping. In these regions, American land investors and settlers wanted relief from raids by Indians in the Ohio Country, who were goaded onward and supplied by the British from Canadian outposts. John Neal's poem about the Battle of Niagara reminds us of the hostilities that ensued from the American attempts to invade Canada, with the intention of defensively stretching the northern border of the new United States.

Almost paradoxically, the chief source of antiwar feeling in 1812 came from New England, where Yankee ship owners, who suffered from an embargo, blockade, and other European harassments of American trade, nonetheless made comfortable profits on their cargoes to Europe and vigorously resisted a politically and economically draining war. In 1812, President Madison sent Joel Barlow to France to negotiate American shipping rights with Napoleon. Barlow was escorted to France by Captain Isaac Hull on the frigate *Constitution*, and went from Paris toward Russia, trying to catch up with Napoleon in Moscow. Barlow's "Advice to a Raven in Russia," his last, best, and most passionately antiwar poem, was written during 1812, while Barlow continued his diplomatic mission in Poland. He was swept up in the chaos of the French army in its flight from Moscow, and died of pneumonia in the village of Zarnowiecz, on the road between Krakow and Warsaw.

An American defeat in the eyes of some historians, the record of the War of 1812 was at the best a mixed success: though the invasion of Canada failed and the nation's capitol at Washington was burned, the Americans could point to a number of naval and land victories in the territory of the Great Lakes and Andrew Jackson's triumph over the British in New Orleans. At the Treaty of Paris, American and English diplomats agreed to a cessation of the fighting even as Andrew Jackson, unaware of the Paris negotiations, was decisively beating the English at New Orleans. The peace treaty has been defined by historians as rather a truce than a treaty: no new rights were acknowledged and no land was exchanged. Yet America, at the conclusion of the War of 1812, had reasserted its independence from Britain, consolidated its continental dominion, and begun to flex its muscles on the global stage.

PHILIP FRENEAU (1752–1832)

ON THE CONFLAGRATIONS AT WASHINGTON

> Jam deiphobi dedit ampla ruinam,
> Vulcano superante, domus; jam proximus ardet
> Ucalegon.[1]
> —Virgil

Now, George the third rules not alone,
For George the vandal shares the throne,
True flesh of flesh and bone of bone.

God save us from the fangs of both;
Or, one a vandal, one a goth,
May roast or boil us into froth.

Like danes, of old, their fleet they man
And rove from *Beersheba* to *Dan*,
To burn, and beard us—where they can.

They say, at George the fourth's command
This vagrant host were sent, to land
And leave in every house—a brand.

An idiot only would require
Such war—the worst they could desire—
The felon's war—the war of fire.

The warfare, now th' invaders make
Must surely keep us all awake,
Or life is lost for freedom's sake.

They said to Cockburn, "honest Cock!
To make a noise and give a shock
Push off, and burn their navy dock:

---

[1] Virgil *Aeneid* 2.310–312: "Now the great house of Deiphobus sank into ruin, destroyed by Vulcan / The fire, and that of Ucalegon, burned nearby."

"Their capitol shall be emblazed!
How will the *buckskins* stand amazed,
And curse the day its walls were raised!"

Six thousand heroes disembark—
Each left at night his floating ark
And *Washington* was made their mark.

That few would fight them—few or none—
Was by their leaders clearly shown—
And "*down*," they said, "*with Madison!*"

How close they crept along the shore!
As closely as if *Rodgers* saw her—
A frigate to a seventy-four.[2]

A veteran host, by veterans led,
With *Ross* and *Cockburn* at their head—
They came—they saw—they burnt—and fled.

But not unpunish'd they retired;
They something paid, for all they fired,
In soldiers kill'd, and chiefs expired.

Five hundred veterans bit the dust,
Who came, inflamed with lucre's lust—
And so they waste—and so they must.

They left our congress naked walls—
Farewell to towers and capitals!
To lofty roofs and splendid halls!

To courtly domes and glittering things,
To folly, that too near us clings,
To courtiers who—'tis well—had wings.

---

[2] A man-of-war carrying seventy-four guns. This type of ship made up the bulk of the Royal Navy.

Farewell to all but glorious war,
Which yet shall guard *Potomac's* shore,
And honor lost, and fame restore.

To conquer armies in the field
Was, once, the surest method held
To make a hostile country yield.

The mode is this, now acted on;
In conflagrating *Washington,*
They held our independence gone!

Supposing *George's* house at Kew
Were burnt, (as we intend to do,)
Would that be burning England too?

Supposing, near the silver *Thames*
We laid in ashes their *saint James,*
Or *Blenheim* palace wrapt in flames;

Made Hampton Court to fire a prey,
And meanly, then, to sneak away,
And never ask them, what's to pay?

Would that be conquering London town?
Would that subvert the english throne,
Or bring the royal system down?

With all their glare of guards or guns,
How would they look like simpletons,
And not at all the *lion's sons!*

Supposing, then, we take our turn
And make it public law, to burn,
Would not old english honor spurn

At such a mean insidious plan
Which only suits some savage clan—
And surely not—the english man!

A doctrine has prevail'd too long;
A king, they hold, *can do no wrong*—
Merely a pitch-fork, without prong:

But de'il may trust such doctrines, more,—
One king, that wrong'd us, long before,
Has wrongs, by hundreds, yet in store.

He wrong'd us forty years ago;
He wrongs us yet, we surely know;
He'll wrong us till he gets a blow

That, with a vengeance, will repay
The mischiefs we lament this day,
This burning, damn'd, infernal play;

Will send *one city* to the sky,
Its buildings low and buildings high,
And buildings—built the lord knows why;

Will give him an eternal check
That breaks his heart or breaks his neck,
And plants our standard on QUEBEC.

FRANCIS SCOTT KEY (1779–1843)

DEFENCE OF FORT MCHENRY

O! say can you see, by the dawn's early light,
   What so proudly we hail'd at the twilight's last gleaming,
Whose broad stripes and bright stars through the perilous fight,
    O'er the ramparts we watch'd, were so gallantly streaming?
      And the rockets' red glare, the bombs bursting in air,
       Gave proof through the night that our flag was still there—
        O! say, does that star-spangled banner yet wave
        O'er the land of the free, and the home of the brave?

On the shore, dimly seen through the mists of the deep,
  Where the foe's haughty host in dread silence reposes,
What is that which the breeze o'er the towering steep,
  As it fitfully blows, half conceals, half discloses?
    Now it catches the gleam of the morning's first beam,
    In full glory reflected now shines on the stream—
      'Tis the star-spangled banner, O! long may it wave
      O'er the land of the free, and the home of the brave.

And where is that band who so vauntingly swore
  That the havock of war and the battle's confusion
A home and a country should leave us no more?
  Their blood has wash'd out their foul foot-steps' pollution.
    No refuge could save the hireling and slave,
    From the terror of flight or the gloom of the grave;
      And the star-spangled banner in triumph doth wave
      O'er the land of the free, and the home of the brave.

O! thus be it ever when freemen shall stand
  Between their lov'd home, and the war's desolation,
Blest with vict'ry and peace, may the heav'n-rescued land
  Praise the power that hath made and preserv'd us a nation!
    Then conquer we must, when our cause it is just,
    And this be our motto—"In God is our trust!"
      And the star-spangled banner in triumph shall wave
      O'er the land of the free, and the home of the brave.

JOHN NEAL (1793–1896)

THE BATTLE OF NIAGARA, FROM CANTO IV[3]

The battle comes again. The charging host
Are Britons—chosen ones—their army's boast.
Reddening they come in martyrdom to Fame;
Shaking their snowy plumes in cloud and flame.
Bravely their banner is abroad outspread—
Alive their meteor, and their shroud when dead.
The tumult deepens. Swell conflicting cries:
Neigh the loud steeds, and hurried sobs arise.
Shakes that dark hill with cataracts of fire:
Up go that army to their blazing pyre!
The cannon's voice is mute. The lightning sheet
Grows dim again. Warriors with warriors meet,—
And wrestle fiercely in their rolling cloud.
Again the mountain shakes! Again the light
Comes thundering loudly down—the blazing flight
Of starry banners are abroad again,
And neighing—plunging—o'er the clouded plain,
Goes many a fiery barb with crimson reeking mane:
Again the meteors of the war are bowed:
Again the mountain heaves beneath its shroud:
Gushes with quenchless light and shakes and storms aloud.

So darkly clouded was that hill with smoke,
Save when the vast artillery day-light broke,
It seemed a midnight altar. From its gloom,
There came the noise of strife as from a tomb.
And then, distinct, amidst the spreading light
Were seen the struggling champions of the fight,
In silent—desperate—dreadful bayonet strife:
The midnight slaughter! When the hero's life—

---

[3] Author's Note: "To the Reader. I have attempted to do justice to the American scenery and American character, not to versify the minutiae of battles—not to give names, titles or geographical references for my authority, for all these may be found in the *newspapers* of the day. I have not attempted to write a history but a poem."

The high—stern summons that he gives his band—
His waving falchion—and extended hand—
His towering plume—his charger's bloody mane—
The battle-anthem and the bugle strain—
Are beamless—lifeless! Heard and seen no more:
Thus 'tis when bayonets hush the cannon's roar.
The blazing would be gone! And with it, lo!
These darkly wrestling groups would come and go,
Like wizard shapes at night upon the snow—
That glitters to the moon upon some mountain's brow.

   So stood the battle. Bravely it was fought.
Lions and Eagles met. That hill was bought,
And sold in desperate combat. Wrapped in flame,
Died these idolaters of bannered Fame.
Three times that meteor hill was bravely lost—
Three times 'twas bravely won; while madly tost,
Encountering red plumes in the dusky air:
While Slaughter shouted in her bloody lair.
And specters blew their horns and shook their whistling hair!

JOEL BARLOW (1754–1812)

ADVICE TO A RAVEN IN RUSSIA

DECEMBER, 1812

   Black fool, why winter here? These frozen skies,
Worn by your wings and deafen'd by your cries,
Should warn you hence, where milder suns invite,
And day alternates with his mother night.
   You fear perhaps your food will fail you there,
Your human carnage, that delicious fare
That lured you hither, following still your friend
The great Napoleon to the world's bleak end.
You fear, because the southern climes pour'd forth
Their clustering nations to infest the north,

Barvarians, Austrians, those who Drink the Po
And those who skirt the Tuscan seas below,
With all Germania, Neustria,[4] Belgia, Gaul,
Doom'd here to wade thro slaughter to their fall,
You fear he left behind no wars, to feed
His feather'd canibals and nurse the breed.

  Fear not, my screamer, call your greedy train,
Sweep over Europe, hurry back to Spain,
You'll find his legions there; the valliant crew
Please best their master when they toil for you.
Abundant there they spread the country o'er
And taint the breeze with every nation's gore,
Iberian, Lussian,[5] British widely strown,
But still more wide and copious flows their own.

  Go where you will; Calabria, Malta, Greece,
Egypt and Syria still his fame increase,
Domingo's[6] fatten'd isle and India's plains
Glow deep with purple drawn from Gallic veins.
No Raven's wing can stretch the flight so far
As the torn bandrols of Napoleon's war.
Choose then your climate, fix your best abode,
He'll make you deserts and he'll bring you blood.

  How could you fear a dearth? have not mankind,
Tho slain by millions, millions left behind?
Has not CONSCRIPTION still the power to weild
Her annual faulchion o'er the human field?
A faithful harvester! or if a man
Escape that gleaner, shall he scape the BAN?
The triple BAN, that like the hound of hell
Gripes with three joles,[7] to hold his victim well.

  Fear nothing then, hatch fast your ravenous brood,
Teach them to cry to Bonaparte for food;
They'll be like you, of all his suppliant train,
The only class that never cries in vain.

[4] Normandy.
[5] Portugese.
[6] The Dominican Republic, ceded to France by Spain in 1795.
[7] Jaws.

For see what mutual benefits you lend!
(The surest way to fix the mutual friend)
While on his slaughter'd troops your tribes are fed,
You cleanse his camp and carry off his dead.
Imperial Scavenger! but now you know
Your work is vain amid these hills of snow.
His tentless troops are marbled thro with frost
And change to crystal when the breath is lost.
Mere trunks of ice, tho limb'd like human frames
And lately warm'd with life's endearing flames,
They cannot taint the air, the world impest,
Nor can you tear one fiber from their breast.
No! from their visual sockets, as they lie,
With beak and claws you cannot pluck an eye.
The frozen orb, preserving still its form,
Defies your talons as it braves the storm,
But stands and stares to God, as if to know
In what curst hands he leaves his world below.

Fly then, or starve; tho all the dreadful road
From Minsk to Moskow with their bodies strow'd
May count some Myriads, yet they can't suffice
To feed you more beneath these dreary skies.
Go back, and winter in the wilds of Spain;
Feast there awhile, and in the next campaign
Rejoin your master; for you'll find him then,
With his new million of the race of men,
Clothed in his thunders, all his flags unfurl'd,
Raging and storming o'er the prostrate world.

War after war his hungry soul requires,
State after State shall sink beneath his fires,
Yet other Spains in victim smoke shall rise
And other Moskows suffocate the skies,
Each land lie reeking with its people's slain
And not a stream run bloodless to the main.
Till men resume their souls, and dare to shed
Earth's total vengeance on the monster's head,
Hurl from his blood-built throne this king of woes,
Dash him to dust, and let the world repose.

OLIVER WENDELL HOLMES (1809–1894)

OLD IRONSIDES

Ay, tear her tattered ensign down!
    Long has it waved on high,
And many an eye has danced to see
    That banner in the sky;
Beneath it rung the battle shout,
    And burst the cannon's roar;—
The meteor of the ocean air
    Shall sweep the clouds no more!

Her deck, once red with heroes' blood
    Where knelt the vanquished foe,
When winds were hurrying o'er the flood
    And waves were white below,
No more shall feel the victor's tread,
    Or know the conquered knee;—
The harpies of the shore shall pluck
    The eagle of the sea!

O better that her shattered hulk
    Should sink beneath the wave;
Her thunders shook the mighty deep,
    And there should be her grave;
Nail to the mast her holy flag,
    Set every thread-bare sail,
And give her to the god of storms,—
    The lightning and the gale!

THE ALAMO AND THE

MEXICAN-AMERICAN WAR

1836 AND 1846–1848

It has been alleged as a reason why Texas should not be annexed, that we have too much territory already. Such an argument may hold good where a government is compelled to maintain its right to territory by force; but here, under our free government, where every man's voice can be heard, the whole continent, or the whole world would not be sufficient. I go for the re-annexation of Texas, even if it should involve us in a war with Mexico, or with England, or with the whole world!

—Mike Walsh, journalist, from William S. Henry's *Campaign Sketches* (1847)

The poems of this section include vivid contrasts in ironic and exalted modes of commemoration, from James Russell Lowell's reluctant Bay State enlistee Birdafredum Sawin pitting himself against the mythic loyalties of Texan soldiers at the Alamo, to Joaquin Miller's "The Defense of the Alamo," representing the mystique invoked ten years later to stoke American pride. Feelings about the war ran high: it was the Mexican-American War which triggered Henry David Thoreau's essay "On Civil Disobedience," a work which became canonical for future American political dissenters. The poems of this war reveal the regional and national divisions of loyalty that continue to have latter-day parallels. They also introduce the ongoing American conflict between strategies of containment versus strategies of expansion.

Joaquin Miller, whose reputation has subsided since the nineteenth century, uses a florid diction alien to the modern ear, while John Greenleaf Whittier thumps out his poem "The Angels of Buena Vista" in a heroic Finnish dactyl, to say roundly that in war all mothers suffer alike. Just as

Francis Scott Key and Henry Wadsworth Longfellow have put in place indelible national icons for earlier wars, Emerson's "Concord Hymn" performs a similar patriotic service, although his "Ode, Inscribed to W. H. Channing," is much sterner about the forces that will unleash an American empire where "Things are in the saddle, /And ride mankind." James Russell Lowell, in response to the doctrine of manifest destiny, draws on feelings that help to define the resolute antimilitarism and anti-imperialism that erupts in subsequent wars. But despite this poetic opposition to expansionism, by February 2, 1848, Mexico had agreed, urged by a money payment and losses on the field, to cede over one million square miles of territory to the United States, including California and New Mexico, and obliging Mexico to recognize the Rio Grande as the southern boundary of Texas.

JOAQUIN MILLER (1841–1913)

THE DEFENSE OF THE ALAMO

Santa Ana came storming, as a storm might come;
There was rumble of cannon; there was rattle of blade;
There was cavalry, infantry, bugle and drum—
Full seven proud thousand in pomp and parade,
The chivalry, flower of all Mexico;
And a gaunt two hundred in the Alamo!

And thirty lay sick, and some were shot through;
For the siege had been bitter, and bloody, and long.
"Surrender, or die!"—"Men, what will *you* do?"
And Travis,[1] great Travis, drew sword, quick and strong;
Drew a line at his feet. . . . "Will you come? Will you go?
I die with my wounded, in the Alamo."

Then Bowie gasped, "Guide me over that line!"
Then Crockett, one hand to the sick, one hand to his gun.
Crossed with him; then never a word or a sign
Till all, sick or well, all, all, save but one,
One man. Then a woman stopped praying, and slow
Across, to die with the heroes of the Alamo.

Then that one coward fled, in the night, in that night,
When all men silently prayed and thought
Of home; of tomorrow; of God and the right;
Till dawn; then Travis sent his single last cannon-shot,
In answer to insolent Mexico,
From the old bell-tower of the Alamo.

Then came Santa Ana; a crescent of flame:
Then the red *escalade*; then the fight hand to hand:
Such an unequal fight as never had name
Since the Persian hordes butchered that doomed Spartan band.

---

[1] William Barret Travis, commander of the Texas defenders of the fort.

All day—all day and all night, and the morning? so slow,
Through the battle smoke mantling the Alamo.

Then silence! Such silence! Two thousand lay dead
In a crescent outside! And within? Not a breath
Save the gasp of a woman, with gory, gashed head,
All alone, with her dead there, waiting for death;
And she but a nurse. Yet when shall we know
Another like this of the Alamo?

Shout "Victory, victory, victory ho!"
I say, 'tis not always with the hosts that win;
I say that the victory, high or low,
Is given the hero who grapples with sin,
Or legion or single; just asking to know
When duty fronts death in his Alamo.

MARTÍN ESPADA (B. 1957)

THE OTHER ALAMO

SAN ANTONIO, TEXAS, 1990

In the Crockett Hotel dining room,
a chalk-faced man in medaled uniform
growls a prayer
at the head of the veterans' table.
Throughout the map of this saint-hungry city,
hands strain for the touch of shrines,
genuflection before cannon and memorial plaque,
grasping the talisman of Bowie knife replica
at the souvenir shop, visitors
in white biblical quote T-shirts.

The stones in the walls are smaller
than the fists of Texas martyrs;
their cavernous mouths could drink the canal to mud.

The Daughters of the Republic
print brochures dancing with Mexican demons,
Santa Anna's leg still hopping
to conjunto accordions.[2]
The lawyers who conquered farmland
by scratching on parchment in an oil lamp haze,
the cotton growers who kept the time
of Mexican peasant lives dangling from their watch chains,
the vigilantes hooded like blind angels
hunting with torches for men the color of night,
gathering at church, the capitol, or the porch
for a century all said this: Alamo.

In 1949, three boys
in Air Force dress khaki
ignored the whites-only sign
at the diner by the bus station:
A soldier from Baltimore, who heard nigger sung here
more often than his name, but would not glance away;
another blond and solemn as his Tennessee
of whitewashed spires;
another from distant Puerto Rico, cap tipped at an angle
in a country where brown skin
could be boiled for the leather of a vigilante's wallet.

The waitress squinted a glare and refused their contamination,
the manager lost his crewcut politeness
and blustered about local customs,
the police, with surrounding faces,
jeered about tacos and senoritas
on the Mexican side of town.
"We're not leaving," they said,
and hunched at their stools
till the manager ordered the cook,
sweat-burnished black man unable to hide his grin,

[2] Versions of polkas and other dances picked up in the United States by Mexican musicians, played on a three-row button-style accordion.

to slide cheeseburgers on plates
across the counter.
"We're not hungry," they said,
and left a week's pay for the cook.
One was my father; his word for fury
is Texas.

This afternoon, the heat clouds the air like bothered gnats.
The lunch counter was wrecked for the dump years ago.
In the newspapers, a report of vandals
scarring the wooden doors
of the Alamo
in black streaks of fire.

RALPH WALDO EMERSON (1803–1882)

ODE, INSCRIBED TO W. H. CHANNING

Though loath to grieve
The evil time's sole patriot,
I cannot leave
My honied thought
For the priest's cant,
Or statesman's rant.

If I refuse
My study for their politique,
Which at the best is trick,
The angry Muse
Puts confusion in my brain.

But who is he that prates
Of the culture of mankind,
Of better arts and life?
Go, blindworm, go,
Behold the famous States

Harrying Mexico
With rifle and with knife!

Or who, with accent bolder,
Dare praise the freedom-loving mountaineer?
I found by thee, O rushing Contoocook![3]
And in thy valleys, Agiochook![4]
The jackals of the negro-holder.

The God who made New Hampshire
Taunted the lofty land
With little men;—
Small bat and wren
House in the oak:—
If earth-fire cleave
The upheaved land, and bury the folk,
The southern crocodile would grieve.
Virtue palters; Right is hence;
Freedom praised, but hid;
Funeral eloquence
Rattles the coffin-lid.

What boots thy zeal,
O glowing friend,
That would indignant rend
The northland from the south?
Wherefore? to what good end?
Boston Bay and Bunker Hill
Would serve things still;—
Things are of the snake.

The horseman serves the horse,
The neatherd serves the neat,
The merchant serves the purse,

[3] A river in New Hampshire.
[4] The White Mountains of New Hampshire.

The eater serves his meat;
'Tis the day of the chattel,
Web to weave, and corn to grind;
Things are in the saddle,
And ride mankind.

There are two laws discrete,
Not reconciled,—
Law for man, and law for thing;
The last builds town and fleet,
But it runs wild,
And doth the man unking.

'Tis fit the forest fall,
The steep be graded,
The mountain tunnelled,
The sand shaded,
The orchard planted,
The glebe tilled,
The prairie granted,
The steamer built.

Let man serve law for man;
Live for friendship, live for love,
For truth's and harmony's behoof;
The state may follow how it can,
As Olympus follows Jove.

    Yet do not I implore
The wrinkled shopman to my sounding woods,
Nor bid the unwilling senator
Ask votes of thrushes in the solitudes.
Every one to his chosen work;—
Foolish hands may mix and mar;
Wise and sure the issues are.
Round they roll till dark is light,
Sex to sex, and even to odd;—
The over-god

Who marries Right to Might,
Who peoples, unpeoples,—
He who exterminates
Races by stronger races,
Black by white faces,—
Knows to bring honey
Out of the lion;
Grafts gentlest scion
On pirate and Turk.

The Cossack eats Poland,
Like stolen fruit;
Her last noble is ruined,
Her last poet mute:
Straight, into double band
The victors divide;
Half for freedom strike and stand;—
The astonished Muse finds thousands at her side.

JOHN GREENLEAF WHITTIER (1807–1892)

THE ANGELS OF BUENA VISTA

A letter-writer from Mexico during the Mexican war, when detailing some of the incidents at the terrible fight of Buena Vista, mentioned that Mexican women were seen hovering near the field of death, for the purpose of giving aid and succor to the wounded. One poor woman was found surrounded by the manned and suffering of both armies, ministering to the wants of Americans as well as Mexicans with impartial tenderness.

Speak and tell us, our Ximena, looking
        northward far away,
O'er the camp of the invaders, o'er the Mex-
        ican array,
Who is losing? who is winning? are they
        far or come they near?
Look abroad, and tell us, sister, whither
        rolls the storm we hear.

"Down the hills of Angostura still the storm
     of battle rolls;
Blood is flowing, men are dying; God have
     mercy on their souls!"
Who is losing? who is winning? "Over
     hill and over plain,
I see but smoke of cannon clouding through
     the mountain rain."

Holy Mother! keep our brothers! Look,
     Ximena, look once more.
"Still I see the fearful whirlwind rolling
     darkly as before,
Bearing on, in strange confusion, friend and
     foeman, foot and horse,
Like some wild and troubled torrent sweep-
     ing down its mountain course."

Look forth once more, Ximena! "Ah! the
     smoke has rolled away;
And I see the Northern rifles gleaming down
     the ranks of gray.
Hark! that sudden blast of bugles! there
     the troop of Minon wheels;
There the Northern horses thunder, with
     the cannon at their heels.

"Jesu, pity! how it thickens! now retreat
     and now advance!
Right against the blazing cannon shivers
     Puebla's charging lance!
Down they go, the brave young riders;
     horse and foot together fall;
Like a ploughshare in the fallow, through
     them ploughs the Northern ball."

Nearer came the storm and nearer, rolling
     fast and frightful on!

Speak, Ximena, speak and tell us, who has
      lost, and who has won?
"Alas! alas! I know not; friend and foe
      together fall,
O'er the dying rush the living: pray, my
      sisters, for them all!

"Lo! the wind the smoke is lifting.
      Blessed Mother, save my brain!
I can see the wounded crawling slowly out
      from heaps of slain.
Now they stagger, blind and bleeding; now
      they fall, and strive to rise;
Hasten, sisters, haste and save them, lest
      they die before our eyes!

"O my heart's love! O my dear one! lay
      thy poor head on my knee;
Dost thou know the lips that kiss thee?
      Canst thou hear me? canst thou see?
O my husband, brave and gentle! O my
      Bernal, look once more
On the blessed cross before thee! Mercy!
      Mercy! all is o'er!"

Dry thy tears, my poor Ximena; lay thy
      dear one down to rest;
Let his hands be meekly folded, lay the cross
      upon his breast;
Let his dirge be sung hereafter, and his
      funeral masses said;
To-day, thou poor bereaved one, the living
      ask thy aid.

Close beside her, faintly moaning, fair and
      young, a soldier lay,
Torn with shot and pierced with lances,
      bleeding slow his life away;

But, as tenderly before him the lorn Ximena
      knelt,
She saw the Northern eagle shining on his
      pistol-belt.

With a stifled cry of horror straight she
      turned away her head;
With a sad and bitter feeling looked she
      back upon her dead;
But she heard the youth's low moaning, and
      his struggling breath of pain,
And she raised the cooling water to his
      parching lips again.

Whispered low the dying soldier, pressed
      her hand and faintly smiled;
Was that pitying face his mother's? did
      she watch beside her child?
All his stranger words with meaning her
      woman's heart supplied;
With her kiss upon his forehead, "Mother!"
      murmured he, and died!

"A bitter curse upon them, poor boy, who
      led thee forth,
From some gentle, sad-eyed mother, weep-
      ing, lonely, in the North!"
Spake the mournful Mexic woman, as she
      laid him with her dead,
And turned to soothe the living, and bind
      the wounds which bled.

Look forth once more, Ximena! "Like a
      cloud before the wind
Rolls the battle down the mountains, leav-
      ing blood and death behind;
Ah! they plead in vain for mercy; in the
      dust the wounded strive;

Hide your faces, holy angels! O thou
    Christ of God, forgive!"

Sink, O Night, among thy mountains! let
    the cool, gray shadows fall;
Dying brothers, fighting demons, drop thy
    curtain over all!
Through the thickening winter twilight,
    wide apart the battle rolled,
In its sheath the sabre rested, and the can-
    non's lips grew cold.

But the noble Mexic women still their holy
    task pursued,
Through that long, dark night of sorrow,
    worn and faint and lacking food.
Over weak and suffering brothers, with a
    tender care they hung,
And the dying foeman blessed them in a
    strange and Northern tongue.

Not wholly lost, O Father! is this evil
    world of ours;
Upward, through its blood and ashes, spring
    afresh the Eden flowers;
From its smoking hell of battle, Love and
    Pity send their prayer,
And still thy white-winged angels hover
    dimly in our air!

JAMES RUSSELL LOWELL (1819–1891)

FROM THE BIGLOW PAPERS

Thrash away, you'll *hev* to rattle
    On them kittle drums o' yourn,—
'Taint a knowin' kind o' cattle
    Thet is ketched with mouldy corn;
Put in stiff, you fifer feller,
    Let folks see how spry you be,—
Guess you'll toot till you are yeller
    'Fore you git ahold o' me!

Thet air flag's a leetle rotten,
    Hope it aint your Sunday's best;—
Fact! it takes a sight o' cotton
    To stuff out a soger's chest:
Sence we farmers hev to pay fer 't,
    Ef you must wear humps like these,
Sposin' you should try salt hay fer 't,
    It would du ez slick ez grease.

'T wouldn't suit them Southern fellers,
    They're a dreffle graspin' set,
We must ollers blow the bellers
    Wen they want their irons het;
May be it's all right ez preachin',
    But *my* narves it kind o' grates,
Wen I see the overreachin'
    O' them nigger-drivin' States.

Them thet rule us, them slave-traders,
    Haint they cut a thunderin' swarth,
(Helped by Yankee renegaders,)
    Thru the vartu o' the North!
We begin to think it's nater
    To take sarse an' not be riled
Who'd expect to see a tater
    All on eend at bein' biled?

Ez fer war, I call it murder,—
 There you hev it plain an' flat
I don't want to go no furder
 Than my Testyment fer that
God hez sed so plump an' fairly.
 It's ez long ez it is broad,
An' you 've gut to git up airly
 Ef you want to take in God.

'Taint your eppyletts an' feathers
 Make the thing a grain more right;
'Taint afollerin' your bell-wethers
 Will excuse ye in His sight;
Ef you take a sword an' dror it,
 An' go stick a feller thru,
Guv'ment aint to answer for it,
 God'll send the bill to you.

Wut's the use o' meetin-goin'
 Every Sabbath, wet or dry,
Ef it's right to go amowin'
 Feller-men like oats an' rye?
I dunno but wut it's pooty
 Trainin' round in bobtail coats,—
But it's curus Christian dooty
 This ere cuttin' folks's throats.

They may talk o' Freedom's airy
 Tell they're pupple in the face,—
It's a grand gret cemetary
 Fer the barthrights of our race;
They jest want this Californy
 So's to lug new slave-states in
To abuse ye, an' to scorn ye,
 An' to plunder ye like sin.

Aint it cute to see a Yankee
 Take sech everlastin' pains

All to git the Devil's thankee,
    Helpin' on 'em weld their chains?
Wy, it's jest ez clear ez figgers,
    Clear ez one an' one make two,
Chaps thet make black slaves o' niggers
    Want to make wite slaves o' you.

Tell ye jest the eend I've come to
    Arter cipherin' plaguy smart,
An' it makes a handy sum, tu,
    Any gump could larn by heart;
Laborin' man an' laborin' woman
    Hev one glory an' one shame,
Ev'y thin' thet's done inhuman
    Injers all on 'em the same.

'Taint by turnin' out to hack folks
    You're agoin' to git your right,—
Nor by lookin' down on black folks
    Coz you're put upon by wite;
Slavery aint o' nary color,
    'Taint the hide thet makes it wus,
All it keers fer in a feller
    'S jest to make him fill its pus.

Want to tackle *me* in, du ye?
    I expect you'll hev to wait;
Wen cold lead puts daylight thru ye
    You'll begin to kal'late;
'Spose the crows wun't fall to pickin'
    All the carkiss from your bones,
Coz you helped to give a lickin'
    To them poor half-Spanish drones?

Jest go home an' ask our Nancy
    Wether I'd be sech a goose
Ez to jine ye—guess you'd fancy
    The etarnal bung wuz loose!

She wants me fer home consumption,
    Let alone the hay's to mow,—
Ef you're arter folks o' gumption,
    You've a darned long row to hoe.

Take them editors thet's crowin'
    Like a cockerel three months old,—
Don't ketch any on 'em goin',
    Though they *be* so blasted bold;
Aint they a prime set o' fellers?
    'Fore they think on 't they will sprout,
(Like a peach thet's got the yellers,)
    With the meanness bustin' out.

Wal, go 'long to help 'em stealin'
    Bigger pens to cram with slaves,
Help the men thet's ollers dealin'
    Insults on your fathers' graves;
Help the strong to grind the feeble,
    Help the many agin the few,
Help the men thet call your people
    Witewashed slaves an' peddlin' crew!

Massachusetts, God forgive her,
    She's akneelin' with the rest,
She, thet ough' to ha' clung fer ever
    In her grand old eagle-nest;
She thet ough' to stand so fearless
    Wile the wracks are round her hurled,
Holdin' up a beacon peerless
    To the oppressed of all the world!

Haint they sold your colored seamen?
    Haint they made your env'ys wiz¯?
Wut'll make ye act like freemen?
    Wut'll git your dander riz?
Come, I'll tell ye wut I'm thinkin'
    Is our dooty in this fix,

They'd ha' done 't ez quick ez winkin'
    In the days o' seventy-six.

Clang the bells in every steeple,
    Call all true men to disown
The tradoocers of our people,
    The enslavers o' their own;
Let our dear old Bay State proudly
    Put the trumpet to her mouth,
Let her ring this messidge loudly
    In the ears of all the South:—

"I'll return ye good fer evil
    Much ez we frail mortils can,
But I wun't go help the Devil
    Makin' man the cus o' man;
Call me coward, call me traiter,
    Jest ez suits your mean idees,—
Here I stand a tyrant-hater,
    An' the friend o' God an' Peace!"

Ef I'd *my* way I hed ruther
    We should go to work an' part,—
They take one way, we take t'other,—
    Guess it wouldn't break my heart;
Man hed ough' to put asunder
    Them thet God, has noways jined;
An' I shouldn't gretly wonder
    Ef there's thousands o' my mind.

HENRY DAVID THOREAU (1817–1862)

"WHEN WITH PALE CHEEK AND SUNKEN EYE I SANG"

When with pale cheek and sunken eye I sang
Unto the slumbering world at midnight's hour,
How it no more resounded with war's clang,
And virtue was decayed in Peace's bower;

How in these days no hero was abroad,
But puny men, afraid of war's alarms,
Stood forth to fight the battles of their Lord,
Who scarce could stand beneath a hero's arms;

A faint, reproachful, reassuring strain,
From some harp's string touched by unskillful hands
Brought back the days of chivalry again,
And the surrounding fields made holy lands.

A bustling camp and an embattled host
Extending far on either hand I saw,
For I alone had slumbered at my post,
Dreaming of peace when all abroad was war.

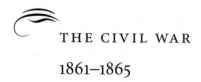

THE CIVIL WAR

1861–1865

The dead in this war—there they lie, strewing the fields and woods and valleys and battlefields of the South—Virginia, the Peninsula, Malvern Hill and Fair Oaks, the banks of the Chickahominy, the terraces of Fredericksburg, Antietam Bridge, the grisly ravines of Manassas, the bloody promenade of the Wilderness; the varieties of the strayed dead (the estimate of the War Department is twenty-five thousand national soldiers killed in battle and never buried at all; three thousand drowned; fifteen thousand inhumed by strangers or on the march in haste, in hitherto unfound localities; two thousand graves covered by sand and mud, by Mississippi freshets; three thousand carried away by caving-in of banks, etc.; Gettysburg, the West, Southwest, Vicksburg, Chattanooga, the trenches of Petersburg; the numberless battles, camps, hospitals everywhere; the crop reaped by the mighty reapers—typhoid, dysentery, inflammations; and—blackest and loathsomest of all—the dead and living burial pits—the prison pens of Andersonville, Salisbury, Belle Isle, etc.). . . . The dead, the dead, the dead, our dead—

—Walt Whitman, "The Million Dead, Too, Summed Up," from *Walt Whitman's Civil War*, edited by Walter Lowenfels (1960)

By the time Robert E. Lee surrendered to Ulysses Grant in 1865 at the courthouse in Appomattox, 618,000 soldiers had died in the Civil War, or nearly as many as would die in the whole of all other American wars. Approximately 1,500,000 men served as long-term Union soldiers, and the Confederacy mustered 900,000 such men out of a white population of six million. Roughly 180,000 black troops enlisted for the Union cause, about 65 percent of their number from the South. On both sides, these were armies of citizen soldiers, although on either side exemption from service could be purchased or substitutes arranged for by the well-to-do; a move to draft soldiers, however, resulted in a four-day race riot in New York City, with over a hundred killed, including at least eleven black men, eight soldiers, and two policemen. For both Union and Confederate sides, sickness killed troops in larger numbers than armed combat.

Of the first of our modern wars, Howard Mumford Jones wrote that it "dramatized ingenuity, it accustomed people to mass and size and uniformity and national action," and it got them used to "ruthlessness," all of which in T. Harry Williams's eyes gave "shape and size" to our institutions. Mobilizing for a protracted, massive engagement changed our finance, transport, communications, and manufacturing industries forever. Militarily, it meant the introduction of armored ships, new forms of gunnery including a prototype of the machine gun, land and sea mines, submarines, and trench warfare. Casualties from traditional frontal engagement in rigid lines were overwhelming: many units on both sides sustained losses of 40 to 80 percent in a single fight. In the trench warfare of the final year, in T. Harry Williams's words, "armies disappeared into the earth," as both attackers and defenders dug in deep in an attempt to evade the withering onslaught of artillery. The final, strung-out engagements prefigured the war of attrition that was World War I. General William T. Sherman ripped across Georgia, burning and pillaging in an attempt to break the civilian will that supported resistance, waging what would later be defined as "total war."

While it is true that many on the Union side cared nothing about freeing slaves, and that many on the Southern side fought simply to repel the invaders of their own soil, the Civil War still remained a war of competing ideologies. In the North, hundreds of thousands understood that they were at war for the preservation of the Union, and yes, finally to end the institution of slavery; on the Southern side, hundreds of thousands fought for their right to have their own autonomous government and maintain slavery. By 1862, President Lincoln had suspended the writ of habeas corpus, and during the course of the war arrested over 13,000 people who were accused of discouraging enlistment, resisting the draft, or other "disloyal practices." Nevertheless, he remains one of the most iconic and articulate of American presidents.

The commemoration of a horrific bloodletting dominates the literature of the period. This was the major war of American history, and the shock waves of its fratricidal passage can still be felt in our history and in our imaginative literature. The poetry of the Civil War includes a copious lyric description and reflection by a major novelist, Herman Melville, and by Walt Whitman, who is recognized by all readers of English as not only a great poet, but as one who was signally American. Yet even Whitman could only point to the unspeakable and incommensurable elements of this war—to the "real war" he said that would never get into the history books. All were aided in their hunt for the look of the "real war" by the first combat photographs, taken by Matthew Brady and his numerous colleagues. Death and grief flow unstoppably over these poems.

I have attempted a balance between Northern and Southern perspectives. However, most of the book writers and book buyers in mid-nineteenth-century America lived in the Northeast, clustered around cities. As a result, the North produced more writers for their side of the war. While flags and other emblems of war still appear in the poems, and poets include sights of encampments and of armies on the move, the memory of wounds and death, and of an enduring and widespread sorrow, pervade the literature of both sides. Commemorative attempts continue to glorify as well as to demystify the action, rendering its complex cultural and national meanings in language both formal and vernacular. In these reworkings of people, events, and even the idea of glory itself, poets continue to connect and reconnect this war to its present descendants.

This section includes a group of twentieth-century writers. When Andrew Hudgins, an ex-Marine, drew on a memoir by Confederate soldier and poet Sidney Lanier to write a sequence of poems on the Civil War, an extract of which is provided in this section, he joins two memories and two traditions of war and literary experience. Poignantly, one of the chief boosters of the military ardor of the Northern forces, Julia Ward Howe, followed her far more famous "Battle Hymn of the Republic" with a wholly pacifistic postwar document issued as the "Mothers' Day Proclamation." In the poems of this war, not just the soldiers, not just the mourners, but the civilians who tend to the broken bodies of the war come into view. Abraham Lincoln, his face, voice, and person prominent in the literature and the documents of the age, remains an icon of both the grief and triumph of the war.

WILLIAM GILMORE SIMMS (1806–1870)

THE VOICE OF MEMORY IN EXILE, FROM A HOME IN ASHES

Ever a voice is pleading at my heart,
    With mournful pleading, ever soft and low,
    Yet deep as with an ocean's overflow,
"Depart! depart! Why wilt thou not depart?
Here are no blossoms such as live; no flowers,
    Such as with sacred scent and happy glow,
Recall Elysian homes, and those dear hours,
When with the breezes sporting in our bowers,
And the soft moonlight sweet'ning the old towers,
There was no tree that sheltered not its bird,
    No shrub without its song and summer bloom,
And never a fate was nigh, with threatening word,
    Articulate of the terror and the doom.
Were not the wings contented there in home
    That never lacked its sunshine and its songs?
We did not lack, beneath the grand old dome,
    The joy of solitude, though bless'd with throngs,
Coming and going; blessing as they came,
    And having solace in the bliss they found:
Depart! depart! and ye shall find the same,
    Nor wither in this cold and foreign ground!"
Alas! alas! for the poor home and heart
That still from out their ashes cry "depart!"

HENRY WADSWORTH LONGFELLOW (1807–1882)

THE ARSENAL AT SPRINGFIELD

This is the Arsenal. From floor to ceiling,
    Like a huge organ, rise the burnished arms;
But from their silent pipes no anthem pealing
    Startles the villages with strange alarms.

Ah! what a sound will rise, how wild and dreary,
    When the death-angel touches those swift keys!
What loud lament and dismal Miserere
    Will mingle with their awful symphonies!

I hear even now the infinite fierce chorus,
    The cries of agony, the endless groan,
Which, through the ages that have gone before us,
    In long reverberations reach our own.

On helm and harness rings the Saxon hammer,
    Through Cimbric[1] forest roars the Norseman's song,
And loud, amid the universal clamor,
    O'er distant deserts sounds the Tartar gong.

I hear the Florentine, who from his palace
    Wheels out his battle-bell with dreadful din,
And Aztec priests upon their teocallis[2]
    Beat the wild war-drums made of serpent's skin;

The tumult of each sacked and burning village;
    The shout that every prayer for mercy drowns;
The soldiers' revels in the midst of pillage;
    The wail of famine in beleaguered towns;

The bursting shell, the gateway wrenched asunder,
    The rattling musketry, the clashing blade;
And ever and anon, in tones of thunder
    The diapason of the cannonade.

Is it, O man, with such discordant noises,
    With such accursed instruments as these,
Thou drownest Nature's sweet and kindly voices,
    And jarrest the celestial harmonies?

---

[1] An ancient tribe (Cimbrii) inhabiting Northern Germany.
[2] Literally, "god's house": a temple, usually pyramidal in form.

Were half the power, that fills the world with terror,
    Were half the wealth bestowed on camps and courts,
Given to redeem the human mind from error,
    There were no need of arsenals or forts:

The warrior's name would be a name abhorred!
    And every nation, that should lift again
Its hand against a brother, on its forehead
    Would wear forevermore the curse of Cain!

Down the dark future, through long generations,
    The echoing sounds grow fainter and then cease;
And like a bell, with solemn, sweet vibrations,
    I hear once more the voice of Christ say, "Peace!"

Peace! and no longer from its brazen portals
    The blast of War's great organ shakes the skies!
But beautiful as songs of the immortals,
    The holy melodies of love arise.

JOHN GREENLEAF WHITTIER (1807–1892)

BARBARA FRIETCHIE

Up from the meadows rich with corn,
Clear in the cool September morn,

The clustered spires of Frederick stand
Green-walled by the hills of Maryland.

Round about them orchards sweep,
Apple and peach tree fruited deep,

Fair as the garden of the Lord
To the eyes of the famished Rebel horde,

On that pleasant morn of the early fall
When Lee marched over the mountain-wall;

Over the mountains winding down,
Horse and foot, into Frederick town.

Forty flags with their silver stars,
Forty flags with their crimson bars,

Flapped in the morning wind: the sun
Of noon looked down, and saw not one.

Up rose old Barbara Frietchie then,
Bowed with her fourscore years and ten;

Bravest of all in Frederick town,
She took up the flag the men hauled down;

In her attic window the staff she set,
To show that one heart was loyal yet.

Up the street came the rebel tread,
Stonewall Jackson riding ahead.

Under his slouched hat left and right
He glanced; the old flag met his sight.

"Halt!"—the dust-brown ranks stood fast.
"Fire!"—out blazed the rifle-blast.

It shivered the window, pane and sash;
It rent the banner with seam and gash.

Quick, as it fell, from the broken staff
Dame Barbara snatched the silken scarf.

She learned far out on the window-sill,
And shook it forth with a royal will.

"Shoot, if you must, this old gray head,
But spare your country's flag," she said.

A shade of sadness, a blush of shame,
Over the face of the leader came;

The nobler nature within him stirred
To life at that woman's deed and word;

"Who touches a hair of yon gray head
Dies like a dog! March on!" he said.

All day long through Frederick street
Sounded the tread of marching feet:

All day long that free flag tossed
Over the heads of the Rebel host.

Ever its torn folds rose and fell
On the loyal winds that loved it well;

And through the hill-gaps sunset light
Shone over it with a warm good-night.

Barbara Frietchie's work is o'er,
And the Rebel rides on his raids no more.

Honor to her! and let a tear
Fall, for her sake, on Stonewall's bier.

Over Barbara Frietchie's grave,
Flag of Freedom and Union, wave!

Peace and order and beauty draw
Round thy symbol of light and law;

And ever the stars above look down
On thy stars below in Frederick town!

THE BATTLE AUTUMN OF 1862

The flags of war like storm-birds fly,
    The charging trumpets blow,
Yet rolls no thunder in the sky,
    No earthquake strives below.

And, calm and patient, Nature keeps
    Her ancient promise well,
Though o'er her bloom and greenness sweeps
    The battle's breath of hell.

And still she walks in golden hours
    Through harvest-happy farms,
And still she wears her fruits and flowers
    Like jewels on her arms.

What mean the gladness of the plain,
    This joy of eve and morn,
The mirth that shakes the beard of grain
    And yellow locks of corn?

Oh, eyes may be full of tears,
    And hearts with hate are hot;
But even-paced come round the years,
    And Nature changes not.

She meets with smiles our bitter grief,
    With songs our groans of pain;
She mocks with tint of flower and leaf
    The war-field's crimson stain.

Still, in the cannon's pause, we hear
    Her sweet thanksgiving-psalm;
Too near to God for doubt or fear,
    She shares the eternal calm.

She knows the seed lies safe below
    The fires that blast and burn;
For all the tears of blood we sow
    She waits the rich return.

She sees with clearer eye than ours
    The good of suffering born—
The hearts that blossom like her flowers,
    And ripen like her corn.

Oh, give to us, in times like these,
    The vision of her eyes;
And make her fields and fruited trees
    Our golden prophecies.

Oh, give to us her finer ear,
    Above this stormy din.
We too would hear the bells of cheer
    Ring peace and freedom in.

HERMAN MELVILLE (1819–1891)

THE MARCH INTO VIRGINIA, ENDING IN THE FIRST MANASSAS

JULY, 1861

Did all the lets and bars appear
    To every just or larger end,
Whence should come the trust and cheer?
    Youth must its ignorant impulse lend—
Age finds place in the rear.
    All wars are boyish, and are fought by boys,

The champions and enthusiasts of the state:
  Turbid ardors and vain joys
    Not barrenly abate—
  Stimulants to the power mature,
    Preparatives of fate.

Who here forecasteth the event?
What heart but spurns at precedent
And warnings of the wise,
Contemned foreclosures of surprise?
The banners play, the bugles call,
The air is blue and prodigal.
  No berrying party, pleasure-wooed,
No picnic party in the May,
Ever went less loth than they
  Into that leafy neighborhood.
In Bacchic glee they file toward Fate,
Moloch's uninitiate;
Expectancy, and glad surmise
Of battle's unknown mysteries.
All they feel is this: 'tis glory,
A rapture sharp, though transitory,
Yet lasting in belaureled story.
So they gayly go to fight,
Chatting left and laughing right.

But some who this blithe mood present,
  As on in lightsome files they fare,
Shall die experienced ere three days are spent—
  Perish, enlightened by the vollied glare;
Or shame survive, and, like to adamant,
  The throe of Second Manassas share.

BALL'S BLUFF[3]

A REVERIE

OCTOBER, 1861

One noonday, at my window in the town,
   I saw a sight—saddest that eyes can see—
   Young soldiers marching lustily
      Unto the wars,
With fifes, and flags in mottoed pageantry;
    While all the porches, walks, and doors
Were rich with ladies cheering royally.

They moved like Juny morning on the wave,
   Their hearts were fresh as clover in its prime
   (It was the breezy summer time),
      Life throbbed so strong,
How should they dream that Death in a rosy clime
    Would come to thin their shining throng?
Youth feels immortal, like the gods sublime.

Weeks passed; and at my window, leaving bed,
   By night I mused, of easeful sleep bereft,
   On those brave boys (Ah War! thy theft);
      Some marching feet
Found pause at last by cliffs Potomac cleft;
    Wakeful I mused, while in the street
Far footfalls died away till none were left.

---

[3] Ball's Bluff is the site of a Confederate victory. The Union army's badly coordinated attempt to cross the Potomac and capture Leesburg resulted in the army being driven over the bluff and into a river.

A UTILITARIAN VIEW OF THE MONITOR'S FIGHT

Plain be the phrase, yet apt the verse,
    More ponderous than nimble;
For since grimed War here laid aside
His Orient pomp, 'twould ill befit
        Overmuch to ply
    The rhyme's barbaric cymbal.

Hail to victory without the gaud
    Of glory; zeal that needs no fans
Of banners; plain mechanic power
Plied cogently in War now placed—
        Where War belongs—
    Among the trades and artisans.

Yet this was battle, and intense—
    Beyond the strife of fleets heroic;
Deadlier, closer, calm 'mid storm;
No passion; all went on by crank,
        Pivot, and screw,
    And calculations of caloric.

Needless to dwell; the story's known.
    The ringing of those plates on plates
Still ringeth round the world—
The clangor of that blacksmith's fray.
        The anvil-din
    Resounds this message from the Fates:

War shall yet be, and to the end;
    But war-paint shows the streaks of weather;
War yet shall be, but warriors
Are now but operatives; War's made
        Less grand than Peace,
    And a singe runs through lace and feather.

SHILOH

A REQUIEM

Skimming lightly, wheeling still,
    The swallows fly low
Over the field in clouded days,
    The forest-field of Shiloh—
Over the field where April rain
Solaced the parched ones stretched in pain
Through the pause of night
That followed the Sunday fight
    Around the church of Shiloh—
The church so lone, the log-built one,
That echoed to many a parting groan
        And natural prayer
    Of dying foemen mingled there—
Foemen at morn, but friends at eve—
    Fame or country least their care:
(What like a bullet can undeceive!)
    But now they lie low,
While over them the swallows skim,
    And all is hushed at Shiloh.

THE COLLEGE COLONEL

He rides at their head;
    A crutch by his saddle just slants into view,
One slung arm is in splints, you see,
    Yet he guides his strong steed—how coldly too.

He brings his regiment home—
    Not as they filed two years before,
But a remnant half-tattered, and battered, and worn,
Like castaway sailors, who—stunned
    By the surf's loud roar,
    Their mates dragged back and seen no more—
Again and again breast the surge,
    And at last crawl, spent, to shore.

A still rigidity and pale—
   An Indian aloofness lones his brow;
He has lived a thousand years
Compressed in battle's pains and prayers,
   Marches and watches slow.
There are welcoming shouts, and flags;
   Old men off hat to the Boy,
Wreaths from gay balconies fall at his feet,
   But to *him*—there comes alloy.

It is not that a leg is lost,
   It is not that an arm is maimed,
It is not that the fever has racked—
   Self he has long disclaimed.

But all through the Seven Days' Fight,
   And deep in the Wilderness grim,
And in the field-hospital tent,
   And Petersburg crater, and dim
Lean brooding in Libby,[4] there came—
   Ah heaven!—what *truth* to him.

JULIA WARD HOWE (1819–1910)

THE BATTLE HYMN OF THE REPUBLIC

Mine eyes have seen the glory of the coming of the Lord;
He is trampling out the vintage where the grapes of wrath are stored;
He hath loosed the fatal lightning of His terrible swift sword:
   His truth is marching on.

I have seen Him in the watch-fires of a hundred circling camps.
They have builded Him an altar in the evening dews and damps;

[4] An infamous Confederate prison in Richmond, Virginia, used by the Union Army after the war.

I can read His righteous sentence by the dim and flaring lamps:
   His day is marching on.

I have read a fiery gospel writ in burnished rows of steel:
"As ye deal with my contemners, so with you my grace shall deal;
Let the Hero, born of woman, crush the serpent with his heel,
   Since God is marching on."

He has sounded forth the trumpet that shall never call retreat;
He is sifting out the hearts of men before his judgment seat:
Oh, be swift, my soul, to answer Him! Be jubilant, my feet!
   Our God is marching on.

In the beauty of the lilies Christ was born across the sea,
With a glory in his bosom that transfigures you and me:
As he died to make men holy, let us die to make men free,
   While God is marching on.

WALT WHITMAN (1819–1892)

CAVALRY CROSSING A FORD

A line in long array where they wind betwixt green islands,
They take a serpentine course, their arms flash in the sun—hark to the
   musical clank,
Behold the silvery river, in it the splashing horses loitering stop to drink,
Behold the brown-faced men, each group, each person a picture, the
   negligent rest on the saddles,
Some emerge on the opposite bank, others are just entering the ford—
   while,
Scarlet and blue and snowy white,
The guidon[5] flags flutter gayly in the wind.

---

[5] A pennant marking a military unit.

By the Bivouac's Fitful Flame

By the bivouac's fitful flame,
A procession winding around me, solemn and sweet and slow—but first
    I note,
The tents of the sleeping army, the fields' and woods' dim outline,
The darkness lit by spots of kindled fire, the silence,
Like a phantom far or near an occasional figure moving,
The shrubs and trees, (as I lift my eyes they seem to be stealthily watch-
    ing me,)
While wind in procession thoughts; O tender and wondrous thoughts,
Of life and death, of home and the past and loved, and of those that are
    far away;
A solemn and slow procession there as I sit on the ground,
By the bivouac's fitful flame.

Come Up from the Fields Father

Come up from the fields father, here's a letter from our Pete,
And come to the front door mother, here's a letter from thy dear son.

Lo, 'tis autumn,
Lo, where the trees, deeper green, yellower and redder,
Cool and sweeten Ohio's villages with leaves fluttering in the moderate
    wind,
Where apples ripe in the orchards hang and grapes on the trellis'd vines,
(Smell you the smell of the grapes on the vines?
Smell you the buckwheat where the bees were lately buzzing?)
Above all, lo, the sky so calm, so transparent after the rain, and with
    wondrous clouds,
Below too, all calm, all vital and beautiful, and the farm prospers well.

Down in the fields all prospers well,
But now from the fields come father, come at the daughter's call,
And come to the entry mother, to the front door come right away.

Fast as she can she hurries, something ominous, her steps trembling,
She does not tarry to smooth her hair nor adjust her cap.

Open the envelope quickly,
O *this* is not our son's writing, yet his name is sign'd,
O a strange hand writes for our dear son, O stricken mother's soul!
All swims before her eyes, flashes with black, she catches the main words
   only,
Sentences broken, *gunshot wound in the breast, cavalry skirmish, taken to
   hospital,*
At present low, but will soon be better.

Ah now the single figure to me,
Amid all teeming and wealthy Ohio with all its cities and farms,
Sickly white in the face and dull in the head, very faint,
By the jamb of a door leans.

Grieve not so, dear mother, (the just-grown daughter speaks through her
   sobs,
The little sisters huddle around speechless and dismay'd,)
See, dearest mother, the letter says Pete will soon be better.

Alas poor boy, he will never be better, (nor may-be needs to be better,
   that brave and simple soul,)
While they stand at home at the door he is dead already,
The only son is dead.

But the mother needs to be better,
She with thin form presently drest in black,
By day her meals untouch'd, then at night fitfully sleeping, often waking,
In the midnight waking, weeping, longing with one deep longing,
O that she might withdraw unnoticed, silent from life escape and with-
   draw,
To follow, to seek, to be with her dear dead son.

A MARCH IN THE RANKS HARD-PREST, AND THE ROAD UNKNOWN

A march in the ranks hard-prest, and the road unknown,
A route through a heavy wood with muffled steps in the darkness,
Our army foil'd with loss severe, and the sullen remnant retreating,

Till after midnight glimmer upon us the lights of a dim-lighted building.
We come to an open space in the woods, and halt by the dim-lighted
  building,
'Tis a large old church at the crossing roads, now an impromptu hospi-
  tal,
Entering but for a minute I see a sight beyond all the pictures and poems
  ever made,
Shadows of deepest, deepest black, just lit by moving candles and lamps,
And by one great pitchy torch stationary with wild red flame and clouds
  of smoke,
By these, crowds, groups of forms vaguely I see on the floor, some in the
  pews laid down,
At my feet more distinctly a soldier, a mere lad, in danger of bleeding to
  death, (he is shot in the abdomen,)
I stanch the blood temporarily, (the youngster's face is white as a lily,)
Then before I depart I sweep my eyes o'er the scene fain to absorb it all,
Faces, varieties, postures beyond description, most in obscurity, some of
  them dead,
Surgeons operating, attendants holding lights, the smell of ether, the
  odor of blood,
The crowd, O the crowd of the bloody forms, the yard outside also fill'd,
Some on the bare ground, some on planks or stretchers, some in the
  death-spasm sweating,
An occasional scream or cry, the doctor's shouted orders or calls,
The glisten of the little steel instruments catching the glint of the
  torches,
These I resume as I chant, I see again the forms, I smell the odor,
Then hear outside the orders given, *Fall in, my men, fall in;*
But first I bend to the dying lad, his eyes open, a half-smile gives he me,
Then the eyes close, calmly close, and I speed forth to the darkness,
Resuming, marching, ever in darkness marching, on in the ranks,
The unknown road still marching.

THE WOUND-DRESSER

1

An old man bending I come among new faces,
Years looking backward resuming in answer to children,

Come tell us old man, as from young men and maidens that love me,
(Arous'd and angry, I'd thought to beat the alarum, and urge relentless
 war,
But soon my fingers fail'd me, my face droop'd and I resign'd myself
To sit by the wounded and soothe them, or silently watch the dead;)
Years hence of these scenes, of these furious passions, these chances,
Of unsurpass'd heroes, (was one side so brave? the other was equally
 brave;)
Now be witness again, paint the mightiest armies of earth,
Of those armies so rapid so wondrous what saw you to tell us?
What stays with you latest and deepest? of curious panics,
Of hard-fought engagements or sieges tremendous what deepest
 remains?

2

O maidens and young men I love and that love me,
What you ask of my days those the strangest and sudden your talking
 recalls,
Soldier alert I arrive after a long march cover'd with sweat and dust,
In the nick of time I come, plunge in the fight, loudly shout in the rush
 of successful charge,
Enter the captur'd works—yet lo, like a swift-running river they fade,
Pass and are gone they fade—I dwell not on soldiers' perils or soldiers'
 joys,
(Both I remember well—many of the hardships, few the joys, yet I was
 content;)

But in silence, in dreams' projections,
While the world of gain and appearance and mirth goes on,
So soon what is over forgotten, and waves wash the imprints off the
 sand,
With hinged knees returning I enter the doors, (while for you up there,
Whoever you are, follow without noise and be of strong heart.)

Bearing the bandages, water and sponge,
Straight and swift to my wounded I go,
Where they lie on the ground after the battle brought in,
Where their priceless blood reddens the grass the ground,
Or to the rows of the hospital tent, or under the roof'd hospital,

To the long rows of cots up and down each side I return,
To each and all one after another I draw near, not one do I miss,
An attendant follows holding a tray, he carries a refuse pail,
Soon to be fill'd with clotted rags and blood, emptied, and fill'd again.

I onward go, I stop,
With hinged knees and steady hand to dress wounds,
I am firm with each, the pangs are sharp yet unavoidable,
One turns to me his appealing eyes—poor boy! I never knew you,
Yet I think I could not refuse this moment to die for you, if that would
    save you.

3

On, on I go, (open doors of time! open hospital doors!)
The crush'd head I dress, (poor crazed hand tear not the bandage away,)
The neck of the cavalry-man with the bullet through and through I
    examine,
Hard the breathing rattles, quite glazed already the eye, yet life struggles
    hard,
(Come sweet death! be persuaded O beautiful death!
In mercy come quickly.)

From the stump of the arm, the amputated hand,
I undo the clotted lint, remove the slough, wash off the matter and
    blood,
Back on his pillow the soldier bends with curv'd neck and side falling
    head,
His eyes are closed, his face is pale, he dares not look on the bloody
    stump,
And has not yet look'd on it.

I dress a wound in the side, deep, deep,
But a day or two more, for see the frame all wasted and sinking,
And the yellow-blue countenance see.

I dress the perforated shoulder, the foot with the bullet-wound,
Cleanse the one with a gnawing and putrid gangrene, so sickening, so
    offensive,
While the attendant stands behind aside me holding the tray and pail.

I am faithful, I do not give out,
The fractur'd thigh, the knee, the wound in the abdomen,
These and more I dress with impassive hand, (yet deep in my breast a
    fire, a burning flame.)

4

Thus in silence in dreams' projections,
Returning, resuming, I thread my way through the hospitals,
The hurt and wounded I pacify with soothing hand,
I sit by the restless all the dark night, some are so young,
Some suffer so much, I recall the experience sweet and sad,
(Many a soldier's loving arms about this neck have cross'd and rested,
Many a soldier's kiss dwells on these bearded lips.)

RECONCILIATION

Word over all, beautiful as the sky,
Beautiful that war and all its deeds of carnage must in time be utterly
    lost,
That the hands of the sisters Death and Night incessantly softly wash
    again, and ever again, this soil'd world;
For my enemy is dead, a man divine as myself is dead,
I look where he lies white-faced and still in the coffin—I draw near,
Bend down and touch lightly with my lips the white face in the coffin.

O CAPTAIN! MY CAPTAIN!

O Captain! my Captain! our fearful trip is done,
The ship has weather'd every rack, the prize we sought is won,
The port is near, the bells I hear, the people all exulting,
While follow eyes the steady keel, the vessel grim and daring;
        But O heart! heart! heart!
        O the bleeding drops of red,
            Where on the deck my Captain lies,
                Fallen cold and dead.

O Captain! my Captain! rise up and hear the bells;
Rise up—for you the flag is flung—for you the bugle trills,

For you bouquets and ribbon'd wreaths—for you the shores a-crowding,
For you they call, the swaying mass, their eager faces turning;
 Here Captain! dear Father!
  This arm beneath your head!
   It is some dream that on the deck,
    You've fallen cold and dead.

My Captain does not answer, his lips are pale and still,
My father does not feel my arm, he has no pulse nor will,
The ship is anchor'd safe and sound, its voyage closed and done,
From fearful trip the victor ship comes in with object won:
 Exult O shores, and ring O bells!
  But I with mournful tread,
   Walk the deck my Captain lies,
    Fallen cold and dead.

HENRY TIMROD (1829–1867)

CHARLESTON

Calm as that second summer which precedes
 The first fall of the snow,
In the broad sunlight of heroic deeds,
 The city bides the foe.

As yet, behind their ramparts, stern and proud,
 Her bolted thunders sleep,—
Dark Sumter, like a battlemented cloud,
 Looms o'er the solemn deep.

No Calpe[6] frowns from lofty cliff or scaur
 To guard the holy strand;
But Moultrie[7] holds in leash her dogs of war
 Above the level sand.

[6] The ancient name of Gibraltar.
[7] A fort defending the coast of South Carolina.

And down the dunes a thousand guns lie couched,
    Unseen, beside the flood,—
Like tigers in some Orient jungle crouched
    That wait and watch for blood.

Meanwhile, through streets still echoing with trade,
    Walk grave and thoughtful men,
Whose hands may one day wield the patriot's blade
    As lightly as the pen.

And maidens, with such eyes as would grow dim
    Over a bleeding hound,
Seem each one to have caught the strength of him
    Whose sword she sadly bound.

Thus girt without and garrisoned at home,
    Day patient following day,
Old Charleston looks from roof and spire and dome,
    Across her tranquil bay.

Ships, through a hundred foes, from Saxon lands
    And spicy Indian ports,
Bring Saxon steel and iron to her hands,
    And Summer to her courts.

But still, along yon dim Atlantic line,
    The only hostile smoke
Creeps like a harmless mist above the brine,
    From some frail, floating oak.

Shall the Spring dawn, and she, still clad in smiles,
    And with an unscathed brow,
Rest in the strong arms of her palm-crowned isles,
    As fair and free as now?

We know not; in the temple of the Fates
    God has inscribed her doom;
And, all untroubled in her faith, she waits
    The triumph or the tomb.

THE UNKNOWN DEAD

The rain is plashing on my sill,
But all the winds of Heaven are still;
And so, it falls with that dull sound
Which thrills us in the churchyard ground,
When the first spadeful drops like lead
Upon the coffin of the dead.
Beyond my streaming window-pane,
I cannot see the neighboring vane,
Yet from its old familiar tower
The bell comes, muffled, through the shower.
What strange and unsuspected link
Of feeling touched has made me think—
While with a vacant soul and eye
I watch that gray and stony sky—
Of nameless graves on battle plains,
Washed by a single winter's rains,
Where, some beneath Virginian hills,
And some by green Atlantic rills,
Some by the waters of the West,
A myriad unknown heroes rest?
Ah! not the chiefs who, dying, see
Their flag's in front of victory,
Or, at their life-blood's noblest cost
Pay for a battle nobly lost,
Claim from their monumental beds
The bitterest tears a nation sheds.
Beneath yon lonely mound—the spot,
By all save some fond few forgot—
Lie the true martyrs of the fight,
Which strikes for freedom and for right.
Of them, their patriot zeal and pride,
The lofty faith that with them died,
No grateful page shall further tell
Than that so many bravely fell;
And we can only dimly guess
What worlds of all this world's distress,

What utter woe, despair, and dearth,
Their fate has brought to many a hearth.
Just such a sky as this should weep
Above them, always, where they sleep;
Yet, haply, at this very hour,—
Their graves are like a lover's bower;
And Nature's self, with eyes unwet,
Oblivious of the crimson debt
To which she owes her April grace,
Laughs gayly o'er their burial place.

JOHN WILLIAM DE FOREST (1826–1909)

In Louisiana

THIBODEAUX, LA., MARCH, 1863.

Without a hillock stretched the plain;
    For months we had not seen a hill;
    The endless, flat Savannahs still
Wearied our eyes with waving cane.

One tangled cane-field lay before
    The ambush of the cautious foe;
    Behind a black bayou, with low
Reed-hidden, miry, treacherous shore;

A sullen swamp along the right,
    Where alligators slept and crawled,
    And moss-robed cypress giants sprawled
Athwart the noontide's blistering light.

Quick, angry spite of musketry
    Proclaimed our skirmishers at work;
    We saw their crouching figures lurk
Through thickets firing from the knee.

Our Parrotts[8] felt the distant wood
 With humming, shrieking, growling shell;
 When suddenly the mouth of hell
Gaped fiercely for its human food.

A long and low blue roll of smoke
 Curled up a hundred yards ahead,
 And deadly storms of driving lead
From rifle-pits and cane-fields broke.

Then, while the bullets whistled thick,
 And hidden batteries boomed and shelled,
 "Charge bayonets!" the colonel yelled;
"Battalion forward,—double quick!"

With even slopes of bayonets
 Advanced—a dazzling, threatening crest—
 Right toward the rebels' hidden nest,
The dark blue, living billow sets.

The color-guard was at my side;
 I heard the color-sergeant groan;
 I heard the bullet crush the bone;
I might have touched him as he died.

The life-blood spouted from his mouth
 And sanctified the wicked land;
 Of martyred saviors what a band
Has suffered to redeem the South!

I had no malice in my mind;
 I only cried: "Close up! guide right!"
 My single purpose in the fight
Was steady march with eyes aligned.

[8] A cannon with a rifled bore.

I glanced along the martial rows,
    And marked the soldiers' eyeballs burn;
    Their eager faces hot and stern,—
The wrathful triumph on their brows.

The traitors saw; they reeled and fled:
    Fear-stricken, gray-clad multitudes
    Streamed wildly toward the covering woods,
And left us victory and their dead.

Once more the march, the tiresome plain,
    The Father River fringed with dykes,
    Gray cypresses, palmetto spikes,
Bayous and swamps and yellowing canes;

With here and there plantations rolled
    In flowers, bananas, orange groves,
    Where laugh the sauntering negro droves,
Reposing from the task of old;

And rarer, half-deserted towns,
    Devoid of men, where women scowl,
    Avoiding us as lepers foul
With sidling gait and flouting gowns.

EMILY DICKINSON (1830–1886)

"IT FEELS A SHAME TO BE ALIVE"

It feels a shame to be Alive—
When Men so brave—are dead—
One envies the Distinguished Dust—
Permitted—such a Head—

The Stone—that tells defending Whom
This Spartan put away
What little of Him we—possessed
In Pawn for Liberty—

The price is great—Sublimely paid—
Do we deserve—a Thing—
That lives—like Dollars—must be piled
Before we may obtain?

Are we that wait—sufficient worth—
That such Enormous Pearl
As life—dissolved be—for Us—
In Battle's—horrid Bowl?

It may be—a Renown to live—
I think the Men who die—
Those unsustained—Saviours—
Present Divinity—

THOMAS BAILEY ALDRICH (1836–1907)

ACCOMPLICES

The soft new grass is creeping o'er the graves
   By the Potomac; and the crisp ground-flower
   Lifts its blue cup to catch the passing shower;
The pine-cone ripens, and the long moss waves
Its tangled gonfalons[9] above our braves.
   Hark, what a burst of music from yon bower!—
   The southern nightingale that, hour by hour,
In its melodious summer madness raves.
Ah, with what delicate touches of her hand,
   With what sweet voices, Nature seeks to screen

---

[9] A banner suspended from a crosspiece.

The awful Crime of this distracted land,—
    Sets her birds singing, while she spreads her green
Mantle of velvet where the Murdered lie,
As if to hide the horror from God's eye.

FREDERICKSBURG

The increasing moonlight drifts across my bed,
    And on the churchyard by the road, I know
    It falls as white and noiselessly as snow.
'Twas such a night two weary summers fled;
The stars, as now, were waning overhead.
    Listen! Again the shrill-lipped bugles blow
    Where the swift currents of the river flow
Past Fredericksburg,—far off the heavens are red
With sudden conflagration; on yon height,
    Linstock[10] in hand, the gunners hold their breath:
A signal-rocket pierces the dense night,
    Flings its spent stars upon the town beneath:
Hark—the artillery massing on the right,
    Hark—the black squadrons wheeling down to Death!

INNES RANDOLPH (1837–1887)

THE REBEL

Oh, I'm a good old Rebel,
    Now that's just what I am;
For this "fair Land of Freedom"
I do not care a dam.
I'm glad I fit against it—
    I only wish we'd won,
And I don't want no pardon
    For anything I've done.

---

[10] A long forked stick to hold a match with which to light a cannon.

I hates the Constitution,
    This great Republic, too;
I hates the Freedmen's Buro,
    In uniforms of blue.
I hates the nasty eagle,
    With all his brag and fuss;
The lyin', thievin' Yankees,
    I hates 'em wuss and wuss.

I hate the Yankee Nation
    And everything they do;
I hate the Declaration
    Of Independence, too.
I hates the glorious Union,
    'Tis dripping with our blood;
I hates the striped banner—
    I fit it all I could.

I followed old Mars' Robert
    For four year, near about,
Got wounded in three places,
    And starved at Pint Lookout.
I cotch the roomatism
    A-campin' in the snow,
But I killed a chance of Yankees—
    I'd like to kill some mo'.

Three hundred thousand Yankees
    Is stiff in Southern dust;
We got three hundred thousand
    Before they conquered us.
They died of Southern fever
    And Southern steel and shot;
I wish it was three millions
    Instead of what we got.

I can't take up my musket
    And fight 'em now no more,
But I ain't agoin' to love 'em,
    Now that is sartin sure.
And I don't want no pardon
    For what I was and am;
I won't be reconstructed,
    And I don't care a dam.

CHARLOTTE L. FORTEN GRIMKE
(1837–1914)

THE GATHERING OF THE GRAND ARMY

Through all the city's streets there poured a flood,
    A flood of human souls, eager, intent;
One thought, one purpose stirred the people's blood,
    And through their veins its quickening current sent.

The flags waved gayly in the summer air,
    O'er patient watchers 'neath the clouded skies;
Old age, and youth, and infancy were there,
    The glad light shining in expectant eyes.

And when at last our country's saviors came,—
    In proud procession down the crowded street,
Still brighter burned the patriotic flame,
    And loud acclaims leaped forth their steps to greet.

And now the veterans scarred and maimed appear,
    And now the tattered battle-flags uprise;
A silence deep one moment fills the air,
    Then shout on shout ascends unto the skies.

Oh, brothers, ye have borne the battle strain,
      And ye have felt it through the ling'ring years;
For all your valiant deeds, your hours of pain,
      We can but give to you our grateful tears!

And now, with heads bowed low, and tear-filled eyes
      We see a Silent Army passing slow;
For it no music swells, no shouts arise,
      But silent blessings from our full hearts flow.

The dead, the living,—All,—a glorious host,
      A "cloud of witnesses,"—around us press—
Shall we, like them, stand faithful at our post,
      Or weakly yield, unequal to the stress?

Shall it be said the land they fought to save,
      Ungrateful now, proves faithless to her trust?
Shall it be said the sons of sires so brave
      Now trail her sacred banner in the dust?

Ah, no! again shall rise the people's voice
      As once it rose in accents clear and high—
"Oh, outraged brother, lift your head, rejoice!
      Justice shall reign,—Insult and Wrong shall die!"

So shall this day the joyous promise be
      Of golden days for our fair land in store;
When Freedom's flag shall float above the free,
      And Love and Peace prevail from shore to shore.

                  (August 12, 1890, Boston)

SIDNEY LANIER (1842–1881)

LAUGHTER IN THE SENATE

In the South lies a lonesome, hungry Land:
He huddles his rags with a cripple's hand;
He mutters, prone on the barren sand,
    What time his heart is breaking.

He lifts his bare head from the ground;
He listens through the gloom around:
The winds have brought him a strange sound
    Of distant merrymaking.

Comes now the Peace, so long delayed?
Is it the cheerful voice of Aid?
Begins the time, his heart has prayed,
    When men may reap and sow?

Ah, God! Back to the cold earth's breast!
The sages chuckle o'er their jest;
Must they, to give a people rest,
    Their dainty wit forego?

The tyrants sit in a stately hall;
They jibe at a wretched people's fall;
The tyrants forget how fresh is the pall
    Over their dead and ours.

Look how the senators ape the clown,
And don the motley and hide the gown,
But yonder a fast-rising frown
    On the people's forehead lowers.

AMBROSE BIERCE (1842–1914?)

THE CONFEDERATE FLAGS

Tut-tut! give back the flags—how can you care,
    You veterans and heroes?
Why should you at a kind intention swear
    Like twenty Neros?

Suppose the act was not so overwise—
    Suppose it was illegal;
Is't well on such a question to arise
    And punch the Eagle?

Nay, let's economize his breath to scold
    And terrify the alien
Who tackles him, as Hercules of old
    The bird Stymphalian.

Among the rebels when we made a breach
    Was it to get the banners?
That was but incidental—'twas to teach
    Them better manners.

They know the lessons well enough to-day;
    Now, let us try to show them
That we're not only stronger far than they,
    (How we did mow them!)

But more magnanimous. My lads, 'tis plain
    'Twas an uncommon riot;
The warlike tribes of Europe fight for gain;
    We fought for quiet.

If we were victors, then we all must live
    With the same flag above us;
'Twas all in vain unless we now forgive
    And make them love us.

Let kings keep trophies to display above
    Their doors like any savage;
The freeman's trophy is the foeman's love,
    Despite war's ravage.

"Make treason odious?" My friends, you'll find
    You can't, in right and reason,
While "Washington" and "treason" are combined—
    "Hugo" and "treason."

All human governments must take the chance
    And hazard of sedition.
O wretch! to pledge your manhood in advance
    To blind submission.

It may be wrong, it may be right, to rise
    In warlike insurrection:
The loyalty that fools so dearly prize
    May mean subjection.

Be loyal to your country, yes—but how
    If tyrants hold dominion?
The South believed they did; can't you allow
    For that opinion?

He who will never rise though rulers plot,
    His liberties despising—
He is he manlier than the *sans-culottes*
    Who's always rising?

Give back the foolish flags whose bearers fell,
    Too valiant to forsake them.
Is it presumptuous, this counsel? Well,
    I helped to take them.

LIZETTE WOODWORTH REESE (1856–1935)

A War Memory

God bless this house and keep us all from hurt.
She led us gravely up the straight long stair;
We were afraid; two held her by the skirt,
One by the hand, and so to bed and prayer.
How frail a thing the little candle shone!
Beneath its flame looked dim and soft and high
The chair, the drawers; she like a tall flower blown
In a great space under a shadowy sky.
God bless us all and Lee and Beauregard—
Without, a soldier paced, in hated blue,
The road betwixt the tents in pale array
And our gnarled gate. But in the windy yard
White tulips raced along the drip of dew;—
Our mother with her candle went away.

PAUL LAURENCE DUNBAR (1872–1906)

The Unsung Heroes

A song for the unsung heroes who rose in the country's need,
When the life of the land was threatened by the slaver's cruel greed,
For the men who came from the cornfield, who came from the plough
    and the flail,
Who rallied round when they heard the sound of the mighty man of the
    rail.

They laid them down in the valleys, they laid them down in the wood,
And the world looked on at the work they did, and whispered, "It is
    good."
They fought their way on the hillside, they fought their way in the glen,
And God looked down on their sinews brown, and said, "I have made
    them men."

They went to the blue lines gladly, and the blue lines took them in,
And the men who saw their muskets' fire thought not of their dusky
    skin.
The gray lines rose and melted beneath their scathing showers,
And they said, "T is true, they have force to do, these old slave boys of
    ours."

Ah, Wagner saw their glory, and Pillow knew their blood,
That poured on a nation's altar, a sacrificial flood.
Port Hudson heard their war-cry that smote its smoke-filled air,
And the old free fires of their savage sires again were kindled there.

They laid them down where the rivers, the greening valleys gem.
And the song of the thund'rous cannon was their sole requiem,
And the great smoke wreath that mingled its hue with the dusky cloud,
Was the flag that furled o'er a saddened world, and the sheet that made
    their shroud.

Oh, Mighty God of the Battles Who held them in Thy hand,
Who gave them strength through the whole day's length, to fight for
    their native land,
They are lying dead on the hillsides, they are lying dead on the plain,
And we have not fire to smite the lyre and sing them one brief strain.

Give, Thou, some seer the power to sing them in their might,
The men who feared the master's whip, but did not fear the fight;
That he may tell of their virtues as minstrels did of old,
Till the pride of face and the hate of race grow obsolete and cold.

A song for the unsung heroes who stood the awful test,
When the humblest host that the land could boast went forth to meet
    the best;
A song for the unsung heroes who fell on the bloody sod,
Who fought their way from night to day and struggled up to God.

ALLEN TATE (1899–1979)

ODE TO THE CONFEDERATE DEAD

Row after row with strict impunity
The headstones yield their names to the element,
The wind whirrs without recollection;
In the riven troughs the splayed leaves
Pile up, of nature the casual sacrament
To the seasonal eternity of death.
Then driven by the fierce scrutiny
Of heaven to their business in the vast breath,
They sough the rumor of mortality.

Autumn is desolation in the plot
Of a thousand acres where these memories grow
From the inexhaustible bodies that are not
Dead, but feed the grass row after rich row:
Remember now the autumns that have gone!—
Ambitious November with the humors of the year,
With a particular zeal for every slab,
Staining the uncomfortable angels that rot
On the slabs, a wing chipped here, an arm there:
The brute curiosity of an angel's stare
Turns you like them to stone,
Transforms the heaving air,
Till plunged to a heavier world below
You shift your sea-space blindly,
Heaving, turning like the blind crab.

    Dazed by the wind, only the wind
    The leaves flying, plunge

You know who have waited by the wall
The twilit certainty of an animal;
Those midnight restitutions of the blood
You know—the immitigable pines, the smoky frieze
Of the sky, the sudden call: you know the rage—

The cold pool left by the mounting flood—
Of muted Zeno and Parmenides.
You who have waited for the angry resolution
Of those desires that should be yours tomorrow,
You know the unimportant shrift of death
And praise the vision
And praise the arrogant circumstance
Of those who fall
Rank upon rank, hurried beyond decision
Here by the sagging gate, stopped by the wall.

   Seeing, seeing only the leaves
   Flying, plunge and expire

Turn your eyes to the immoderate past
Turn to the inscrutable infantry rising
Demons out of the earth—they will not last.
Stonewall, Stonewall, and the sunken fields of hemp,
Shiloh, Antietam, Malvern Hill, Bull Run.
Lost in that orient of the thick and fast
You will curse the setting sun.

   Cursing only the leaves crying
   Like an old man in a storm

You hear the shout—the crazy hemlocks point
With troubled fingers to the silence which
Smothers you, a mummy, in time. The hound bitch
Toothless and dying, in a musty cellar
Hears the wind only.

        Now that the salt of their blood
Stiffens the saltier oblivion of the sea,
Seals the malignant purity of the flood,
What shall we, who count our days and bow
Our heads with a commemorial woe,
In the ribboned coats of grim felicity,
What shall we say of the bones, unclean

Whose verdurous anonymity will grow?
The ragged arms, the ragged heads and eyes
Lost in these acres of the insane green?
The gray lean spiders come, they come and go;
In a tangle of willows without light
The singular screech-owl's bright
Invisible lyric seeds the mind
With the furious murmur of their chivalry.

    We shall say only, the leaves
    Flying, plunge and expire

We shall say only, the leaves whispering
In the improbable mist of nightfall
That flies on multiple wing;
Night is the beginning and the end,
And in between the ends of distraction
Waits mute speculation, the patient curse
That stones the eyes, or like the jaguar leaps
For his own image in a jungle pool, his victim.

What shall we say who have knowledge
Carried to the heart? Shall we take the act
To the grave? Shall we, more hopeful, set up the grave
In the house? The ravenous grave?

                                Leave now
The shut gate and the decomposing wall:
The gentle serpent, green in the mulberry bush,
Riots with his tongue through the hush—
Sentinel of the grave who counts us all!

ELIZABETH BISHOP (1911–1979)

FROM TROLLOPE'S JOURNAL

WINTER, 1861

As far as statues go, so far there's not
much choice: they're either Washingtons
or Indians, a whitewashed, stubby lot,
His country's Father or His foster sons.
The White House in a sad, unhealthy spot
just higher than Potomac's swampy brim,
—they say the present President has got
ague or fever in each backwoods limb.
On Sunday afternoon I wandered,—rather,
I floundered,—out alone. The air was raw
and dark; the marsh half-ice, half-mud. This weather
is normal now: a frost, and then a thaw,
and then a frost. A hunting man, I found
the Pennsylvania Avenue heavy ground . . .
There all around me in the ugly mud,
—hoof-pocked, uncultivated,—herds of cattle,
numberless, wond'ring steers and oxen, stood:
beef for the Army, after the next battle.
Their legs were caked the color of dried blood;
their horns were wreathed with fog. Poor, starving, dumb
or lowing creatures, never to chew the cud
or fill their maws again! Th' effluvium
made that damned anthrax on my forehead throb.
I called a surgeon in, a young man, but,
with a sore throat himself, he did his job.
We talked about the War, and as he cut
away, he croaked out, "Sir, I do declare
everyone's sick! The soldiers poison the air."

ROBERT PENN WARREN (1905–1989)

A CONFEDERATE VETERAN TRIES TO EXPLAIN THE EVENT

"But why did he do it, Grandpa?" I said
to the old man sitting under the cedar,
who had come a long way to that place, and that time
when that younger man lay down in the hay

to arrange himself. And now the old man
lifted his head to stare at me.
"It's one of those things," he said, and stopped.
"What things?" I said. And he said: "Son—

"son, one of those things you never know."
"But there must be a *why*," I said. Then he
said: "Folks—yes, folks, they up and die."
"But, Grandpa—" I said. And he: "They die."

Said: "Yes, by God, and I've seen 'em die.
I've seen 'em die and I've seen 'em dead.
I've seen 'em die hot and seen 'em die cold.
Hot lead and cold steel—" The words, they stopped.

The mouth closed up. The eyes looked away.
Beyond the lawn where the fennel throve,
beyond the fence where the whitewash peeled,
beyond the cedars along the lane,

the eyes fixed. The land, in sunlight,
swam, with the meadow the color of rust,
and distance the blue of Time, and nothing—
oh, nothing—would ever happen, and

in the silence my breath did not happen. But
the eyes, they happened, they found me, I
stood there and waited. "Dying," he said,
"hell, dying's a thing any fool can do."

"But what made him do it?" I said, again.
Then wished I hadn't, for he stared at me.
He stared at me as though I weren't there,
or as though I were dead, or had never been born,

and I felt like dandelion fuzz blown away,
or a word you'd once heard but never could spell,
or only an empty hole in the air.
From the cedar shade his eyes burned red.

Darker than shade, his mouth opened then.
Spit was pink on his lips, I saw the tongue move
beyond the old teeth, in the dark of his head.
It moved in that dark. Then, "Son—" the tongue said.

"For some folks the world gets too much," it said.
In that dark, the tongue moved. "For some folks," it said.

ROBERT LOWELL (1917–1977)

FOR THE UNION DEAD

Relinquunt Omnia Servare Rem Publicam.[11]

The old South Boston Aquarium stands
in a Sahara of snow now. Its broken windows are boarded.
The bronze weathervane cod has lost half its scales.
The airy tanks are dry.

Once my nose crawled like a snail on the glass;
my hand tingled
to burst the bubbles
drifting from the noses of the cowed, compliant fish.

My hand draws back. I often sigh still
for the dark downward and vegetating kingdom

---

[11] "They give up everything to serve the Republic." Latin.

of the fish and reptile. One morning last March,
I pressed against the new barbed and galvanized

fence on the Boston Common. Behind their cage,
yellow dinosaur steamshovels were grunting
as they cropped up tons of mush and grass
to gouge their underworld garage.

Parking spaces luxuriate like civic
sandpiles in the heart of Boston.
A girdle of orange, Puritan-pumpkin colored girders
braces the tingling Statehouse,

shaking over the excavations, as it faces Colonel Shaw[12]
and his bell-cheeked Negro infantry
on St. Gauden's shaking Civil War relief,
propped by a plank splint against the garage's earthquake.

Two months after marching through Boston,
half the regiment was dead;
at the dedication,
William James could almost hear the bronze Negroes breathe.

Their monument sticks like a fishbone
in the city's throat.
Its Colonel is as lean
as a compass-needle.

He has an angry wrenlike vigilance,
a greyhound's gentle tautness;
he seems to wince at pleasure,
and suffocate for privacy.

He is out of bounds now. He rejoices in man's lovely,
peculiar power to choose life and die—

---

[12] Colonel Robert Gould Shaw (1837–1863) was commander of the first all-black Civil War
regiment, the Massachusetts Fifty-fourth, many of whom were killed along with him in the
nearly suicidal assault on the well-defended Fort Wagner.

when he leads his black soldiers to death,
he cannot bend his back.

On a thousand small town New England greens,
the old white churches hold their air
of sparse, sincere rebellion; frayed flags
quilt the graveyards of the Grand Army of the Republic.

The stone statues of the abstract Union Soldier
grow slimmer and younger each year—
wasp-waisted, they doze over muskets
and muse through their sideburns . . .

Shaw's father wanted no monument
except the ditch,
where his son's body was thrown
and lost with his "niggers."

The ditch is nearer.
There are no statues for the last war here;
on Boylston Street, a commercial photograph
shows Hiroshima boiling

over a Mosler Safe, the "Rock of Ages"
that survived the blast. Space is nearer.
When I crouch to my television set,
the drained faces of Negro school-children rise like balloons.

Colonel Shaw
is riding on his bubble,
he waits
for the blessèd break.

The Aquarium is gone. Everywhere,
giant finned cars nose forward like fish;
a savage servility
slides by on grease.

ALAN DUGAN (1923–2003)

FABRICATION OF ANCESTORS

(FOR OLD BILLY DUGAN, SHOT IN THE ASS IN THE CIVIL WAR,
MY FATHER SAID)

The old wound in my ass
has opened up again, but I
am past the prodigies
of youth's campaigns, and weep
where I used to laugh
in war's red humors, half
in love with silly-assed pains
and half not feeling them.
I have to sit up with
an indoor unsittable itch
before I go down late
and weeping to the storm-
cellar on a dirty night
and go to bed with the worms.
So pull the dirt up over me
and make a family joke
for Old Billy Blue Balls,
the oldest private in the world
with two ass-holes and no
place more to go to for a laugh
except the last one. Say:
The North won the Civil War
without much help from me
although I wear a proof
of the war's obscenity.

JAMES DICKEY (1923–1997)

HUNTING CIVIL WAR RELICS AT NIMBLEWILL CREEK

As he moves the mine detector
A few inches over the ground,
Making it vitally float
Among the ferns and weeds,
I come into this war
Slowly, with my one brother,
Watching his face grow deep
Between the earphones,
For I can tell
If we enter the buried battle
Of Nimblewill
Only by his expression.

Softly he wanders, parting
The grass with a dreaming hand.
No dead cry yet takes root
In his clapped ears
Or can be seen in his smile.
But underfoot I feel
The dead regroup,
The burst metals all in place,
The battle lines be drawn
Anew to include us
In Nimblewill,
And I carry the shovel and pick
More as if they were
Bright weapons that I bore.
A bird's cry breaks
In two, and into three parts.
We cross the creek; the cry
Shifts into another,
Nearer, bird, and is
Like the shout of a shadow—
Lived-with, appallingly close—

Or the soul, pronouncing
"Nimblewill":
Three tones; your being changes.

We climb the bank;
A faint light glows
On my brother's mouth.
I listen, as two birds fight
For a single voice, but he
Must be hearing the grave,
In pieces, all singing
To his clamped head,
For he smiles as if
He rose from the dead within
Green Nimblewill
And stood in his grandson's shape.

ANDREW HUDGINS (B. 1951)

THE ROAD HOME

My boots stayed damp with suppuration,
sweat, blood, body ooze. But what
began in soggy steps moved on
to something much like grace, as if
my will, floating six feet off the earth,
dragged my worn body after it
as a kite will drag a tail of rags
into the air. I can't recall
the order of events. They happened but
they really didn't, since I don't
remember when. Like dreams, but dreams
you can't dismiss as simply dreams.
These are my actual life: Once, hungry,
I left the road to beg for food.
As I approached the door, a small dog

exploded from an open window,
jumped on a nearby shed, then pulled
himself, barely, onto the roof
and howled. Because I wore my old
slouch hat and thin hair swept my neck,
the lady let him bark. I yelled
to be heard over him, asking for food.
While I stood in the yard and chewed
a yellow slab of cornbread,
he never once let up. I said,
"Thank you." She nodded once. The dog
raced back and forth along the roof,
yapping. I would have paid in gold
for that damn dog—to strangle it—
but no more coins popped from my flesh.
The moment my foot touched the road,
she said, "Hush, Boots," and then, at last,
the goddamn dog shut up. I loathed
Boots more than any soldier whom
I killed. I even knew his name,
which helps. Before or after that,
a farmer I met on the road
shared with me half a pan of pork
so rank it smelled like frying sweat.
I knelt to wash my mouth and saw,
wrinkling their fluted edges in
the white reflection of my face,
leeches. I reached into the pond
to pluck them from my face. They seized
my hand. I hadn't thought there was
enough blood left inside my skin
to lure a leech, the veal-white heart
bent backward on itself by all
the death it takes to stay alive.
I bit four leeches from my hand
and spat them in the pond. Amused,
the farmer said, "Them leeches are
a nasty piece of work." I laughed,

but the sharp taste of blood flushed out
the bad meat that had fouled my mouth
with rot.
        Another time, I'm sure
a red fox trotted, tippy-toed, by me.
His black paws made him seem to float
above the red dirt road. *Human,* he said,
there's danger on the road through here.

"Ah, Fox," I said, "you have acquired
a reputation as a sweet
deceiver."
        He grinned. *I know. I know.*
But there is nothing I can gain
from you, Human.
           "Nothing that I can see."
His sharp head twisting up at me,
he grinned. *I like the way you think,*
he said. He led me down a path
he claimed was safer than the road.
When our trail joined the road again
I offered him a piece of pork
the farmer had given me.
           It stinks,
the fox replied.
          "It's all I have."
And I have lived on worse, he said,
and gulped it down with three quick jerks.
Take this. He coughed, then spat a tooth
between my boots. "I thank thee, Fox."

You are most welcome, Human, said
the fox, as formally as I.
He trotted back into the woods.
I walked and didn't think too much
since I was safe. But safe from what,
if anything? Or had I played a part
in some larger design the fox

had put together? I trusted it
—the tooth—because its point was sharp,
because it bore a stain of blood,
because it pricked my finger when
I picked it up. Before or after that,
a deer behind me whispered, *Run!*
I even ran a step or two
before I figured out that *run*
is deer's advice for everything.
I walked two weeks. You're halfway there,
then half of that, then half again,
until you're never there, or till
—May I?—you take a giant step
as in the children's game, cut out
philosophy, and there you are: at home.
Just as my body hit the bed
—in that one instant, flesh on linen—
the whole world shuddered, hesitated, bloomed
so violently, so all-at-once, the house
trembled, and I was frightened that
the walls would fall apart, the roof
explode, the floor dissolve. They held.
The whole house trembled, held—as when,
a child, I sassed my pa in church.
His hand drew back. His whole body
trembled as he kept from hitting me.
And on the fourteenth day, I sagged
into my father's arms. He caught
my weight. I never touched the floor.

THE INDIAN WARS

1620–1911

Brother!—Listen to what we say. There was a time when our forefathers owned this great island [continental America]. Their seats extended from the rising to the setting sun. The Great Spirit had made it for the use of Indians. He had created the buffalo, the deer, and other animals for food. He made the bear and the beaver, and their skins served us for clothing. He had scattered them over the country and taught us to take them. He had caused the earth to produce corn for bread. All this he had done for his red children because he loved them. If we had any disputes about hunting-grounds, they were generally settled without the shedding of much blood. But an evil day came upon us. Your forefathers crossed the great waters, and landed on this island. Their numbers were small. They found friends and not enemies. They told us they had fled from their own country for fear of wicked men, and come here to enjoy their religion. They asked for a small seat. We took pity on them, granted their request, and they sat down amongst us. We gave them corn and meat. They gave us poison in return [spirituous liquor]. The white people had now found our country. Tidings were carried back, and more came amongst us. Yet we did not fear them. We took them to be friends. They called us brothers. We believed them, and gave them a larger seat. At length their numbers had greatly increased. They wanted more land. They wanted our country. Our eyes were opened, and our minds became uneasy. Wars took place . . .

—The Senecan chief, Red Jacket, 1812, from *Thatcher's Indian Biography* (1834)

Violent clashes marked contact between European explorers and indigenous tribes on the North American continent from the onset of their meeting in the fifteenth century, but in the initial phase of European conquest, these clashes died away when Columbus and other explorers went home. In the seventeenth century, however, when the Europeans came not only to map but to live on, and possess exclusively, the land that had been claimed by Indian hunters, fishermen, and farmers, the bursts of warfare spread across the whole of what was to be the United States, and lasted for approximately three hundred years.

In Virginia in 1644, Powhatan's brother, Opechancanough, massacred nearly five hundred English colonists: men, women, and children. The colonists retaliated. King Philip's War, or Metacom's war, raged through southern New England in 1675 and 1676. After 1630, the Iroquois Confederacy made war on the Hurons for more than forty years, but by 1675, their powers reduced, they became pawns in the imperial wars between French Catholic and English Protestants, and lost their broad territorial sway. Later intertribal hostilities, as well as hostilities against colonists, were subsumed in the French and Indian War from 1756 to 1763; tribes took different sides, depending on where they thought their interests lay. Pontiac's War erupted in 1763 in the Great Lakes region, but again, the idea of a Pan-Indian community went down to defeat. Indians continued to fight one another, as well as the settlers, although the number of intertribal wars accelerated after contact, when Indians, taking a leaf from the European book, discovered the value of selling the captives that they had taken in raids for slaves.

In the Revolutionary War, Indians fought mostly for the British, foreseeing their eventual defeat and extinction in the relentless push toward western settlement by the victorious American colonists. They lined up variously with different allies, however, throughout the War of 1812; a last attempt at maintaining Indian dominance in the Great Lakes region broke down with the death of Tecumseh. In both successive Seminole Wars in Florida in 1821 and then in 1835 through 1837, Indians fought to maintain their territorial control. By 1842, through a final treaty, the Seminoles were largely moved west: over their protests, they were resettled—minus their mixed black and Seminole relations. The Cherokee nation, seen as an inconvenience lying between Georgian consumers and northeastern manufacturers, were evacuated by General Winfield Scott in 1838, over what became known as the Trail of Tears. And so it continued, on into the gold rush of 1849, where once again Indians sat in possession of what whites wanted for themselves.

The nineteenth century saw an accelerated collision of all these forces competing for possession and domination, and this section of poems on

Indian wars and Indian warfare, from both within and without Indian communities, indicates the complexity and longevity of the Amerindian role in American history. In the last stages of envelopment and displacement, Indians fought the U.S. Army. From 1850 on, even after the demobilization that occurred after the Civil War, the Army enlarged and redefined itself through these encounters with hostile Indians, despite both a strong national prejudice against standing armies and the growing dismay at the treatment of Indians. For a period beginning roughly after the Civil War and extending into the 1880s, U.S. soldiers engaged in over a thousand combat actions and suffered 2,000 soldier casualties. In even larger proportion, 5,000 Indians died. In league with the soldiers, the settlers and hunters eradicated the buffalo herds vital to the culture and ecosystem of the Indians. Settlers battled the arid and difficult soils of the grassland, the sweltering summers and bitter winters, and eventually, through blind obstinacy and dogged will, seasoned by violence and governmental chicanery, succeeded in taking the Great Plains and the Rockies away from their original inhabitants.

After a last flare-up of resistance by the Shoshones in Nevada in 1911, and a renewed clash between FBI agents and Indian activists at Wounded Knee, South Dakota, in the 1970s, the native populations had been subjugated. Cannon and howitzer, the cozening and cajoling of Indian tribes by peace treaties representing false intentions about land use or hunting rights, and the often forcible removal to reservations had done their work. Indians remained on a drastically shrunken portion of their original domain. The centuries from 1500 to 1900 saw the original Indian population, calculated at around 1,850,000 at the time of Columbus, and having the free run of nearly two billion acres, decrease to 248,253 people by 1890. A little more than a century later, the population climbed slowly back to 1,873,536 self-declared Indians, who are now herded onto forty million acres of reservation land, with twelve million in private Indian hands. This represents a net loss of 1.882 billion acres for the Indians. To put the figures in another perspective, while the Indian population was being decimated, immigration figures for 1873 alone showed 459,803 people arriving in America. The rise of the immigrant population and the decline of the American Indian, as recorded by both Euro-Americans and Native Americans, indicates one way of life vanishing in the ascendancy of another.

The Indian wars were to become the United States' most protracted conflict. Many of the doomed chiefs of these tribes, from Pontiac and

Tecumseh to Black Hawk and Chief Joseph and to Crazy Horse and Sitting Bull, became household names, and represented idealized courage and steadfast loyalty to a warrior code. As the problem of land transfer resolved itself in favor of the incoming Europeans, more and more did the doomed and demolished Indian way of life assert itself in the formative American imagination as precious and vital, perhaps the manifestation of a Freudian return of the repressed. The Indian was seen to possess an untamed, internal, and portable wilderness that the increasingly domesticated and urbanized heir to frontier settlement would value.

While awareness of the injustice dealt to Indians sparked in nineteenth-century texts like Helen Hunt Jackson's *A Century of Dishonor: A Sketch of the United States Government's Dealings with Some of the North American Tribes* (1881) and flared again in twentieth-century accounts like David E. Stannard's *American Holocaust* (1992), interest in and appreciation of Indian culture was nothing new. From the seventeenth century on, European settlers attempted to record a Native American culture that intrigued them, and this continued even through periods of intensifying hostilities. The first translation of an Indian war song was published in the eighteenth century, when Lieutenant Henry Timberlake arranged the Cherokee sounds that he had transcribed into heroic couplets. These couplets roughly simulated the Indian meaning and loosely approximated what he thought to be "extremely pretty, and very like the Scotch."

Modern translators like Brian Swann admit the difficulties of this enterprise: first, what is traditionally sung or accompanied by music cannot be fairly represented in print. Yet elsewhere we face this difficulty willingly, as when hearing Greek tragedy spoken, rather than sung in the modes and meters for which the original Greeks had designed it. Because of the immense divide between cultural values, and between aesthetic and linguistic practice, it is also hard to make the target words match meanings in the host language. The elaborate Augustan or the florid Victorian diction of earlier attempts at translation fit awkwardly; Euro-Americans interested in amplified description and characterization often supplement their translations with such detail. Arnold Krupat notes that some earlier translators dismissive of Indian cultural values are nonetheless better and more accurate transcribers, more so than translators who embellish their efforts in an attempt to house Indian poetry in literary forms more recognizable to their readers and themselves. In any event, the translations presented here indicate the compromises that reader and translator alike inevitably make in their effort to approach these texts. Besides translations, this section includes poems about Indians as seen by the dominant white American culture, often through idealizing and romanticizing filters, and closes with a selection of poems by twentieth-century Indians themselves, which often display an ironic and wrenching discontinuity with the splendors of lost traditions.

WILLIAM CULLEN BRYANT (1794–1878)

THE DISINTERRED WARRIOR

Gather him to his grave again,
   And solemnly and softly lay,
Beneath the verdure of the plain,
   The warrior's scattered bones away.
Pay the deep reverence, taught of old,
   The homage of man's heart to death;
Nor dare to trifle with the mould
   Once hallowed by the Almighty's breath.

The soul hath quickened every part—
   That remnant of a martial brow,
Those ribs that held the mighty heart,
   That strong arm—strong no longer now.
Spare them, each mouldering relic spare,
   Of God's own image, let them rest,
Till not a trace shall speak of where
   The awful likeness was impressed.

For he was fresher from the hand
   That formed of earth the human face,
And to the elements did stand
   In nearer kindred than our race.
In many a flood to madness tossed,
   In many a storm has been his path;
He hid him not from heat or frost,
   But met them, and defied their wrath.

Then they were kind—the forests here,
   Rivers, and stiller waters paid
A tribute to the net and spear
   Of the red ruler of the shade.
Fruits on the woodland branches lay,
   Roots in the shaded soil below,
The stars looked forth to teach his way,
   The still earth warned him of the foe.

A noble race! but they are gone,
   With their old forests wide and deep,
And we have built our homes upon
   Fields where their generations sleep.
Their fountains slake our thirst at noon,
   Upon their fields our harvest waves,
Our lovers woo beneath their moon—
   Ah, let us spare, at least, their graves!

JOHN GREENLEAF WHITTIER (1807–1892)

METACOM

METACOM, OR PHILIP, THE CHIEF OF THE WAMPANOAGS,[1] WAS
THE MOST POWERFUL AND SAGACIOUS SACHEM WHO EVER
MADE WAR UPON THE ENGLISH.

Red as the banner which enshrouds
   The warrior-dead, when strife is done,
A broken mass of crimson clouds
   Hung over the departed sun.
The shadow of the western hill
Crept swiftly down, and darkly still,
As if a sullen wave of night
Were rushing on the pale twilight;
The forest-openings grew more dim,
   As glimpses of the arching blue
   And waking stars came softly through
The rifts of many a giant limb.
Above the wet and tangled swamp
White vapors gathered thick and damp,

[1] Metacom (King Philip) led a war against the settlers provoked by the takeover of lands that exceeded their agreements. The war began in 1675 and ended with his death the following year, when his alliance fell apart after being attacked by the Mohawks from New York. The Wampanoags were a tribe of southeastern Massachusetts, Nantucket, and Martha's Vineyard.

And through their cloudy curtaining
Flapped many a brown and dusky wing—
Pinions that fan the moonless dun,
But fold them at the rising sun!

Beneath the closing veil of night,
    And leafy bough and curling fog,
With his few warriors ranged in sight—
Scarred relics of his latest fight—
    Rested the fiery Wampanoag,
He leaned upon his loaded gun,
Warm with its recent work of death,
And, save the struggling of his breath,
That, slow and hard and long-repressed,
Shook the damp folds around his breast,
An eye that was unused to scan
The sterner moods of that dark man;
Had deemed his tall and silent form
With hidden passion fierce and warm,
With that fixed eye, as still and dark
As clouds which veil their lightning spark,
That of some forest-champion,
Whom sudden death had passed upon—
A giant frozen into stone!
Son of the thronëd Sachem!—Thou,
The sternest of the forest kings,—
Shall the scorned pale-one trample now,
Unambushed on thy mountain's brow,
Yea, drive his vile and hated plough
    Among thy nation's holy things,
Crushing the warrior-skeleton
In scorn beneath his armed heel,
And not a band be left to deal
A kindred vengeance fiercely back,
And cross in blood the Spoiler's track?

He turned him to his trustiest one,
The old and war-tried Annawon—

"Brother!"—The favored warrior stood
In hushed and listening attitude—
"This night the Vision-Spirit hath
    Unrolled the scroll of fate before me;
And ere the sunrise cometh, Death
    Will wave his dusky pinion o'er me!
Nay, start not—well I know thy faith—
Thy weapon now may keep its sheath;
But, when the bodeful morning breaks,
And the green forest widely wakes
    Unto the roar of English thunder,
Then trusted brother, be it thine
To burst upon the foeman's line,
And rend his serried strength asunder.
Perchance thyself and yet a few
Of faithful ones may struggle through,
And, rallying on the wooded plain,
Strike deep for vengeance once again,
And offer up in pale-face blood
An offering to the Indian's God."

A musket shot—a sharp, quick yell—
    And then the stifled groan of pain,
Told that another red man fell,—
    And blazed a sudden light again
Across that kingly brow and eye,
Like lightning on a clouded sky,—
And a low growl, like that which thrills
The hunter of the Eastern hills,
    Burst through clenched teeth and rigid lip—
And, when the great chief spoke again
His deep voice shook beneath its rein,
    As wrath and grief held fellowship.

"Brother! methought when as but now
    I pondered on my nation's wrong,
With sadness on his shadowy brow
    My father's spirit passed along!

He pointed to the far south-west,
    Where sunset's gold was growing dim,
    And seemed to beckon me to him,
And to the forests of the blest!—
My father loved the white men, when
They were but children, shelterless,
For his great spirit at distress
Melted to woman's tenderness—
Nor was it given him to know
    That children whom he cherished then
    Would rise at length, like armed men,
To work his people's overthrow.
Yet thus it is;—the God before
    Whose awful shrine the pale ones bow
Hath frowned upon, and given o'er
    The red man to the stranger now!

A few more moons, and there will be
No gathering to the council tree;
The scorchëd earth—the blackened log—
    The naked bones of warriors slain,
    Be the sole relics which remain
Of the once mighty Wampanoag!
The forests of our hunting-land,
    With all their old and solemn green,
Will bow before the Spoiler's axe—
The plough displace the hunter's tracks,
And the tall prayer-house steeple stand
    Where the Great Spirit's shrine hath been!

"Yet, brother, from this awful hour
    The dying curse of Metacom
Shall linger with abiding power
    Upon the spoilers of my home.
    The fearful veil of things to come,
    By Kitchtan's hand is lifted from
The shadows of the embryo years;
    And I can see more clearly through

Than ever visioned Powwah did,
For all the future comes unbid
    Yet welcome to my trancëd view,
As battle-yell to warrior-ears!
From stream and lake and hunting-hill
    Our tribes may vanish like a dream,
    And even my dark curse may seem
Like idle winds when Heaven is still,
    No bodeful harbinger of ill;
But, fiercer than the downright thunder,
When yawns the mountain-rock asunder,
And riven pine and knotted oak
Are reeling to the fearful stroke,
    That curse shall work its master's will!
The bed of yon blue mountain stream
Shall pour a darker tide than rain—
The sea shall catch its blood-red stain,
And broadly on its banks shall gleam
    The steel of those who should be brothers;
Yea, those whom one fond parent nursed
Shall meet in strife, like fiends accursed,
And trample down the once loved form,
While yet with breathing passion warm,
    As fiercely as they would another's!"

The morning star sat dimly on
The lighted eastern horizon—
The deadly glare of levelled gun.
    Came streaking through the twilight haze
    And naked to its reddest blaze,
A hundred warriors sprang in view;
    One dark red arm was tossed on high,
One giant shout came hoarsely through
    The clangor and the charging cry,
Just as across the scattering gloom,
Red as the naked hand of Doom,
    The English volley hurtled by—

The arm—the voice of Metacom!—
    One piercing shriek—one vengeful yell,
Sent like an arrow to the sky,
    Told when the hunter-monarch fell!

ANONYMOUS

"PRAYER OF A WARRIOR" (ASSINIBOINE)[2]

TRANSLATED BY EDWIN T. DENIG, *INDIAN TRIBES OF THE
UPPER MISSOURI*, CA. 1854

O Wakonda,[3] you see me a poor man.
Have pity on me.
I go to war to revenge the death of my brother.
Have pity upon me.
I smoke this tobacco taken from my medicine sack,
where it has been enveloped with the remains of my
dead brother [a lock of his hair]. I smoke it to my
tutelary, to you; aid me in revenge.
    On my path preserve me from mad wolves.
    Let no enemies surprise me.
    I have sacrificed, I have smoked, my heart is low,
have pity upon me. Give me the bows and arrows of
my enemies. Give me their guns. Give me their horses.
Give me their bodies. Let me have my face blackened
on my return. Let good weather come that I can see.
Good dreams give that I can judge where they are. I
have suffered. I wish to live. I wish to be revenged. I
am poor. I want horses. I will sacrifice. I will smoke.
I will remember. Have pity on me.

[2] A tribe of the upper Missouri.
[3] A tribal deity, now a city in South Dakota.

"CHEROKEE[4] WAR-SONG," VERSION 1

FROM HENRY ROWE SCHOOLCRAFT, *ARCHIVES OF ORIGINAL KNOWLEDGE*, 1860

From the south they come,
The birds, the warlike birds,
    With sounding wings.

I wish to change myself
To the body of that swift bird.

I throw away my body in the strife.

"CHEROKEE WAR-SONG," VERSION 2

From the south they came, Birds of War—
Hark! To their passing scream.
I wish the body of the fiercest,
As swift, as cruel, as strong.
I cast my body to the chance of fighting.
Happy shall I be to lie in that place,
In that place where the fight was,
Beyond the enemy's line.

"SONG FOR A FALLEN WARRIOR" (BLACKFEET)[5]

TRANSLATED BY JOHN MASON BROWNE, 1866

O my son, farewell!
You have gone beyond the great river,
Your spirit is on the other side of the Sand Buttes;
I will not see you for a hundred winters;

[4] A tribe originally of the southern Appalachians, now concentrated in eastern Oklahoma.
[5] Plains Indians of the Algonquin family.

You will scalp the enemy in the green prairie,
Beyond the great river.
When the warriors of the Blackfeet meet,
When they smoke the medicine-pipe and dance the war-dance,
They will ask, "Where is Isthumaka?—
Where is the bravest of the Mannikappi?"
He fell on the war-path.
      Mai-ram-bo, mai-ram-bo.

Many scalps will be taken for your death;
The Crows will lose many horses;
Their women will weep for their braves,
They will curse the spirit of Isthumaka.
O my son! I will come to you
And make moccasins for the war-path,
As I did when you struck the lodge
Of the "Horse-Guard" with the tomahawk.
Farewell, my son! I will see you
Beyond the broad river.
      Mai-ram-bo, mai-ram-bo.

"*I WILL ARISE WITH MY TOMAHAWK*" (PASSAMAQUODDY)

TAKEN FROM J. W. FEWKES, "A CONTRIBUTION TO PASSAMOQUODDY FOLKLORE" (1890)

I will arise with my tomahawk in my hand
And I must have revenge on that nation that has slain my poor people.
I arise with war-club in my hand,
And follow the bloody track of that nation that has killed my people.
I will sacrifice my own life and the lives of my warriors.
I arise with war-club in my hand and follow the track of my enemy.
When I overtake him I will take his scalp and string it on a long pole,
And I will stick it in the ground, and my warriors will dance around it
for many days;
Then I will sing my song for the victory over my enemy.

"Warpath Song"

From Maurice Boyd, *Kiowa Voices*

I ran to the brook to do my hair.
I painted my face with colors of the evening skies.
My aunt chose a bright blue shawl for me, blue as the sky.
But then we heard the cry that meant
darkness to all my people.

I ran back to my tent.
I washed off all the paint
with my tears.

"Last Song of Sitting Bull" (teton sioux)

From Frances Densmore. Sitting Bull[6] sang this, his last song, after he had surrendered to the United States authorities, some time after the Custer massacre.

A warrior
I have been.
Now
It is all over.
A hard time
I have.

---

[6] Sitting Bull was chief and holy man of the Teton Sioux Lakota, one of the greatest of the Indian leaders, and killed by tribal police sent to arrest him during a bloody melee with his supporters. The Teton Sioux were the largest and most powerful of the Sioux tribes, located in the upper Midwest.

WALT WHITMAN (1819–1892)

FROM FAR DAKOTA'S CAÑONS

JUNE 25, 1876

From far Dakota's cañons,
Lands of the wild ravine, the dusky Sioux, the lonesome stretch, the
 silence,
Haply to-day a mournful wail, haply a trumpet-note for heroes.

The battle-bulletin,
The Indian ambuscade, the craft, the fatal environment,
The cavalry companies fighting to the last in sternest heroism,
In the midst of their little circle, with their slaughter'd horses for breast-
 works,
The fall of Custer and all his officers and men.

Continues yet the old, old legend of our race,
The loftiest of life upheld by death,
The ancient banner perfectly maintain'd,
O lesson opportune, O how I welcome thee!

As sitting in dark days,
Lone, sulky, through the time's thick murk looking in vain for light, for
 hope,
From unsuspected parts a fierce and momentary proof,
(The sun there at the centre though conceal'd,
Electric life forever at the centre,)
Breaks forth a lightning flash.
Thou of the tawny flowing hair in battle,
I erewhile saw, with erect head, pressing ever in front, bearing a bright
 sword in thy hand,
Now ending well in death the splendid fever of thy deeds,
(I bring no dirge for it or thee, I bring a glad triumphal sonnet,)
Desperate and glorious, aye in defeat most desperate, most glorious,
After thy many battles in which never yielding up a gun or a color,
Leaving behind thee a memory sweet to soldiers,
Thou yieldest up thyself.

ANONYMOUS

"*THE TAKING OF LIFE BRINGS SERIOUS THOUGHTS*" (PIMA)

TRANSLATED BY FRANK RUSSELL, 1904–1905

We have come thus far, my brothers. We have already laid our plans.
   With magic power the trail is made easy, bordered with flowers, grass,
   and trees.
The enemy saw the apparent bounty of nature and assembled, laughing,
   to gather the seeds and plants. It was the power of the distant magi-
   cian which made the enemy enjoy his fancied prosperity.
In the center of our council ground the fire burned and, lighting a ciga-
   rette I puffed smoke toward the east. Slowly a vision arose before
   me . . .
On the mountain tops was a yellow-spider magician, upon whom I
   called for help. He went to the enemy, darkened their hearts, tied their
   hands and their bows, and made them grow weak as women.
Then he pushed us on to destroy the enemy. We rushed upon the
   Apaches and killed them without difficulty.
With gladness in my heart I gathered the evidences of my victory and
   turned toward home.
You may think this over, my relatives. The taking of life brings serious
   thoughts of the waste; the celebration of victory may become riotous.

"*WAR SONG*" (PAPAGO)[7]

FROM RUTH UNDERHILL, *SINGING FOR POWER, THE SONG MAGIC OF THE PAPAGO INDIANS OF SOUTHERN ARIZONA*, 1938

   Is it for me to eat what food I have
And all day sit idle?
Is it for me to drink the sweet water poured out
And all day sit idle?
Is it for me to gaze upon my wife
And all day sit idle?

---

[7] A tribe of the desert regions of northern Arizona.

Is it for me to hold my child in my arms
And all day sit idle?

   My desire was uncontrollable.
It was the dizziness [of battle];
I, ground it to powder and therewith I painted my face.
It was the drunkenness of battle;
I ground it to powder and therewith I tied my hair in a war knot.
Then did I hold firm my well-strung bow and my smooth, straight-
   flying arrow.
To me did I draw my far-striding sandals, and fast I tied them.

   Over the flat land did I then go striding,
Over the embedded stones did I then go stumbling,
Under the trees in the ditches did I go stooping,
Through the trees on the high ground did I go hurtling,
Through the mountain gullies did I go brushing quickly.

   In four halts did I reach the shining white eagle, my guardian,
And I asked power.
Then favorable to me he felt
And did bring forth his shining white stone.
Our enemy's mountain he made white as with moonlight
And brought them close,
And across them I went striding.

   In four halts did I reach the blue hawk, my guardian,
And I asked power.
The hawk favorable to me he felt
And did bring forth his blue stone.
Our enemy's waters he made white as with moonlight,
And around them I went striding.
There did I seize and pull up and make into a bundle
Those things which were my enemy's,
All kinds of seeds and beautiful clouds and beautiful winds.

Then came forth a thick stalk and a thick tassel,
And the undying seed did ripen.

This I did on behalf of my people.
Thus should you also think and desire,
All you my kinsmen.

ARCHIBALD MACLEISH (1892–1982)

WILDWEST

There were none of my blood in this battle:
There were Minneconjous, Sans Arcs, Brules,[8]
Many nations of Sioux: they were few men galloping.

This would have been in the long days in June:
They were galloping well deployed under the plum-trees:
They were driving riderless horses: themselves they were few.

Crazy Horse had done it with few numbers.
Crazy Horse was small for a Lakota.[9]
He was riding always alone thinking of something:

He was standing alone by the picket lines by the ropes:
He was young then, he was thirty when he died:
Unless there were children to talk he took no notice

When the soldiers came for him there on the other side
On the Greasy Grass in the villages we were shouting
"Hoka Hey! Crazy Horse will be riding!"

They fought in the water: horses and men were drowning:
They rode on the butte: dust settled in sunlight:
Hoka Hey! they lay on the bloody ground.

[8] The Minneconjous: a division of the Sioux; the Sans Arcs: a band of the Teton Sioux, close to the Minneconjous; the Brules: a tribe related to the Dakotas.
[9] Part of the Sioux Nation.

No one could tell of the dead which man was Custer . . .
That was the end of his luck: by that river.
The soldiers beat him at Slim Buttes once:

They beat him at Willow Creek when the snow lifted:
That last time they beat him was the Tongue.
He had only the meat he had made and of that little.

Do you ask why he should fight? It was his country:
My God should he not fight? It was his.
But after the Tongue there were no herds to be hunting:

He cut the knots of the tails and he led them in:
He cried out "I am Crazy Horse! Do not touch me!"
There were many soldiers between and the gun glinting . . .

And a Mister Josiah Perham of Maine had much of the
land Mister Perham was building the Northern Pacific
railroad that is Mister Perham was saying at lunch that

forty say fifty millions of acres in gift and
government grant outright ought to be worth a
wide price on the Board at two-fifty and

later a Mister Cooke had relieved Mister Perham and
later a Mister Morgan relieved Mister Cooke:
Mister Morgan converted at prices current:

It was all prices to them: they never looked at it:
why should they look at the land? they were Empire Builders:
it was all in the bid and the asked and the ink on their books . . .

When Crazy Horse was there by the Black Hills
His heart would be big with the love he had for that country
And all the game he had seen and the mares he had ridden

And how it went out from you wide and clean in the sunlight

JAMES WRIGHT (1927–1980)

A CENTENARY ODE

INSCRIBED TO LITTLE CROW,[10] LEADER OF THE SIOUX REBELLION IN MINNESOTA, 1862

I had nothing to do with it. I was not here.
I was not born.
In 1862, when your hotheads
Raised hell from here to South Dakota,
My own fathers scattered into West Virginia
And southern Ohio.
My family fought the Confederacy
And fought the Union.
None of them got killed.
But for all that, it was not my fathers
Who murdered you.
Not much.

I don't know
Where the fathers of Minneapolis finalized
Your flayed carcass.
Little Crow, true father
Of my dark America,
When I close my eyes I lose you among
Old lonelinesses.
My family were a lot of singing drunks and good carpenters.
We had brothers who loved one another no matter what they did
And they did plenty.

I think they would have run like hell from your Sioux.
And when you caught them you all would have run like hell
From the Confederacy and from the Union
Into the hills and hunted for a few things,

---

[10] Leader of the Dakotas in a vain effort to resist the takeover of Indian land and culture. About five hundred whites were killed before the warriors were scattered and destroyed.

Some bull-cat under the stones, a gar maybe,
If you were hungry, and if you were happy,
Sunfish and corn.

If only I knew where to mourn you,
I would surely mourn.

But I don't know.
I did not come here only to grieve
For my people's defeat.
The troops of the Union, who won,
Still outnumber us.
Old Paddy Beck, my great-uncle, is dead
At the old soldiers home near Tiffen, Ohio.
He got away with every last stitch
Of his uniform, save only
The dress trousers.

Oh all around us,
The hobo jungles of America grow wild again.
The pick handles bloom like your skinned spine.
I don't even know where
My own grave is.

CARTER REVARD (B. 1931)

PARADING WITH THE V. F. W.

Apache, Omaha, Osage, Choctaw, Micmac, Cherokee, Oglala
Our place was ninety-fifth,
and when we got there with our ribbon shirts
and drum and singers on the trailer,
women in shawls and traditional dresses,
we looked into the muzzle of
an Army howitzer in front of us.
"Hey, Cliff," I said, "haven't seen guns that big

since we were in Wounded Knee."
Cliff carried the new American flag
donated by another post; Cliff prays
in Omaha for us, being chairman
of our Pow-Wow Committee, and his prayers
keep us together, helped
by hard work from the rest of course.
"They'll move that 105 ahead," Cliff said.
They did, but then the cavalry arrived.
No kidding, there was this troop outfitted
with Civil War style uniforms and carbines
on horseback, metal clopping on
the asphalt street, and there
on jackets were the insignia:
the 7th Cavalry, George Custer's bunch.
"Cliff," Walt said, "they think you're Sitting Bull."
"Just watch out where you're stepping, Walt,"
Cliff said. "Those pooper-scoopers
will not be working when the parade begins."
"Us women walking behind the trailer
will have to step around it all
so much, they'll think we're dancing,"
was all that Sherry said.
                         We followed
the yellow line, and here and there
some fake war-whoops came out to us
from sidewalk faces, but applause
moved with us when the singers started,
and we got our banner seen announcing
this year's Pow-Wow in June,
free to the public in Jefferson Barracks Park,
where the dragoons were quartered for the Indian Wars.
When we had passed the judging stand
and pulled off to the little park all
green and daffodilly under the misting rain,
we put the shawls and clothing in the car
and went back to the Indian Center, while

Cliff and George Coon went out and got
some chicken from the Colonel
that tasted great, given the temporary
absence of buffalo here in the
Gateway to the West, St. Louis.

DUANE NIATUM (B. 1938)

A TRIBUTE TO CHIEF JOSEPH[11]

Never reaching the promised land in Canada,
HIN-MAH-TOO-YAH-LAT-KET:
"Thunder-rolling-in-the-mountains,"
the fugitive chief sits in a corner
of the prison car headed for Oklahoma,
chained to his warriors,
a featherless hawk in exile.

He sees out the window
geese rise from the storm's center
and knows more men died
by snow blizzard
than by cavalry shot.

Still his father's shield
of Wallowa Valley deer and elk
flashes in his eyes
and coyote runs the circles
and a cricket swallows the dark.

How many songs this elder
sang to break the cycle

---

[11] Chief Joseph (1840–1904) tried to resist the removal of his people from their traditional
lands to a reservation.

of cold weather and disease
his people coughed and breathed
in this land of drifting ice.
Now sleepless as the door-guard,
the train rattles like dirt in his teeth,
straw in his eyes.

Holding rage in the palm of his fist,
his people's future spirals to red-forest dust,
leaves his bones on the track,
his soul in the whistle.

WILLIAM HEYEN (B. 1940)

THE STEADYING

Where we are, & at what speed: I know
we're spinning 14 miles a minute around the axis
of the earth; 1080 miles a minute in orbit
around our sun; 700 miles a second
straight out toward the constellation Virgo,
& now Custer is charging maybe a half-
mile a minute into an Indian village; but
from many eye-witnesses we know
Crazy Horse dismounted to fire his gun.
He steadied himself, & did not waste ammo.

Where we are, & at what speed: I saw
on display at Ford's Theatre in Washington, D.C.,
the black boots & tophat Lincoln wore that night;
at Auschwitz, a pile of thousands of eyeglasses also
behind glass to slow their disintegration;
in a Toronto museum, ancient mummies, ditto;
in Waikiki, some glittering duds once worn by Elvis; but
from many eye-witnesses we know
Crazy Horse dismounted to fire his gun.
He steadied himself, & did not waste ammo.

Where we are, & at what speed: I remember,
in Montana, a tumbleweed striking the back of my knees;
when I was a boy, a flock of blackbirds & starlings
beating past Nesconset for the whole morning;
at Westminster Abbey, in the stone corner, a poet's rose
for just a second drinking a streak of snow;
cattlecars of redwoods vowelling to gotham in my dream; but
from many eye-witnesses we know
Crazy Horse dismounted to fire his gun.
He steadied himself, & did not waste ammo.

JOY HARJO (B. 1941)

I GIVE YOU BACK

I release you, my beautiful and terrible
fear. I release you. You were my beloved
and hated twin, but now, I don't know you
as myself. I release you with all the
pain I would know at the death of
my daughters.

You are not my blood anymore.

I give you back to the white soldiers
who burned down my home, beheaded my children,
raped and sodomized my brothers and sisters.
I give you back to those who stole the
food from our plates when we were starving.

I release you, fear, because you hold
these scenes in front of me and I was born
with eyes that can never close.

I release you, fear, so you can no longer
keep me naked and frozen in the winter,
or smothered under blankets in the summer.

I release you
I release you
I release you
I release you

I am not afraid to be angry.
I am not afraid to rejoice.
I am not afraid to be black.
I am not afraid to be white.
I am not afraid to be hungry.
I am not afraid to be full.
I am not afraid to be hated.
I am not afraid to be loved.
to be loved, to be loved, fear.

Oh, you have choked me, but I gave you the leash.
You have gutted me but I gave you the knife.
You have devoured me, but I laid myself across the fire.
You held my mother down and raped her, but I gave you the heated
    thing.

I take myself back, fear.
You are not my shadow any longer.
I won't hold you in my hands.
You can't live in my eyes, my ears, my voice
my belly, or in my heart my heart
my heart   my heart

But come here, fear
I am alive and you are so afraid
                              of dying.

RAYNA GREEN (B. 1942)

COOSAPONAKEESA (MARY MATHEWS MUSGROVE BOSOMSWORTH)[12]

LEADER OF THE CREEKS, 1700–1783

what kind of lovers could they have been
these colonists

good enough to marry them everyone
or was it something else that made her take them on

all woman
part swamp rat
half horse
she rode through Georgia
It was hers and the Creeks'
and Oglethorpe wanted it all

But she rolled with him too
and kept them at bay
for too long
'til they said
she'd sold out for the goods

the money and velvet was what she loved
sure enough
but Ossabaw and Sapelo and Savannah more

so she fought them with sex and war
and anything that worked
until they rolled over her

---

[12] Daughter of an English trader and Creek Indian mother, she smoothed relations between the Indians and the settlers and fought to keep her claim to the Georgia Sea Islands that she had been granted by the Creeks, Ossabough, Sapelo, and St. Catherine's.

The Creeks say Mary came back as Sherman
just to see what they'd taken away
burned to the ground
and returned to her once more

The Creek girls in Oklahoma
laugh like Mary now
wild and good
they'll fight you for it
and make you want everything all over again

no deals this time though
it's all
or nothing

WENDY ROSE (B. 1948)

THREE THOUSAND DOLLAR DEATH SONG

> Nineteen American Indian skeletons from Nevada . . . valued at $3,000.
> —invoice received at a museum as normal business, 1975

Is it in cold hard cash? the kind
that dusts the insides of mens' pockets
laying silver-polished surface along the cloth.
Or in bills? papering the wallets of they
who thread the night with dark words. Or
checks? paper promises weighing the same
as words spoken once on the other side
of the mown grass and dammed rivers
of history. However it goes, it goes.
Through my body it goes
assessing each nerve, running its edges
along my arteries, planning ahead
for whose hands will rip me
into pieces of dusty red paper,

whose hands will smooth or smatter me
into traces of rubble. Invoiced now
it's official how our bones are valued
that stretch out pointing to sunrise
or are flexed into one last fetal bend,
that are removed and tossed about,
cataloged, numbered with black ink
on newly-white foreheads.
As we were formed to the white soldier's voice,
so we explode under white students' hands.
Death is a long trail of days
in our fleshless prison.
From this distant point
we watch our bones auctioned
with our careful quillwork,
beaded medicine bundles, even the bridles
of our shot-down horses. You who have priced us,
you who have removed us—at what cost?
What price the pits
where our bones share
a single bit of memory,
how one century has turned
our dead into specimens,
our history into dust,
our survivors into clowns.
Our memory might be catching, you know.
Picture the mortars, the arrowheads, the labrets
shaking off their labels like bears suddenly awake
to find the seasons ended while they slept.
Watch them touch each other, measure reality,
march out the museum door!
Watch as they lift their faces
and smell about for us. Watch our bones rise
to meet them and mount the horses once again!
The cost then will be paid
for our sweetgrass-smelling having-been
in clam-shell beads and steatite, dentalia

and woodpecker scalp, turquoise and copper,
blood and oil, coal and uranium,
children, a universe
of stolen things.

LOUISE ERDRICH (B. 1954)

DEAR JOHN WAYNE

August and the drive-in picture is packed.
We lounge on the hood of the Pontiac
surrounded by the slow-burning spirals they sell
at the window, to vanquish the hordes of mosquitoes.
Nothing works. They break through the smoke screen for blood.

Always the lookout spots the Indians first,
spread north to south, barring progress.
The Sioux or some other Plains bunch
in spectacular columns, ICBM missiles,
feathers bristling in the meaningful sunset.

The drum breaks. There will be no parlance.
Only the arrows whining, a death-cloud of nerves
swarming down on the settlers
who die beautifully, tumbling like dust weeds
into the history that brought us all here
together: this wide screen beneath the sign of the bear.

The sky fills, acres of blue squint and eye
that the crowd cheers. His face moves over us,
a thick cloud of vengeance, pitted
like the land that was once flesh. Each rut,
each scar makes a promise: *It is
not over, this fight, not as long as you resist.*

Everything we see belongs to us.

A few laughing Indians fall over the hood
slipping in the hot spilled butter.
The eye sees a lot, John, but the heart is so blind.
Death makes us owners of nothing.
He smiles, a horizon of teeth
the credits reel over, and then the white fields

again blowing in the true-to-life dark.
The dark films over everything.
We get into the car
scratching our mosquito bites, speechless and small
as people are when the movie is done.
We are back in our skins.

How can we help but keep hearing his voice,
the flip side of the sound track, still playing:
Come on, boys, we got them
where we want them, drunk, running.
They'll give us what we want, what we need.
Even his disease was the idea of taking everything.
Those cells, burning, doubling, splitting out of their skins.

CAPTIVITY

> He (my captor) gave me a bisquit, which I put in my pocket, and not
> daring to eat it, buried it under a log, fearing he had put something
> in it to make me love him.
>
> —From the narrative of the captivity of Mrs. Mary Rowlandson,[13]
> who was taken prisoner by the Wampanoag when Lancaster, Mas-
> sachusetts, was destroyed, in the year 1676

The stream was swift, and so cold
I thought I would be sliced in two.
But he dragged me from the flood
by the ends of my hair.

---

[13] Mary Rowlandson (1637–1710/11) was captured with three of her children close to the end of
King Philip's War. She and then her children were ransomed after three months of captivity.
Her narrative of her experience is an American classic.

I had grown to recognize his face.
I could distinguish it from the others.
There were times I feared I understood
his language, which was not human,
and I knelt to pray for strength.

We were pursued by God's agents
or pitch devils, I did not know.
Only that we must march.
Their guns were loaded with swan shot.
I could not suckle and my child's wail
put them in danger.
He had a woman
with teeth black and glittering.
She fed the child milk of acorns.
The forest closed, the light deepened.

I told myself that I would starve
before I took food from his hands
but I did not starve.
One night
he killed a deer with a young one in her
and gave me to eat of the fawn.
It was so tender,
the bones like the stems of flowers,
that I followed where he took me.
The night was thick. He cut the cord
that bound me to the tree.

After that the birds mocked.
Shadows gaped and roared
and the trees flung down
their sharpened lashes.
He did not notice God's wrath.
God blasted fire from half-buried stumps.
I hid my face in my dress, fearing He would burn us all
but this, too, passed.

Rescued, I see no truth in things.
My husband drives a thick wedge
through the earth, still it shuts
to him year after year.
My child is fed of the first wheat.
I lay myself to sleep
on a Holland-laced pillowbeer.
I lay to sleep.
And in the dark I see myself
as I was outside their circle.

They knelt on deerskins, some with sticks,
and he led his company in the noise
until I could no longer bear
the thought of how I was.
I stripped a branch
and struck the earth,
in time, begging it to open
to admit me
as he was
and feed me honey from the rock.

THE SPANISH-AMERICAN WAR

1898

The army was dusty, disheveled, its hair matted to its forehead with sweat, its shirts glued to its back with the same, and indescribably dirty, thirsty, hungry, and a-weary from its bundles and its marches and its fights. It sat down on the conquered crest and felt satisfied.
  "Well, hell! here we are."

—Stephen Crane, *War Dispatches* (1898)

These were the wars in which popular journalism played an inflammatory and crucial role, and in which regional congressional ambitions clashed over peace and war, over empire and an isolationist self-sufficiency. The Spanish War, Secretary of State John Hay's "splendid little war," was the most resounding. Initiated in April, 1898, and over by August of the same year, this was the first war fought on terrain not contiguous to the United States. In the name of Cuban independence from Spain, the three-hundred pound General Shafter led troops starved of food, supplies, and water, and sweating in wool through tropical harbors and jungle coastland, while Theodore Roosevelt charged triumphantly up San Juan Hill. Secretary of War Russell Alger reported that while 345 American deaths had been combat related, there had been 2,565 deaths by disease. In an offshoot of the war, Commodore Dewey brought Manila Bay under American control, an engagement referred to by an English historian as "more a military execution than a real contest."

  Stephen Crane filed his gaily nonchalant dispatches from Cuba as a war correspondent—yet two ironic assessments of war, one a poem that Crane had published earlier in "War Is Kind," as well as another, "The Battle Hymn," which lay tucked into his unpublished papers, represent grimmer shades of his opinion.

STEPHEN CRANE (1871–1900)

WAR IS KIND

Do not weep, maiden, for war is kind.
Because your lover threw wild hands toward the sky
And the affrighted steed ran on alone,
Do not weep.
War is kind.

    Hoarse, booming drums of the regiment,
    Little souls who thirst for fight,
    These men were born to drill and die.
    The unexplained glory flies above them,
    Great is the battle-god, great, and his kingdom—
    A field where a thousand corpses lie.

Do not weep, babe, for war is kind.
Because your father tumbled in the yellow trenches,
Raged at his breast, gulped and died,
Do not weep.
War is kind.

    Swift blazing flag of the regiment,
    Eagle with crest of red and gold,
    These men were born to drill and die.
    Point for them the virtue of slaughter,
    Make plain to them the excellence of killing
    And a field where a thousand corpses lie,

Mother whose heart hung humble as a button
On the bright splendid shroud of your son,
Do not weep.
War is kind.

THE BATTLE HYMN

All-feeling God, hear in the war-night
The rolling voices of a nation;
Through dusky billows of darkness
See the flash, the under-light, of bared swords—
—Whirling gleams like wee shells
Deep in the streams of the universe—
Bend and see a people, O, God,
A people rebuked, accursed,
By him of the many lungs
And by him of the bruised weary war-drum
(The chanting disintegrate and the two-faced eagle)
Bend and mark our steps, O, God.
Mark well, mark well, Father of the Never-Ending Circles
And if the path, the new path, lead awry
Then in the forest of the lost standards
Suffer us to grope and bleed apace
For the wisdom is Thine.
Bend and see a people, O, God,
A people applauded, acclaimed,
By him of the raw red shoulders
The manacle-marked, the thin victim
(He lies white amid the smoking cane)
—And if the path, the new path, leads straight—
Then—O, God—then bare the great bronze arm;
Swing high the blaze of the chained stars
And let them look and heed
(The chanting distintegrate and the two-faced eagle)
For we go, we go in a lunge of a long blue corps
And—to Thee we commit our lifeless sons,
The convulsed and furious dead.
(They shall be white amid the smoking cane)
For, the seas shall not bar us;
The capped mountains shall not hold us back
We shall sweep and swarm through jungle and pool,
Then let the savage one bend his high chin
To see on his breast, the sullen glow of the death-medals

For we know and we say our gift.
His prize is death, deep doom.
(He shall be white amid the smoking cane.)

PAUL LAURENCE DUNBAR (1872–1906)

THE CONQUERORS: THE BLACK TROOPS IN CUBA

Round the wide earth, from the red field your valour has won,
Blown with the breath of the far-speaking gun,
    Goes the word.
Bravely you spoke through the battle cloud heavy and dun.
Tossed though the speech toward the mist-hidden sun,
    The world heard.

Hell would have shrunk from you seeking it fresh from the fray,
Grim with the dust of the battle, and gray
    From the fight.
Heaven would have crowned you, with crowns not of gold but of bay,
Owning you fit for the light of her day,
    Men of night.

Far through the cycle of years and of lives that shall come,
There shall speak voices long muffled and dumb,
    Out of fear.
And through the noises of trade and the turbulent hum,
Truth shall rise over the militant drum,
    Loud and clear.

Then on the cheek of the honester nation that grows,
All for their love of you, not for your woes,
    There shall lie
Tears that shall be to your souls as the dew to the rose;
Afterward thanks, that the present yet knows
    Not to ply!

THE WAR OF THE PHILIPPINES

1899–1902

There have been lies; yes, but they were told in a good cause. We have been treacherous; but that was only in order that real good might come out of apparent evil. True, we have crushed a deceived and confiding people; we have turned against the weak and the friendless who trusted us; we have stamped out a just and intelligent and well-ordered republic; we have stabbed an ally in the back and slapped the face of a guest [Emilio Aguinaldo]; we have bought a Shadow from an enemy [Spain] that hadn't it to sell; we have robbed a trusting friend of his land and liberty; we have invited our clean young men to shoulder a discredited musket and do bandit's work under a flag which bandits have been accustomed to fear, not to follow; we have debauched America's honor and blackened her face before the world; but each detail was for the best.

—Mark Twain, "To the Person Sitting in Darkness," *The North American Review* (1901)

In the Philippine War, defenders and attackers alike fought with savagery. At the conclusion of both the Spanish and Philippine wars, American forces had secured control over not only Cuba, but the imperial prizes of the Philippine Islands, Puerto Rico, and Guam. The Philippine independence fighters, led by the Tagalog Emilio Aguinaldo, introduced the term *guerilla*, meaning "little war"; another borrowing from the Tagalog language, *bunduk*, became the familiar American *boondock*. Both William Vaughan Moody's stately elegy for a military death and his angry "Ode in Time of Hesitation" stand in formal contrast to Edgar Lee Masters's more baldly colloquial treatment of American military aims, yet both poets deplore the waste of life engendered by an aggressive expansionism and a false idea of the heroic. Kristin L. Hoganson writes that from 1899 to 1902,

U.S. forces landed 126,468 soldiers in the Philippines, of whom 4,234 died. And on the insurrectionary side: "an estimated sixteen to twenty-thousand Filipino soldiers and two hundred thousand Filipino civilians died in the war."

WILLIAM VAUGHAN MOODY (1869–1910)

ON A SOLDIER FALLEN IN THE PHILIPPINES

Streets of the roaring town,
Hush for him, hush, be still!
He comes, who was stricken down
Doing the word of our will.
Hush! Let him have his state,
Give him his soldier's crown.
The grists of trade can wait
Their grinding at the mill,
But he cannot wait for his honor, now the trumpet has been blown;
Wreathe pride now for his granite brow, lay love on his breast of stone.

Toll! Let the great bells toll
Till the clashing air is dim.
Did we wrong this parted soul?
We will make up it to him.
Toll! Let him never guess
What work we set him to.
Laurel, laurel, yes;
He did what we bade him do.
Praise, and never a whispered hint but the fight he fought was good;
Never a word that the blood on his sword was his country's own heart's-
    blood.

A flag for the soldier's bier
Who dies that his land may live;
O, banners, banners here,
That he doubt not nor misgive!
That he heed not from the tomb
The evil days draw near
When the nation, robed in gloom,
With its faithless past shall strive.

Let him never dream that his bullet's scream went wide of its island
     mark,
Home to the heart of his darling land where she stumbled and sinned in
     the dark.

FROM *ODE IN THE TIME OF HESITATION*

9

Ah no!
We have not fallen so.
We are our fathers' sons: let those who lead us know!
'Twas only yesterday sick Cuba's cry
Came up the tropic wind, "Now help us, for we die!"
Then Alabama heard,
And rising, pale, to Maine and Idaho
Shouted a burning word.
Proud state with proud impassioned state conferred,
And at the lifting of a hand sprang forth,
East, west, and south, and north,
Beautiful armies. Oh, by the sweet blood and young
Shed on the awful hill slope at San Juan,[1]
By the unforgotten names of eager boys
Who might have tasted girls' love and been stung
With the old mystic joys
And starry griefs, now the spring nights come on,
But that the heart of youth is generous—
We charge you, ye who lead us,
Breathe on their chivalry no hint of stain!
Turn not their new-world victories to gain!
One least leaf plucked for chaffer from the bays
Of their dear praise,
One jot of their pure conquest put to hire,

---

[1] The battle of San Juan Hill in Cuba.

The implacable republic will require;
With clamor, in the glare and gaze of noon,
Or subtly, coming as a thief at night,
But surely, very surely, slow or soon
That insult deep we deeply will requite.
Tempt not our weakness, our cupidity!
For save we let the island men[2] go free,
Those baffled and dislaureled ghosts
Will curse us from the lamentable coasts
Where walk the frustrate dead.
The cup of trembling shall be drainèd quite,
Eaten the sour bread of astonishment,
With ashes of the hearth shall be made white
Our hair, and wailing shall be in the tent;
Then on your guiltier head
Shall our intolerable self-disdain
Wreak suddenly its anger and its pain;
For manifest in that disastrous light
We shall discern the right
And do it, tardily.—O ye who lead,
Take heed!
Blindness we may forgive, but baseness we will smite.

EDGAR LEE MASTERS (1869–1950)

HARRY WILMANS

I was just turned twenty-one,
And Henry Phipps, the Sunday-school superintendent,
Made a speech in Bindle's Opera House.
"The honor of the flag must be upheld," he said,

[2] Filipinos.

"Whether it be assailed by a barbarous tribe of Tagalogs[3]
Or the greatest power in Europe."
And we cheered and cheered the speech and the flag he waved
As he spoke.
And I went to the war in spite of my father,
And followed the flag till I saw it raised
By our camp in a rice field near Manila,
And all of us cheered and cheered it.
But there were flies and poisonous things;
And there was deadly water,
And the cruel heat,
And the sickening putrid food;
And the smell of the trench just back of the tents
Where the soldiers went to empty themselves;
And there were the whores who followed us, full of syphilis;
And beastly acts between ourselves or alone,
With bullying, hatred, degradation among us,
And days of loathing and nights of fear
To the hour of the charge through the steaming swamp,
Following the flag,
Till I fell with a scream, shot through the guts.
Now there's a flag over me in Spoon River!
A flag! A flag!

[3] Filipinos.

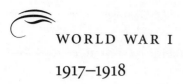

WORLD WAR I

1917–1918

I heard an excited exclamation from a group of Sisters behind me.

"Look! Look! Here are the Americans!"

I pressed forward with the others to watch the United States physically entering the War, so god-like, so splendidly unimpaired in comparison with the tired, nerve-wracked men of the British Army. So these were our deliverers at last, marching up the road to Camiers in the spring sunshine! There seemed to be hundreds of them, and in the fearless swagger of their proud strength they looked a formidable bulwark against the peril looming from Amiens.

—Vera Brittain, *Testament of Youth* (1933)

Americans entered this global conflict in the final years, when exhaustion had already drained the forces of the Allied and the Central Powers. In this war, as well as in World War II, the conclusion of hostilities saw the United States established in an economic position more favorable than that of any other nation. All the other belligerents emerged from war in debt to America, which permanently altered the power balance of the twentieth century. Because the American prewar slump had been eradicated by the stimulus of wartime manufacture, the nation achieved a new status on the postwar scene as the financial center of the Western world, replacing Britain. The United States is still considered the key to the victory of 1918. One hundred and fourteen thousand Americans had died in this war from all causes, and nothing can shrink the tragedy of these numbers. It remains to be said, however, that in comparison to the European dead—the 1,811,000 Russians, the 2,037,000 Germans, the 1,398,000 French, and the 723,000 English—the numbers show that while Americans certainly suffered, they endured less and benefited more from the war than their allies.

During this war, the continental landmass of America, buffered on each side by the vast oceans that for centuries have been its chief defensive feature, lay guarded against attack from any but the most determined and concentrated naval maneuver. Their houses intact, Americans stayed distant from the displacements of population, the blighted cities, the ruined fields, and the mine-laced countryside of Europe. For both world wars, the American civilian's direct experience of combat was nonexistent; Americans had to leave home to see war.

When poets brought home to America the war that they had witnessed, they made clear its devastating character. The new industrial warfare, with its machine-guns and unimaginable quantities of shells and mortars, made a mockery of the tactical wisdom of earlier ideas of chivalric death, in which heroes needed only to duel with heroes or to lead blindly obedient followers to win victory in the field; in modern war, victory derived from mastering not only men but technology. The Civil War had drawn many more soldiers per capita from a much smaller population, but by 1917, the United States had mustered an army of 3.5 million, bringing to France more than two million. Yet the sheer number of men could only account for a part of military dominance: in engagements like St. Mihiel, observers noted that American soldiers fell, as they had fallen in the Civil War, lying in orderly rows, mowed down by pitilessly efficient machine gun fire.

Again, lamentation over the ravages of mass death rules the resulting poetry. While a poem by Malcolm Cowley may delight in raising contrasts of Old and New World culture, Cowley and other poets including E. E. Cummings and Ezra Pound also brought a newly intensified antimilitarism. A heartfelt mourning exists in this poetry, yet the waste of life and the redirection of resources that the new warfare dictated, along with the growing awareness of the misfit of old forms of unthinking patriotic loyalty, also elicited a new, rebellious, and skeptical strain of thought and imagery.

AMY LOWELL (1874–1925)

PATTERNS

I walk down the garden paths,
And all the daffodils
Are blowing, and the bright blue squills.
I walk down the patterned garden paths
In my stiff, brocaded gown.
With my powdered hair and jewelled fan,
I too am a rare
Pattern. As I wander down
The garden paths,
My dress is richly figured,
And the train
Makes a pink and silver stain
On the gravel, and the thrift
Of the borders.
Just a plate of current fashion,
Tripping by in high-heeled, ribboned shoes.
Not a softness anywhere about me,
Only whale-bone and brocade.
And I sink on a seat in the shade
Of a lime tree. For my passion
Wars against the stiff brocade.
The daffodils and squills
Flutter in the breeze
As they please.
And I weep;
For the lime tree is in blossom
And one small flower has dropped upon my bosom.

And the splashing of waterdrops
In the marble fountain
Comes down the garden paths.
The dripping never stops.
Underneath my stiffened gown
Is the softness of a woman bathing in a marble basin,

A basin in the midst of hedges grown
So thick, she cannot see her lover hiding,
But she guesses he is near,
And the sliding of the water
Seems the stroking of a dear
Hand upon her.
What is Summer in a fine brocaded gown!
I should like to see it lying in a heap upon the ground.
All the pink and silver crumpled up on the ground.

I would be the pink and silver as I ran along the paths,
And he would stumble after,
Bewildered by my laughter.
I should see the sun flashing from his sword hilt and the buckles on his
    shoes.
I would choose
To lead him in a maze along the patterned paths,
A bright and laughing maze for my heavy-booted lover,
Till he caught me in the shade,
And the buttons of his waistcoat bruised my body as he clasped me,
Aching, melting, unafraid.
With the shadows of the leaves and the sundrops,
And the plopping of the waterdrops,
All about us in the open afternoon—
I am very like to swoon
With the weight of this brocade,
For the sun sifts through the shade.

Underneath the fallen blossom
In my bosom,
Is a letter I have hid.
It was brought to me this morning by a rider from the Duke.
"Madam, we regret to inform you that Lord Hartwell
Died in action Thursday sen'night."
As I read it in the white, morning sunlight,
The letters squirmed like snakes.
"Any answer, Madam?" said my footman.
"No," I told him.

"See that the messenger takes some refreshment.
No, no answer."
And I walked into the garden,
Up and down the patterned paths,
In my stiff, correct brocade.
The blue and yellow flowers stood up proudly in the sun,
Each one.
I stood upright too,
Held rigid to the pattern
By the stiffness of my gown.
Up and down I walked,
Up and down.

In a month he would have been my husband.
In a month, here, underneath this lime,
We would have broke the pattern;
He for me, and I for him,
He as Colonel, I as Lady,
On this shady seat.
He had a whim
That sunlight carried blessing.
And I answered, "It shall be as you have said."
Now he is dead,

In Summer and in Winter I shall walk
Up and down
The patterned garden paths
In my stiff, brocaded gown.
The squills and daffodils
Will give place to pillared roses, and to asters, and to snow.
I shall go
Up and down,
In my gown.
Gorgeously arrayed,
Boned and stayed.
And the softness of my body will be guarded from embrace
By each button, hook, and lace.

For the man who should loose me is dead,
Fighting with the Duke in Flanders,
In a pattern called a war.
Christ! What are patterns for?

ROBERT FROST (1874–1963)

NOT TO KEEP

They sent him back to her. The letter came
Saying . . . and she could have him. And before
She could be sure there was no hidden ill
Under the formal writing, he was in her sight—
Living.—They gave him back to her alive—
How else? They are not known to send the dead—
And not disfigured visibly. His face?—
His hands? She had to look—to ask
"What was it, dear?" And she had given all
And still she had all—*they* had—they the lucky!
Wasn't she glad now? Everything seemed won,
And all the rest for them permissible ease.
She had to ask "What was it, dear?"
                                          "Enough,
Yet not enough. A bullet through and through,
High in the breast. Nothing but what good care
And medicine and rest—and you a week,
Can cure me of to go again." The same
Grim giving to do over for them both.
She dared no more than ask him with her eyes
How was it with him for a second trial.
And with his eyes he asked her not to ask.
They had given him back to her, but not to keep.

CARL SANDBURG (1878–1967)

BUTTONS

I have been watching the war map slammed up for advertising in front
    of the newspaper office.
Buttons—red and yellow buttons—blue and black buttons—are shoved
    back and forth across the map.

A laughing young man, sunny with freckles,
Climbs a ladder, yells a joke to somebody in the crowd
And then fixes a yellow button one inch west
And follows the yellow button with a black button one inch west.

(Ten thousand men and boys twist on their bodies in a red soak along a
    river edge,
Gasping of wounds, calling for water, some rattling death in their
    throats.)
Who by Christ would guess what it cost to move two buttons one inch
    on the war map here in front of the newspaper office where the
    freckle-faced young man is laughing to us?

GRASS

Pile the bodies high at Austerlitz and Waterloo.
Shovel them under and let me work—
                    I am the grass; I cover all.

And pile them high at Gettysburg
And pile them high at Ypres and Verdun.
Shovel them under and let me work.
Two years, ten years, and passengers ask the conductor:
                    What place is this?
                    Where are we now?

                    I am the grass.
                    Let me work.

WALLACE STEVENS (1879–1955)

THE DEATH OF A SOLDIER

> La mort du soldat est près des choses naturelles.[1]

Life contracts and death is expected,
As in a season of autumn.
The soldier falls.

He does not become a three-days personage,
Imposing his separation,
Calling for pomp.

Death is absolute and without memorial,
As in a season of autumn,
When the wind stops,

When the wind stops and, over the heavens,
The clouds go, nevertheless,
In their direction.

EZRA POUND (1885–1972)

FROM HUGH SELWYN MAUBERLEY

IV

These fought in any case,
and some believing,
               pro domo,[2] in any case . . .

---

[1] "The death of a soldier is close to a natural thing."
[2] "*pro domo*": for home.

Some quick to arm,
some for adventure,
some from fear of weakness,
some from fear of censure,
some for love of slaughter, in imagination,
learning later . . .
some in fear, learning love of slaughter;
Died some, pro patria,
                    non "dulce" non "et decor" . . . [3]
walked eye-deep in hell
believing in old men's lies, then unbelieving
came home, home to a lie,
home to many deceits,
home to old lies and new infamy;
usury age-old and age-thick
and liars in public places.

Daring as never before, wastage as never before.
Young blood and high blood,
fair cheeks, and fine bodies;

fortitude as never before

frankness as never before,
disillusions as never told in the old days,
hysterias, trench confessions,
laughter out of dead bellies.

V

There died a myriad,
And of the best, among them,
For an old bitch gone in the teeth,
For a botched civilization,

[3] These lines play off the famous line of Horace (*Odes* 3.2.13) that became a slogan urged by schoolmasters on their students: "*Dulce et decorum est pro patria mori*," which is translated as "It is sweet and fitting to die for one's country."

Charm, smiling at the good mouth,
Quick eyes gone under earth's lid,

For two gross of broken statues,
For a few thousand battered books.

SARA TEASDALE (1884–1933)

THERE WILL COME SOFT RAINS

There will come soft rains and the smell of the ground,
And swallows circling with their shimmering sound;

And frogs in the pools singing at night,
And wild plum-trees in tremulous white;

Robins will wear their feathery fire
Whistling their whims on a low fence-wire;

And not one will know of the war, not one
Will care at last when it is done.

Not one would mind, neither bird nor tree
If mankind perished utterly;

And Spring herself, when she woke at dawn,
Would scarcely know that we were gone.

T. S. ELIOT (1888–1965)

TRIUMPHAL MARCH—1931

FROM CORIOLAN

Stone, bronze, stone, steel, stone, oakleaves, horses' heels
Over the paving.
And the flags. And the trumpets. And so many eagles.
How many? Count them. And such a press of people.
We hardly knew ourselves that day, or knew the City.
This is the way to the temple, and we so many crowding the way.
So many waiting, how many waiting? what did it matter, on such a day?
Are they coming? No, not yet. You can see some eagles. And hear the
    trumpets.
Here they come. Is he coming?
The natural wakeful life of our Ego is a perceiving.
We can wait with our stools and our sausages.
What comes first? Can you see? Tell us. It is

 5,800,000 rifles and carbines,
  102,000 machine guns,
   28,000 trench mortars,
   53,000 field and heavy guns,
I cannot tell how many projectiles, mines and fuses,
   13,000 aeroplanes,
   24,000 aeroplane engines,
   50,000 ammunition waggons,
now 55,000 army waggons,
   11,000 field kitchens,
   1,150 field bakeries.

What a time that took. Will it be he now? No,
Those are the golf club Captains, these the Scouts,
And now the *société gymnastique de Poissy*
And now come the Mayor and the Liverymen. Look
There he is now, look:
There is no interrogation in his eyes
Or in the hands, quiet over the horse's neck,

And the eyes watchful, waiting, perceiving, indifferent.
O hidden under the dove's wing, hidden in the turtle's breast,
Under the palmtree at noon, under the running water
At the still point of the turning world. O hidden.

Now they go up to the temple. Then the sacrifice.
Now come the virgins bearing urns, urns containing
Dust
Dust
Dust of dust, and now
Stone, bronze, stone, steel, stone, oakleaves, horses' heels
Over the paving.

That is all we could see. But how many eagles! and how many trumpets!
(And Easter Day, we didn't get to the country,
So we took young Cyril to church. And they rang a bell
And he said right out loud, *crumpets.*)
                              Don't throw away that sausage,
It'll come in handy. He's artful. Please, will you
Give us a light?
Light
Light
Et les soldats faisaient la haie? ILS LA FAISAIENT.[4]

ALAN SEEGER (1888–1916)

I HAVE A RENDEZVOUS WITH DEATH

   I have a rendezvous with Death
At some disputed barricade,
When Spring comes back with rustling shade
And apple-blossoms fill the air—
I have a rendezvous with Death
When Spring brings back blue days and fair.

---

[4] "And do the soldiers line the street? THEY LINE IT."

It may be he shall take my hand
And lead me into his dark land
And close my eyes and quench my breath—
It may be I shall pass him still.
I have a rendezvous with Death
On some scarred slope of battered hill,
When Spring comes round again this year
And the first meadow-flowers appear.

God knows 'twere better to be deep
Pillowed in silk and scented down,
Where Love throbs out in blissful sleep,
Pulse nigh to pulse, and breath to breath,
Where hushed awakenings are dear . . .
But I've a rendezvous with Death
At midnight in some flaming town,
When Spring trips north again this year,
And I to my pledged word am true,
I shall not fail that rendezvous.

THE AISNE (1914–15)

We first saw fire on the tragic slopes
Where the flood-tide of France's early gain,
Big with wrecked promise and abandoned hopes,
Broke in a surf of blood along the Aisne.[5]

The charge her heroes left us, we assumed,
What, dying, they reconquered, we preserved,
In the chill trenches, harried, shelled, entombed,
Winter came down on us, but no man swerved.

Winter came down on us. The low clouds, torn
In the stark branches of the riven pines,
Blurred the white rockets that from dusk till morn
Traced the wide curve of the close-grappling lines.

[5] The Aisne is a tributary of the river Oise, and both were the sites of repeated battles from 1914 to 1918.

In rain, and fog that on the withered hill
Froze before dawn, the lurking foe drew down;
Or light snows fell that made forlorner still
The ravaged country and the ruined town;

Or the long clouds would end. Intensely fair,
The winter constellations blazing forth—
Perseus, the Twins, Orion, the Great Bear—
Gleamed on our bayonets pointing to the north.

And the lone sentinel would start and soar
On wings of strong emotion as he knew
That kinship with the stars that only War
Is great enough to lift man's spirit to.

And ever down the curving front, aglow
With the pale rockets' intermittent light,
He heard, like distant thunder, growl and grow
The rumble of far battles in the night,—

Rumours, reverberant, indistinct, remote,
Borne from red fields whose martial names have won
The power to thrill like a far trumpet-note,—
Vic, Vailly, Soupir, Hurtelise, Craonne . . .

Craonne, before thy cannon-swept plateau,
Where like sere leaves lay strewn September's dead,
I found for all things I forfeited
A recompense I would not now forgo.

For that high fellowship was ours then
With those who, championing another's good,
More than dull Peace or its poor votaries could,
Taught us the dignity of being men.

There we drained deeper the deep cup of life,
And on sublimer summits came to learn,
After soft things, the terrible and stern,
After sweet Love, the majesty of Strife;

There where we faced under those frowning heights
The blast that maims, the hurricane that kills;
There where the watch-lights on the winter hills
Flickered like balefire through inclement nights;

There where, firm links in the unyielding chain,
Where fell the long-planned blow and fell in vain—
Hearts worthy of the honour and the trail,
We helped to hold the lines along the Aisne.

ARCHIBALD MACLEISH (1892–1982)

MEMORIAL RAIN

FOR KENNETH MACLEISH, 1894–1918

Ambassador Puser the ambassador
Reminds himself in French, felicitous tongue,
What these (young men no longer) lie here for
In rows that once, and somewhere else were young . . .

   All night in Brussels the wind had tugged at my door:
   I had heard the wind at my door and the trees strung
   Taut, and to me who had never been before
   In that country it was a strange wind, blowing
   Steadily, stiffening the walls, the floor,
   The roof of my room. I had not slept for knowing
He, too, dead, was a stranger in that land
   And felt beneath the earth in the wind's flowing
   A tightening of roots and would not understand,
Remembering lake winds in Illinois,
That strange wind. I had felt his bones in the sand
   Listening.

   . . . *Reflects that these enjoy*
Their country's gratitude, that deep repose,
That peace no pain can break, no hurt destroy,
That rest, that sleep . . .

At Ghent the wind rose.
There was a smell of rain and a heavy drag
Of wind in the hedges but not as the wind blows
Over fresh water when the waves lag
Foaming and the willows huddle and it will rain:
I felt him waiting.

. . . Indicates the flag
Which (may he say) enisles in Flanders plain
This little field these happy, happy dead
Have made America . . .

In the ripe grain
The wind coiled glistening, darted, fled,
Dragging its heavy body: at Waereghem
The wind coiled in the grass above his head:
Waiting—listening . . .

. . . Dedicates to them
This earth their bones have hallowed, this last gift
A Grateful country . . .

Under the dry grass stem
The words are blurred, are thickened, the words sift
Confused by the rasp of the wind, by the thin grating
Of ants under the grass, the minute shift
And tumble of dusty sand separating
From dusty sand. The roots of the grass strain,
Tighten, the earth is rigid, waits—he is waiting—

And suddenly, and all at once, the rain!

The living scatter, they run into houses, the wind
Is trampled under the rain, shakes free, is again
Trampled. The rain gathers, running in thinned
Spurts of water that ravel in the dry sand,
Seeping in the sand under the grass roots, seeping
Between cracked boards to the bones of a clenched hand:
The earth relaxes, loosens; he is sleeping,
He rests, he is quiet, he sleeps in a strange land.

E. E. CUMMINGS (1894–1962)

I SING OF OLAF

i sing of Olaf glad and big
whose warmest heart recoiled at war:
a conscientious object-or.

his wellbelovéd colonel (trig[6]
westpointer most succinctly bred)
took erring Olaf soon in hand;
but—though an host of overjoyed
noncoms (first knocking on the head
him) do through icy waters roll
that helplessness which others stroke
with brushes recently employed
anent this muddy toiletbowl,
while kindred intellects evoke
allegiance per blunt instruments—
Olaf (being to all intents
a corpse and wanting any rag
upon what God unto him gave)
responds, without getting annoyed
"I will not kiss your f-ing flag"

straightway the silver bird looked grave
(departing hurriedly to shave)

but—though all kinds of officers
(a yearning nation's blueeyed pride)
their passive prey did kick and curse
until for wear their clarion
voices and boots were much the worse,
and egged the firstclassprivates on
his rectum wickedly to tease

---

[6] Prim or neat.

by means of skillfully applied
bayonets roasted hot with heat—
Olaf (upon what were once knees)
does almost ceaselessly repeat
"there is some s. I will not eat"

our president,being of which
assertions duly notified
threw the yellowsonofabitch
into a dungeon, where he died

Christ (of His mercy infinite)
i pray to see;and Olaf, too

preponderatingly because
unless statistics lie he was
more brave than me:more blond than you.

LOUISE BOGAN (1897–1970)

TO MY BROTHER KILLED: HAUMONT WOOD: OCTOBER, 1918[7]

O you so long dead,
You masked and obscure,
I can tell you, all things endure:
The wine and the bread;

The marble quarried for the arch;
The iron become steel;
The spoke broken from the wheel;
The sweat of the long march;

[7] Haumont Wood was one of the first sites of the battle of Verdun.

The hay-stacks cut through like loaves
And the hundred flowers from the seed;
All things indeed
Though struck by the hooves

Of disaster, of time due,
Of fell loss and gain,
All things remain,
I can tell you, this is true.

Though burned down to stone
Though lost from the eye,
I can tell you, and not lie,—
Save of peace alone.

MALCOLM COWLEY (1898–1989)

CHATEAU DE SOUPIR, 1917[8]

Jean tells me that the Senator
came here to see his mistresses.
With a commotion at the door
the servants ushered him, Jean says,
through velvets and mahoganies
to where the odalisque was set,
the queen pro tempore, Yvette.

An eighteenth-century chateau
remodeled to his Lydian taste,
painted and gilt fortissimo:
the Germans, grown sardonical,
had used a bust of Cicero
as shield for a machine-gun nest
at one end of the banquet hall.

[8] A site of combat and later an Allied dressing station.

The trenches run diagonally
across the gardens and the lawns,
and jagged wire from tree to tree.
The lake is desolate of swans.
In tortured immobility
the deities of stone or bronze
abide each new catastrophe.

Phantasmagorical at nights,
yellow and white and amethyst,
the star-shells flare, the Verey lights
hiss upward, brighten, and persist
until a tidal wave of mist
rolls over and makes us seem
the drowned creatures of a dream,

ghosts among earlier ghosts. Yvette,
the tight skirt raised above her knees,
beckons her lover *en fillette*,
then nymphlike flits among the trees,
while he, beard streaming in the breeze,
pants after her, a portly satyr,
his goat feet shod in patent leather.

The mist creeps riverward. A fox
barks underneath a blasted tree.
An enemy machine gun mocks
This ante-bellum coquetry
and then falls silent, while a bronze
Silenus, patron of these lawns,
Lies riddled like a pepper box.

ERNEST HEMINGWAY (1899–1961)

CHAMPS D'HONNEUR[9]

Soldiers never do die well;
    Crosses mark the places—
Wooden crosses where they fell,
    Stuck above their faces.
Soldiers pitch and cough and twitch—
    All the world roars red and black;
Soldiers smother in a ditch,
    Choking through the whole attack.

RIPARTO D'ASSALTO[10]

Drummed their boots on the camion floor,
Hob-nailed boots on the camion floor.
Sergeants stiff,
Corporals sore.
Lieutenant thought of a Mestre[11] whore—
Warm and soft and sleepy whore,
Cozy, warm and lovely whore;
Damned cold, bitter, rotten ride,
Winding road up the Grappa[12] side.
Arditi[13] on benches stiff and cold,
Pride of their country stiff and cold,
Bristly faces, dirty hides—
Infantry marches, Arditi rides.
Grey, cold, bitter, sullen ride—
To splintered pines on the Grappa side
At Asalone,[14] where the truck-load died.

---

[9] "Field of Honor," or battlefield.
[10] A battalion.
[11] A harbor near Venice.
[12] Monte Grappa, near Bassano.
[13] Italian storm troops.
[14] Site of a battle.

MURIEL RUKEYSER (1913–1980)

FROM *POEM OUT OF CHILDHOOD*

In adolescence I knew travellers
speakers digressing from the ink-pocked rooms,
bearing the unequivocal sunny word.

 Prinzip's[15] year bore us see us turning at breast
 quietly while the air throbs over Sarajevo
 after the mechanic laugh of that bullet.
 How could they know what sinister knowledge finds
 its way among our brains' wet palpitance,
 what words would nudge and giggle at our spine,
 what murders dance?
 These horrors have approached the growing child;
 now that the factory is sealed-up brick
 the kids throw stones, smashing the windows,
 membranes of uselessness in desolation.

 We grew older quickly, watching the father shave
 and the splatter of lather hardening on the glass,
 playing in sandboxes to escape paralysis,
 being victimized by fataller sly things.
 "Oh, and you," he said, scraping his jaw, "what will you be?"
 "Maybe : something : like : Joan : of : Arc. . . ."
 Allies Advance, we see,
 Six Miles South to Soissons.[16] And we beat the drums.
 Watchsprings snap in the mind, uncoil, relax,
 the leafy years all somber with foreign war.
 How could we know what exposed guts resembled?

 Disturbed by war we pedalled bicycles
 breakneck down the decline, until the treads

[15] Gavril Prinzip was the Serbian nationalist who shot Archduke Ferdinand in Sarajevo and precipitated World War I.
[16] A site of battles in the Verdun region.

conquered our speed and pulled our feet behind them,
and pulled our heads.
We never knew the war, standing so small
looking at eye-level toward the puttees, searching
the picture-books for sceptres, pennants for truth;
see Galahad unaided by puberty.

Ratat a drum upon the armistice,
Kodak As You Go   :   photo   :   they danced late,
and we were a generation of grim children
leaning over the bedroom sills, watching
the music and the shoulders and how the war was over,
laughing until the blow on the mouth broke night
wide out from cover.
The child's curls blow in a forgotten wind,
immortal ivy trembles on the wall:
the sun has crystallized these scenes, and tall
shadows remember time cannot rescind.

THE SPANISH CIVIL WAR

1936–1939

I think now of a boat on which I sailed away from the beginning of a war. It was nighttime, and over the deep fertile sea of night the voices of people talking quietly; some lights of the sea-coast, far-away; some stars.

This was the first moment of stillness in days of fighting. We had seen the primitive beginnings of the open warfare of this period: men running through the silvery groves, the sniper whose gun would speak, as the bullet broke the wall beside you; a child staring upward at a single plane. More would come; in the city, the cars burned and blood streamed over the walls of houses and the horses shrieked; armies formed and marched out; the gypsies, the priests in their purity and violence fought. Word from abroad was coming in as they asked us to meet in the summer leafy Square, and told us what they knew. They had seen how as foreigners, we were deprived; how we were kept from, and wanted, above all things one: our responsibility.

This was a stroke of insight: it was true. "Now you have your responsibility," the voice said, deep, prophetic, direct, "go home: tell your peoples what you have seen."

—Muriel Rukeyser, on leaving Barcelona in 1936, *The Life of Poetry* (1996)

Although the United States did not enter World War II until late 1941, Americans had already seen the Japanese invasion of Manchuria, Mussolini's victory in Ethiopia, and the consolidation of Hitler's power in Germany. In a world of maximum economic distress and political upheaval, the fascist program for world dominance appeared to be gaining. For adherents of democracy, Spain emerged as the one positive change: the new republic favored land reform and secularized education, and meant to unseat an oppressive, entrenched aristocracy and a church and military dedicated to the status quo. When the republic came under attack by Generalissimo Franco, support for Spain coalesced, and the words of Dolores Ibarruri, known as La Pasionaria, became an international slogan: "It is better to die on your feet than live on your knees."

In 1936, the Communist International, or Comintern, put Spain on its list of priorities. By November, 2,000 communist and socialist antifascists from France, Great Britain, Yugoslavia, Belgium, Poland, and Austria were on the streets of Madrid in uniform, many of them political refugees from fascism in their own countries. Ultimately, the volunteers of the Fifteenth International Brigade numbered 40,000, and came from fifty-two different countries. Officially, the U.S. government, protecting its corporate investments in Spain and suspicious of the Popular Front coalition, adopted a nonintervention policy, maintaining neutrality in the face of active aid to Franco by Hitler in Germany, Mussolini in Italy, and Salazar in Portugal. The bombing of Guernica in 1937, aided by the German Luftwaffe, marked the first aerial bombardment of a civilian population in any war. The Russians accounted for the only tanks and weapons given to the Spanish republic.

In the heyday of the Popular Front, in which Communist Party orthodoxy softened enough to include other left-wing organizations in their efforts, Americans flocked to the defense of Spain. More than 150 worked as doctors, nurses, medical technicians, and ambulance drivers in the American Medical Bureau to Aid Spanish Democracy; 2,800 served in the Lincoln and Washington Battalions, who were that part of the International Brigade that, through a support wing, erroneously came to be known as the Abraham Lincoln Brigade. Defying a State Department order forbidding travel to Spain, Americans found their way to France, and by late January, 1937, were walking over the Pyrenees to get to Madrid. Later in the war, badly equipped, undertrained, and suffering heavy combat losses, the remnants of the Lincoln and Washington Battalions combined on the field; about a third of those who volunteered and fought were buried in Spanish earth.

The Lincolns included among their ranks sharecroppers and Ivy League graduates, IWW "Wobblies" and idealistic students, men and women, and blacks and whites. At least 60 percent were members of the Young Communist League or the Communist Party, but beyond party loyalty, the urge to join the loyalist forces came from a deep disregard for a narrow nationalism and from a love of social justice. When Oliver Law took over the command of the Lincoln battalion at Jarama, it was the first time in American history that an integrated military force had been led by an African-American officer. He was killed late in the summer at Brunete.

The poets of this war ardently believed that participation in the arts could matter politically, a conviction that the fall of Madrid shook for many. After 1939, when Stalin signed a nonaggression pact with Hitler, some Lincolns began to question their party loyalties. Some fought American entry into World War II, while others went on to become soldiers; still others were denied active service because of their Communist Party membership. In the 1950s, the rifts of opinion opened further, as evidence of Stalinist purges became widely known. Poet Genevieve Taggard nonetheless wrote to defend those who had fought in the International Brigade against questioning by the House Un-American Activities Committee. Brigade members were harassed by the FBI, blacklisted, and marginalized; others served jail sentences for their refusal to deny the political affiliations of that time or to act as informers about their history and the history of others in the communist movement.

Decades later, the surviving Lincolns marched to protest American involvement in Vietnam.

ROBINSON JEFFERS (1887–1962)

SINVERGUENZA[1]

They snarl over Spain like cur-dogs over a bone, then look at each other
　　and shamelessly
Lie out of the sides of their mouths.
Brag, threat and lie, these are diplomacy; wolf-fierce, cobra-deadly and
　　monkey-shameless,
These are the masters of powerful nations.
I wonder is it any satisfaction to Spaniards to see that their blood is only
The first drops of a forming rain-storm.

EDNA ST. VINCENT MILLAY (1892–1950)

SAY THAT WE SAW SPAIN DIE

Say that we saw Spain die. O splendid bull, how well you fought!
Lost from the first.
　　　　　　. . . the tossed, the replaced, the
　　　　　watchful *torero* with gesture elegant and spry,
Before the dark, the tiring but the unglazed eye deploying the bright
　　cape,
Which hid for once not air, but the enemy indeed, the authentic shape,
A thousand of him, interminably into the ring released . . .
　　　　the turning beast at length between converging colors caught.

Save for the weapons of its skull, a bull
Unarmed, considering, weighing, charging
Almost a world, itself without ally.

Say that we saw the shoulders more than the mind confused, so pro-
　　fusely

---

[1] Literally, "without shame." As a noun it means scoundrel, as an adjective, shameless.

Bleeding from so many more than the accustomed barbs, the game gone
 vulgar, the rules abused.

Say that we saw Spain die from loss of blood, a rustic reason, in a rein-
 forced
And proud punctilious land, no *espada*[2]—
A hundred men unhorsed,
A hundred horses gored, and the afternoon aging, and the crowd grow-
 ing restless (all, all so much later than planned),
And the big head heavy, sliding forward in the sand, and the tongue dry
 with sand,—no *espada*
Toward that hot neck, for the delicate and final thrust, having dared trust
 forth his hand.

GENEVIEVE TAGGARD (1894–1948)

TO THE VETERANS OF THE ABRAHAM LINCOLN BRIGADE[3]

Say of them
They knew no Spanish
At first, and nothing of the arts of war
At first,
   How to shoot, how to attack, how to retreat
How to kill, how to meet killing
At first.
Say they kept the air blue
Grousing and griping,
Arid words and harsh faces. Say
They were young;
The haggard in a trench, the dead on the olive slope
All young. And the thin, the ill and the shattered,
Sightless, in hospitals, all young.

[2] Sword.
[3] The Lincoln Brigade was composed of American volunteers, who fought with the Republicans.

Say of them they were young, there was much they did not
     Know,
They were human. Say it all; it is true. Now say
When the eminent, the great, the easy, the old,
And the men on the make
Were busy bickering and selling,
Betraying, conniving, transacting, splitting hairs,
Writing bad articles, signing bad papers,
Passing bad bills,
Bribing, blackmailing,
Whimpering, meaching, garroting,—they
Knew and acted
           understood and died.
Or if they did not die came home to peace
That is not peace.
          Say of them
They are no longer young, they never learned
The arts, the stealth of peace, this peace, the tricks of fear;
And what they knew, they know.
And what they dared, they dare.

ALEXANDER BERGMAN (1912–1940)

TO EUGENE P. LOVEMAN

On the sea fringe
where the waves
wash umber on the crusted rocks,
sand whispers in scoured shells
and sea gulls poise
to plummet under surf
for silver little fish

Here where Columbus smiles
when steamers vanish
downhill in the east

we lit driftwood fires,
and in the sharkteeth flames
saw naked dancers on a jungle shore
worshipping weird idols and their gods.

We traced the lonely latitudes
where sad Magellan sailed,
and felt the tremor
of the other shore
beneath our feet
when giant combers fell.

The years have curtained down
behind the Jersey hills,
and now while you sleep
in the other shore of Spain
boys, as we were, wander here again

and scan the sea-lanes
where the cargoes ride
to lands where guntongues
bellow heavenward;
and when evening
drifts in from the east
they light perennial fires

And constant watchers
feed the phoenix flames
that flicker on the margins of the world.

EDWIN ROLFE [FISHMAN] (1909–1954)

CITY OF ANGUISH

FOR MILTON WOLFF[4]

At midnight they roused us. In the distance we heard
verberations of thunder. "To the cellar," they ordered.
"It's safest under the stairway." Pointing,
a veteran led us. The children, whimpering,
followed the silent women who would never
sing again strolling in the *Paseo*[5] on Sunday evenings.
In the candle-light their faces were granite.

"Artillery," muttered Enrico, cursing.
Together we turned at the lowest stair.
"Come on," he said. "It's better on the rooftop.
More fireworks, better view." Slowly we ascended
past the stalled lift, felt through the roof door,
squinted in moonless darkness.

We counted the flashes, divided the horizon,
90 degrees for Enrico, 90 for me.
"Four?" "No, five!" We spotted the big guns when
the sounds came crashing, split-seconds after light.
Felt the slight earthquake tremor when shells fell
square on the Gran Via; heard high above our heads
the masculine shriek of the shell descending—
the single sharp rifle-crack, the inevitable dogs
barking, angry, roused from midsummer sleep.
The lulls grew fewer: soon talking subsided
as the cannonade quickened. Each flash in darkness
created horizon, outlined huge buildings.
Off a few blocks to the north, the *Telefónica*[6]

---

[4] Milton Wolff was the last commander of the Lincoln Brigade and the author of three
autobiographical novels.
[5] Promenade.
[6] Telephone building.

reared its massive shoulders, its great symbol profile
in dignity, like the statue of Moses pointing,
agèd but ageless, to the Promised Land.

2

Deafening now, the sky is aflame with
unnatural lightning. The ear—
like the scout's on patrol—gauges each explosion.
The mind—neither ear nor eye is aware of it—
calculates destruction, paints the dark pictures
of beams fallen, ribs crushed beneath them; beds
blown with their innocent sleepers to agonized
death.
      And the great gaping craters in streets
yawn, hypnotic to the terrified madman,
sane a mere hour ago.
          The headless body
stands strangely, totters for a second, falls.
The girl speeds screaming through wreckage; her
      hair is
wilder than torture.
          The solitary foot,
deep-arched, is perfect on the cobbles, naked,
strong, ridged with strong veins, upright, complete . . .

The city weeps. The city shudders, weeping.

The city weeps: for the moment is silent—
the pause in the idiot's symphony, prolonged
beyond the awaited crashing of cymbals, but
the hands are in mid-air, the instruments gleaming:
the swastika'd baton falls! and the clatter of
thunder begins again.
          Enrico beckons me.
Fires there. Where? Toward the *Casa de Campo*.
And closer. There. The *Puerto del Sol*[7] exudes

[7] The *Casa de Campo* and *Puerta del Sol* are famous squares in Madrid.

submarine glow in the darkness, alive with
strange twisting shapes, skyfish of stars,
fireworks of death, mangled lives, silent lips.
In thousands of beds now the muscles of men are
aroused, flexed for springing, quivering, tense,
that moments ago were relaxed, asleep.

3

It is too late for sleep now.
Few hours are left before dawn. We wait for
the sun's coming . . . And it rises, sulphurous
through smoke. It is too late for sleep.

The city weeps. The city wakens, weeping.

And the Madrilenos rise from wreckage, emerge
from shattered doorways.
                              But always the wanderer,
the old woman searching, digging among debris.
In the morning light her crazed face is granite.

And the beggar sings among the ruins:

    All night, all night
    flared in my city the bright
    cruel explosion of bombs.
    All night, all night,
    there, where the soil and stone
    spilled like brains from the sandbag's head,
    the bodiless head lay staring;
    while the anti-aircraft barked,
    barked at the droning plane,
    and the dogs of war, awakened,
    howled at the hidden moon.
    And a star fell, omen of ill,
    and a man fell, lifeless,
    and my wife fell, childless,
    and, friendless, my friend.

And I stumbled away from them, crying
from eyeless lids, blinded.
Trees became torches
lighting the avenues
where lovers huddled in terror
who would be lovers no longer.
All night, all night
flared in my city the bright
cruel explosion of hope—
all night
all night . . .

4

Come for a joyride in Madrid: the August morning
is cleared of smoke and cloud now; the journalists
dip their hard bread in the *Florida* coffee,
no longer distasteful after sour waking.
Listen to Ryan, fresh from the lines, talking
    (Behind you the memory of bombs beats
    the blood in the brain's vessels—the dream broken,
    sleep pounded to bits by the unending roar of
    shells in air, the silvery bombs descending,
    rabid spit of machine guns and the carnival flare
    of fire in the sky):
                "Why is it, why?
when I'm here in the trenches, half-sunk in mud,
blanket drenched, hungry, I dream of Dublin,
of home, of the girls? But give me a safe spot,
clean linen, bed and all, sleep becomes nightmare
of shrapnel hurtling, bombs falling, the screaming of bullets,
their thud on the brain's parapet. Why? Why?"

Exit the hotel. The morning constitutional.
Stroll down the avenues. Did Alfonso's car
detour past barricades? Did broken mains splatter him?
Here's the bellyless building; four walls, no guts.
But the biggest disaster's the wrecking of power:
thirty-six hours and no power: electric

sources are severed. The printer is frantic:
how print the leaflet, the poster, or set
the type for the bulletin?
                              After his food
a soldier needs cigarettes, something to read,
something to think about: words to pull
the war-weary brain back to life from forgetfulness:
spirited words, the gestures of Dolores,
majestic Pasionaria speaking—
mother to men, mother of revolutions,
winner of battles, comforter of defenders;
her figure magnificent as any monument
constructed for heroes; her voice a symphony,
consoling, urging, declaiming in prophecy,
her forehead the wide plateaus of her country,
her eyes constant witness of her words' truth.

5

Needless to catalogue heroes. No man
weighted with rifle, digging with nails in earth,
quickens at the name. Hero's a word for
peacetime. Battle
knows only three realities: enemy, rifle, life.

No man knows war or its meaning who has not
stumbled from tree to tree, desperate for cover,
or dug his face deep in earth, felt the ground pulse with
the ear-breaking fall of death. No man knows war
who never has crouched in his foxhole, hearing
the bullets an inch from his head, nor the zoom of
planes like a Ferris wheel strafing the trenches . . .

War is your comrade struck dead beside you,
his shared cigarette still alive in your lips.

                              1937
                              Madrid

FIRST LOVE

Again I am summoned to the eternal field
green with the blood still fresh at the roots of flowers,
green through the dust-rimmed memory of faces
that moved among the trees there for the last time
before the final shock, the glazed eye, the hasty mound.

But why are my thoughts in another country?
Why do I always return to the sunken road through corroded hills,
with the Moorish castle's shadow casting ruins over my shoulder
and the black-smocked girl approaching, her hands laden with grapes?

I am eager to enter it, eager to end it.
Perhaps this one will be the last one.
And men afterward will study our arms in museums
and nod their heads, and frown, and name the inadequate dates
and stumble with infant tongues over the strange place-names.

But my heart is forever captive of that other war
that taught me first the meaning of peace and of comradeship

and always I think of my friend who amid the apparition of bombs
saw on the lyric lake the single perfect swan.

1943

MURIEL RUKEYSER (1913–1980)

SESTINA

FROM *LETTER TO THE FRONT*

Coming to Spain on the first day of the fighting,
Flame in the mountains, and the exotic soldiers,
I gave up ideas of strangeness, but now, keeping
All I profoundly hoped for, I saw fearing
Travellers and the unprepared and the fast-changing
Foothills. The train stopped in a silver country.

Coast-water lit the valleys of this country—
All mysteries stood human in the fighting.
We came from far. We wondered, were they changing,
Our mild companions, turning into soldiers?
But the cowards were persistent in their fearing,
Each of us narrowed to one wish he was keeping.

There was no change of heart here; we were keeping
Our deepest wish, meeting with hope this country.
The enemies among us went on fearing
The frontier was too far behind. The fighting
Was clear to us all at last. The belted soldiers
Vanished into white hills that dark was changing.

The train stood naked in flowery midnight changing
All complex marvelous hope to war, and keeping
Among us only the main wish, and the soldiers.
We loved each other, believed in the war; this country
Meant to us the arrival of the fighting
At home; we began to know what we were fearing.

As continents broke apart, we saw our fearing
Reflect our nations' fears; we acted as changing
Cities at home would act, with one wish, fighting
This threat or falling under it; we were keeping
The knowledge of fiery promises; this country
Struck at our lives, struck deeper than its soldiers.

Those who among us were sure became our soldiers.
The dreams of peace resolved our subtle fearing.
This was the first day of war in a strange country.
Free Catalonia offered that day our changing
Age's hope and resistance, held in its keeping
The war this age must win in love and fighting.

This first day of fighting showed us all men as soldiers.
It offered one wish for keeping. Hope. Deep fearing.
Our changing spirits awake in the soul's country.

PHILIP LEVINE (B. 1928)

ON THE MURDER OF LIEUTENANT JOSE DEL CASTILLO

BY THE FALANGIST BRAVO MARTINEZ, JULY 12, 1936

When the Lieutenant of the Guardia de Asalto,
heard the automatic go off, he turned
and took the second shot just above
the sternum, the third tore away
the right shoulder of his uniform,
the fourth perforated his cheek. As he
slid out of his comrade's hold
toward the gray cement of the Ramblas
he lost count and knew only
that he would not die and that the blue sky
smudged with clouds was not heaven
for heaven was nowhere and in his eyes
slowly filling with their own light.
The pigeons that spotted the cold floor
of Barcelona rose as he sank below
the waves of silence crashing
on the far shores of his legs, growing
faint and watery. His hands opened
a last time to receive the benedictions
of automobile exhaust and rain
and the rain of soot. His mouth,
that would never again say "I am afraid,"
closed on nothing. The old grandfather
hawking daisies at his stand pressed
a handkerchief against his lips
and turned his eyes away before they held
the eyes of a gunman. The shepherd dogs
on sale howled in their cages
and turned in circles. There is more
to be said, but by someone who has suffered
and died for his sister the earth
and his brothers the beasts and the trees.
The Lieutenant can hear it, the prayer

that comes on the voices of water, today
or yesterday, from Chicago or Valladolid,
and hangs like smoke above this street
he won't walk as a man ever again.

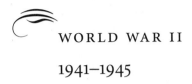

WORLD WAR II

1941–1945

> To remember a battle in which he has taken part, a man must make himself innocent again—innocent of newspapers, books and movies. He must remember his actual life, the life of the body. Everything else is journalism. . . .
>
> I called the next man on guard and went back to my hole. I peeled off my overshoes, my boots and socks, and rubbed my freezing feet. Then I put on a dry pair of socks and my shoes and overshoes, and set about making breakfast. . . . It was then that the shells came in. They were falling around us. The ground shook and fragments of iron went singing by.
>
> Being shelled is the real work of an infantry soldier, which no one talks about. Everyone has his own way of going about it. In general, it means lying face down and contracting your body into as small a space as possible. In novels you read about soldiers, at such moments, fouling themselves. The opposite is true. As all your parts are contracting, you are more likely to be constipated.
>
> —Louis Simpson, on the Battle of the Bulge, *North of Jamaica* (1972)

After the 1941 attack on Pearl Harbor, when war once again was declared an official fact of life, most Americans could be found at home, as they had been during the last world war. Massive numbers of civilians prospered in the defense industry jobs that now lifted them out of the economic doldrums of the depression years, while "our boys" went overseas. The Selective Service Act had drawn fairly comprehensively on manpower, and as a result, the political opinions of both soldier and civilian for this war are quite varied and sophisticated in style and tone, representing a range of classes, ages, education, and literary training. Women, too, joined the war effort at home and overseas, and wrote about what they saw. The poems of Randall Jarrell have always stood out among the many written about World War II, but it is in the whole body of this work that American war poetry came of age. This was a century, as Paul Fussell has remarked, in which the spread of literacy had made the writing and the fighting classes one and the same; additionally, World War II poems took on a more markedly American intonation. In this poetry, the variety of subjects that poets of war now began to include greatly extended literary coverage of the war, and poems were composed in anything from the loose weave of James Dickey's lyricism to the edgy and insouciant meter of Lincoln Kirstein. Poets not only described battles and the minutiae of soldier life in the mechanized mass army, but recorded more particularly their travels in the countries through which so many more of them were passing than in previous wars.

The war poems of Marianne Moore and Jane Cooper speak to home-front concerns. Randall Jarrell attempted to canvas the wide, global nature of the conflict being waged, taking in the soldiers who, like himself, trained but never left home, as well as those who were flying bombers or dying on Pacific atolls. Likewise, his poems included the prisoners who came to American shores, as well as the hapless people dying in concentration camps and under aerial bombardment; for the first time, the children caught in war's meshes appear vividly, recorded with a depth of feeling and observation that goes beyond sentimental portraits of victimization. Poets like Howard Nemerov and Hayden Carruth also contribute a kind of afterthought in which victory is no longer the defining triumph of an era, and war poetry itself slides into a territory in which it is also less certain that a gilding and transcendent heroism awaits the winner.

In this poetry, space and time break up. Total war stretches across hemispheres, and air, sea, and land are invaded; home front and battle-front edges are blurred, as one burns into the other, and European and Asian refugee populations fleeing attack are forced to deal with a war-hammered political map. The tempo of war changes too, as battles and sieges lengthen over days, weeks, and months. Similarly, the time of war's onset, as well as its ceasing, blend the mobilizations of prewar, war, and postwar periods into the rearrangement of borders and the scattering of peoples, as the ongoing and unrelenting work of memory plays over all who remain.

In twentieth-century total war, poets seem less inspired to write odes or formal elegies in praise of their leaders; nothing in World War II poetry on either presidents or generals equals the force of Whitman on Lincoln or of assorted writers on Lee and Grant. Even the bonding of soldiers, a battle-field cliché elsewhere, gains recognition in poetry now as well as fiction for being the many-sided and nuanced relationship that it is. In a society struggling for the egalitarian, the soldierly brotherhood between classes and races begins in Gwendolyn Brooks and others to be examined with more skepticism than formerly, while the unified effect of heroic leader-ship on the conduct of war remains more inscrutable than ever. Fifty mil-lion people died in World War II. As the absolute number of deaths and injuries caused by modern war continues its climb, the complicated search for responsibility and control over past and future outbreaks of violence becomes a larger and continually more anguished element of the war poem.

WALLACE STEVENS (1879–1955)

FROM *NOTES TOWARD A SUPREME FICTION*

Soldier, there is a war between the mind
And sky, between thought and day and night. It is
For that the poet is always in the sun,

Patches the moon together in his room
To his Virgilian cadences, up down,
Up down. It is a war that never ends.

Yet it depends on yours. The two are one.
They are a plural, a right and left, a pair,
Two parallels that meet if only in

The meeting of their shadows or that meet
In a book in a barrack, a letter from Malay.
But your war ends. And after it you return

With six meats and twelve wines or else without
To walk another room . . . Monsieur and comrade,
The soldier is poor without the poet's lines,

His petty syllabi, the sounds that stick,
Inevitably modulating, in the blood.
And war for war, each has its gallant kind.

How simply the fictive hero becomes the real;
How gladly with proper words the soldier dies,
If he must, or lives on the bread of faithful speech.

H.D. [HILDA DOOLITTLE] (1886–1961)

FROM TRILOGY

An incident here and there,
and rails gone (for guns)
from your (and my) old town square:

mist and mist-grey, no colour,
still the Luxor[1] bee, chick and hare
pursue unalterable purpose

in green, rose-red, lapis;
they continue to prophesy
from the stone papyrus:

there, as here, ruin opens
the tomb, the temple; enter,
there as here, there are no doors:

the shrine lies open to the sky,
the rain falls, here, there
sand drifts; eternity endures:

ruin everywhere, yet as the fallen roof
leaves the sealed room
open to the air,

so, through our desolation,
thoughts stir, inspiration stalks us
through gloom:

unaware, Spirit announces the Presence;
shivering overtakes us,
as of old, Samuel:

[1] Site of an ancient Egyptian temple.

trembling at a known street-corner,
we know not nor are known;
the Pythian pronounces—we pass on

to another cellar, to another sliced wall
where poor utensils show
like rare objects in a museum;

Pompeii has nothing to teach us,
we know crack of volcanic fissure,
slow flow of terrible lava,

pressure on heart, lungs, the brain
about to burst its brittle case
(what the skull can endure!):

over us, Apocryphal fire,
under us, the earth sway, dip of a floor,
slope of a pavement

where men roll, drunk
with a new bewilderment,
sorcery, bedevilment:

the bone-frame was made for
no such shock knit within terror,
yet the skeleton stood up to it:

the flesh? it was melted away,
the heart burnt out, dead ember,
tendons, muscles shattered, outer husk dismembered,

yet the frame held:
we passed the flame: we wonder
what saved us? what for?

MARIANNE MOORE (1887–1972)

IN DISTRUST OF MERITS

Strengthened to live, strengthened to die for
    medals and positioned victories?
They're fighting, fighting, fighting the blind
    man who thinks he sees,—
who cannot see that the enslaver is
enslaved; the hater, harmed. O shining O
       firm star, O tumultuous
          ocean lashed till small things go
      as they will, the mountainous
        wave makes us who look, know

depth. Lost at sea before they fought! O
      star of David, star of Bethlehem,
O black imperial lion
    of the Lord—emblem
of a risen world—be joined at last, be
joined. There is hate's crown beneath which all is
      death; there's love's without which none
        is king; the blessed deeds bless
      the halo. As contagion
        of sickness makes sickness, ·

contagion of trust can make trust. They're
      fighting in deserts and caves, one by
one, in battalions and squadrons;
      they're fighting that I
may yet recover from the disease, My
Self; some have it lightly; some will die. "Man's
      wolf to man" and we devour
        ourselves. The enemy could not
      have made a greater breach in our
        defenses. One pilot-

ing a blind man can escape him, but
      Job disheartened by false comfort knew

that nothing can be so defeating
      as a blind man who
can see. O alive who are dead, who are
proud not to see, O small dust of the earth
          that walks so arrogantly,
              trust begets power and faith is
          an affectionate thing. We
            vow, we make this promise

to the fighting—it's a promise—"We'll
      never hate black, white, red, yellow, Jew,
Gentile, Untouchable." We are
      not competent to
make our vows. With set jaw they are fighting,
fighting, fighting,—some we love whom we know,
          some we love but know not—that
            hearts may feel and not be numb.
         It cures me; or am I what
          I can't believe in? Some

in snow, some on crags, some in quicksands,
      little by little, much by much, they
are fighting fighting fighting that where
      there was death there may
be life. "When a man is prey to anger,
he is moved by outside things; when he holds
         his ground in patience patience
           patience, that is action or
        beauty," the soldier's defense
         and hardest armor for

the fight. The world's an orphans' home. Shall
      we never have peace without sorrow?
without pleas of the dying for
      help that won't come? O
quiet form upon the dust, I cannot
look and yet I must. If these great patient
         dyings—all these agonies

and wound bearings and bloodshed—
    can teach us how to live, these
        dyings were not wasted.

Hate-hardened heart, O heart of iron,
    iron is iron till it is rust.
There never was a war that was
    not inward; I must
fight till I have conquered in myself what
causes war, but I would not believe it.
        I inwardly did nothing.
          O Iscariot-like crime!
      Beauty is everlasting
        and dust is for a time.

LANGSTON HUGHES (1902–1967)

BEAUMONT TO DETROIT: 1943

Looky here, America
What you done done—
Let things drift
Until the riots come.

Now your policemen
Let your mobs run free.
I reckon you don't care
Nothing about me.

You tell me that hitler
Is a mighty bad man.
I guess he took lessons
From the ku klux klan.

You tell me mussolini's
Got an evil heart.

Well, it mus-a been in Beaumont
That he had his start—

Cause everything that hitler
And mussolini do,
Negroes get the same
Treatment from you.

You jim crowed me
Before hitler rose to power—
And you're STILL jim crowing me
Right now, this very hour.

Yet you say we're fighting
For democracy.
Then why don't democracy
Include me?

I ask you this question
Cause I want to know
How long I got to fight
BOTH HITLER—AND JIM CROW.

RICHARD EBERHART (1904–2005)

THE FURY OF AERIAL BOMBARDMENT

You would think the fury of aerial bombardment
Would rouse God to relent; the infinite spaces
Are still silent. He looks on shock-pried faces.
History, even, does not know what is meant.

You would feel that after so many centuries
God would give man to repent; yet he can kill
As Cain could, but with multitudinous will,
No farther advanced than in his ancient furies.

Was man made stupid to see his own stupidity?
Is God by definition indifferent, beyond us all?
Is the eternal truth man's fighting soul
Wherein the Beast ravens in its own avidity?

Of Van Wettering I speak, and Averill,
Names on a list, whose faces I do not recall
But they are gone to early death, who late in school
Distinguished the belt feed lever from the belt holding pawl.

LINCOLN KIRSTEIN (1907–1996)

SNATCH

Stained-glass panels shed their red as in a chapel to endow
With rose reflection brass and bench, and bathe the bar in ruddy glow.
Exhausted though still unrelieved, some GI's lounge against the glass
To sip warm beer and drag dead butts and wait their rationed piece of
   ass.

Near two full hours before high noon but in this whore-home's smoky
   air
A stupefied narcotic pulse vibrates the muzzy atmosphere.
Too bright and early to make love; nervous fatigue harasses haste.
We've just been dumped upon this town. We've fucking little time to
   waste,

And vice versa. Here she comes, with nothing on but rhinestone
   drawers,
To toss her tit and wink her twat and cense her scent of musky pores.
Our soldier feels his courage stir, although he'd almost just as soon
Hang around, bull-shit, drink and piss, and make it back to chow by
   noon.

Yet sullen dreams of luxury unspent for starveling months to come
Inspire a blackmail base for lust to activate our beat-up chum.

Though he's no expert, still he can manage five-minute stiff routine
As skillfully as grease a jeep or service other mild machine.

Slips off his brakes; gives her the gas; dog tag and rosary entwine;
Moistures distilled from tenderness lubricates the kinky spine.
Well: up and at 'em. Now downstairs, the other joes have had theirs too;
They're waiting on him. Buzzy and smug, beer makes 'em feel a shade
    less blue.

He slicks his cowlick in the glass; unchanged his mug her mirror shows.
His pecker limp, he pats her ass and blindly back to business goes.

DP's

In boxcars displaced persons howl hymns of home like wolves at bay.
Accordions support their choir: *Praschai.*[2] We're cast on song, away.
For them it seems all holiday. For those in charge, quite something less—
Insuring thirteen hundred souls plus their accumulating mess
Leave a point north of nearly here, a treasure hunt which ends in hell,
For an undetermined turn on a blind gear-stripped carousel,
To hit a siding where ten trucks with bread and blankets lie in wait.
Estimate movement: twenty-eight hours. We are forty-eight hours late.

Paragraph 1, Subsection 1: the hypodermic numbing cold,
Far worse for them in open cars, infant or pregnant, sick or old.
Subsection 2: electric fright. Each scheduled stop an ambush seems
To petrify their timid guard and verify my livid dreams.
Boy with a granulating wound has dropped his pants for Doc to see—
My flashlight white upon his red; my hand that holds it shaking me.
The halts. The starts. The startling stops. Their wailing tunes and tundra
    wails;
Then, to surpass apocalypse, at 2:13 the train derails.

Its shuddered brakes. Disaster sure. It cannot be as bad as this,
While all it means to our dazed mob is one more chance to grab a piss.

[2] Farewell (Russian).

The shy sun, blinded, oversleeps. Dawn, like our train, 's derailed by
    night.
A wrecking crew arrives by five to bang in a blaze of target light.
I do not care who else is slain; from strafing spare the undersigned:
"Where did you put my goddamned gun?" "I'm sorry, sir. I've lost my
    mind."
For cheap insurance let us bet where lucky Jerry's falcon-burst
Can easiest ignite our gas to repay worry with the worst.

The worst is spared us. Nigh on noon, the switch is patched, engines
    put-put.
We're really rolling. Feel them wheels. Sit still, my heart. Unknot, my
    gut—
Thus, o'er eroded Europe's map, her bridges blown, her signals crossed,
Filter ten thousand scrambled trains, unclocked and aimless; shunted,
    lost.
All you who catch the 8:18 to make your office sharp by nine
Consider your timetable may rarely correspond to mine,
Where Mars the testy anarch tortures unscheduled stateless cars
To give thumbscrews the one twist more he keeps for first-class global
    wars.

GEORGE OPPEN (1908–1984)

SURVIVAL: INFANTRY

And the world changed.
There had been trees and people,
Sidewalks and roads

There were fish in the sea.

Where did all the rocks come from?
And the smell of explosives
Iron standing in mud
We crawled everywhere on the ground without seeing the earth again

We were ashamed of our half life and our misery: we saw that everything
    had died.

And the letters came. People who addressed us thru our lives
They left us gasping. And in tears
In the same mud in the terrible ground

FROM OF BEING NUMEROUS

14

I cannot even now
Altogether disengage myself
From those men

With whom I stood in emplacements, in mess tents,
In hospitals and sheds and hid in the gullies
Of blasted roads in a ruined country,

Among them many men
More capable than I—

Muykut and a sergeant
Named Healy,
That lieutenant also—

How forget that? How talk
Distantly of "The People"

Who are that force
Within the walls
Of cities

Wherein their cars

Echo like history
Down walled avenues
In which one cannot speak.

18

It is the air of atrocity,
An event as ordinary
As a President.

A plume of smoke, visible at a distance
In which people burn.

19

Now in the helicopters the casual will
Is atrocious

Insanity in high places,
If it is true we must do these things
We must cut our throats

The fly in the bottle

Insane, the insane fly

Which, over the city
Is the bright light of shipwreck

20

—They await

War, and the news
Is war

As always

That the juices may flow in them
Tho the juices lie.

Great things have happened
On the earth and given it history, armies
And the ragged hordes moving and the passions

Of that death. But who escapes
Death

Among these riders
Of the subway,

They know
By now as I know

Failure and the guilt
Of failure.
As in Hardy's poem of Christmas

We might half-hope to find the animals
In the sheds of a nation
Kneeling at midnight,

Farm animals,
Draft animals, beasts for slaughter
Because it would mean they have forgiven us,
Or which is the same thing,
That we do not altogether matter.

KARL SHAPIRO (1913–2000)

TROOP TRAIN

It stops the town we come through. Workers raise
Their oily arms in good salute and grin.
Kids scream as at a circus. Business men
Glance hopefully and go their measured way.
And women standing at their dumbstruck door
More slowly wave and seem to warn us back,
As if a tear blinding the course of war
Might once dissolve our iron in their sweet wish.

Fruit of the world, O clustered on ourselves
We hang as from a cornucopia.
In total friendliness, with faces bunched
To spray the streets with catcalls and with leers.
A bottle smashes on the moving ties
And eyes fixed on a lady smiling pink
Stretch like a rubber-band and snap and sting
The mouth that wants the drink-of-water kiss.

And on through crummy continents and days,
Deliberate, grimy, slightly drunk we crawl,
The good-bad boys of circumstance and chance,
Whose bucket-helmets bang the empty wall
Where twist the murdered bodies of our packs
Next to the guns that only seem themselves.
And distance like a strap adjusted shrinks,
Tightens across the shoulder and holds firm.

Here is a deck of cards; out of this hand
Dealer, deal me my luck, a pair of bulls,
The right draw to a flush, the one-eyed jack.
Diamonds and hearts are red but spades are black,
And spades are spades and clubs are clovers—black,
But deal me winners, souvenirs of peace.
This stands to reason and arithmetic,
Luck also travels and not all come back.

Trains lead to ships and ships to death or trains,
And trains to death or trucks, and trucks to death,
Or trucks lead to the march, the march to death,
Or that survival which is all our hope;
And death leads back to trucks and trains and ships,
But life leads to the march, O flag! at last
The place of life found after trains and death
—Nightfall of nations brilliant after war.

RANDALL JARRELL (1914–1965)

LOSSES

It was not dying: everybody died.
It was not dying: we had died before
In the routine crashes—and our fields
Called up the papers, wrote home to our folks,
And the rates rose, all because of us.
We died on the wrong page of the almanac,
Scattered on mountains fifty miles away;
Diving on haystacks, fighting with a friend,
We blazed up on the lines we never saw.
We died like aunts or pets or foreigners.
(When we left high school nothing else had died
For us to figure we had died like.)

In our new planes, with our new crews, we bombed
The ranges by the desert or the shore,
Fired at towed targets, waited for our scores—
And turned into replacements and woke up
One morning, over England, operational.
It wasn't different: but if we died
It was not an accident but a mistake
(But an easy one for anyone to make).
We read our mail and counted up our missions—
In bombers named for girls, we burned
The cities we had learned about in school—
Till our lives wore out; our bodies lay among
The people we had killed and never seen.
When we lasted long enough they gave us medals;
When we died they said, "Our casualties were low."
They said, "Here are the maps"; we burned the cities.

It was not dying—no, not ever dying;
But the night I died I dreamed that I was dead,
And the cities said to me: "Why are you dying?
We are satisfied, if you are; but why did I die?"

PRISONERS

Within the wires of the post, unloading the cans of garbage,
The three in soiled blue denim (the white *P* on their backs
Sending its chilly *North* six yards to the turning blackened
Sights of the cradled rifle, to the eyes of the yawning guard)
Go on all day being punished, go on all month, all year
Loading, unloading; give their child's, beast's sigh—of despair,
Of endurance and of existence; look unexpectingly
At the big guard, dark in his khaki, at the dust of the blazing plain,
At the running or crawling soldiers in their soiled and shapeless green.

The prisoners, the guards, the soldiers—they are all, in their way, being
    trained.
From these moments, repeated forever, our own new world will be made.

THE DEATH OF THE BALL TURRET GUNNER[3]

From my mother's sleep I fell into the State,
And I hunched in its belly till my wet fur froze.
Six miles from earth, loosed from its dream of life,
I woke to black flak and the nightmare fighters.
When I died they washed me out of the turret with a hose.

PROTOCOLS

(BIRKENAU, ODESSA;[4] THE CHILDREN SPEAK ALTERNATELY.)

We went there on the train. *They had big barges that they towed,*
We stood up, there were so many I was squashed.
There was a smoke-stack, then they made me wash.

[3] *Jarrell's note*: A ball turret was a plexiglass sphere set into the belly of a B-17 or B-24, and inhabited by two .50 caliber machine-guns and one man, a short, small man. When this gunner tracked with his machine-guns a fighter attacking his bomber from below, he revolved with the turret; hunched upside-down in his little sphere, he looked like a foetus in the womb. The fighters which attacked him were armed with cannon firing explosive shells. The hose was a steam hose.

[4] *Birkenau*: the extermination camp that was an extension of Auschwitz; *Odessa*: a city in the Ukraine on the Black Sea that had a large Jewish population before World War II.

It was a factory, I think. *My mother held me up*
And I could see the ship that made the smoke.

When I was tired my mother carried me.
She said, "Don't be afraid." But I was only tired.
Where we went there is no more Odessa.
They had water in a pipe—like rain, but hot;
The water there is deeper than the world

And I was tired and fell in in my sleep
And the water drank me. That is what I think
And I said to my mother, "Now I'm washed and dried,"
My mother hugged me, and it smelled like hay
And that is how you die. And that is how you die.

THE TRUTH[5]

When I was four my father went to Scotland.
They *said* he went to Scotland.

When I woke up I think I thought that I was dreaming—
I was so little then that I thought dreams
Are in the room with you, like the cinema.
That's why you don't dream when it's still light—
They pull the shades down when it is, so you can sleep.
I thought that then, but that's not right.
Really it's in your head.

And it was light then—light at *night.*
I heard Stalky bark outside.
But really it was Mother crying—
She coughed so hard she cried.
She kept shaking Sister,

[5] Citing the sources for "The Truth," Jarrell writes that his poem was inspired by "a number . . . of case histories in a book by Anna Freud. One child in the book said, 'I'm nobody's nothing.'" The book Jarrell referred to was Anna Freud and Dorothy Burlingame, *War and Children* (New York: Medical War Books, 1943).

She shook her and shook her.
I thought Sister had had her nightmare.
But he wasn't barking, he had died.
There was dirt all over Sister.
It was all streaks, like mud. I cried.
She didn't, but she was older.
                              I thought she didn't
Because she was older, I thought Stalky had just gone.
I got *everything* wrong.
I didn't get one single thing right.
It seems to me that I'd have thought
It didn't happen, like a dream,
Except that it was light. At night.

They burnt our house down, they burnt down London.
Next day my mother cried all day, and after that
She said to me when she would come to see me:
"Your father has gone away to Scotland.
He will be back after the war."

The war then was different from the war now.
The war now is *nothing.*

I used to live in London till they burnt it.
What was it like? It was just like here.
No, that's the truth.
My mother would come here, some, but she would cry.
She said to Miss Elise, "He's not himself";
She said, "Don't you love me any more at all?"
I was *my*self.
Finally she wouldn't come at all.
She never said one thing my father said, or Sister,
Sometimes she did,
Sometimes she was the same, but that was when I dreamed it.
I could tell I was dreaming, she was just the same.

That Christmas she bought me a toy dog.

I asked her what was its name, and when she didn't know
I asked her over, and when she didn't know
I said, "You're not my mother, you're not my mother.
She *hasn't* gone to Scotland, she is dead!"
And she said, "Yes, he's dead, he's dead!"
And cried and cried; she *was* my mother,
She put her arms around me and we cried.

JOHN CIARDI (1916–1986)

ELEGY JUST IN CASE

Here lie Ciardi's pearly bones
In their ripe organic mess.
Jungle blown, his chromosomes
Breed to a new address.

Was it bullets or a wind
Or a rip cord fouled on chance?
Artifacts the natives find
Decorate them when they dance.

Here lies the sgt.'s mortal wreck
Lily spiked and termite kissed,
Spiders pendant from his neck
And a beetle on his wrist.

Bring the tick and southern flies
Where the land crabs run unmourning
Through a night of jungle skies
To a climeless morning.

And bring the chalked eraser here
Fresh from rubbing out his name.
Burn the crew-board for a bier.
(Also Colonel what's-his-name.)

Let no dice be stored and still.
Let no poker deck be torn.
But pour the smuggled rye until
The barracks threshold is outworn.

File the papers, pack the clothes,
Send the coded word through air—
"We regret and no one knows
Where the sgt. goes from here."

"Missing as of inst. oblige,
Deepest sorrow and remain—"
Shall I grin at persiflage?
Could I have my skin again

Would I choose a business form
Stilted mute as a giraffe,
Or a pinstripe unicorn
On a cashier's epitaph?

Darling, darling, just in case
Rivets fail or engines burn,
I forget the time and place
But your flesh was sweet to learn.

Swift and single as a shark
I have seen you churn my sleep
Now if beetles hunt my dark
What will beetles find to keep?

Fractured meat and open bone—
Nothing single or surprised.
Fragments of a written stone
Undeciphered but surmised.

A BOX COMES HOME

I remember the United States of America
As a flag-draped box with Arthur in it
And six marines to bear it on their shoulders.

I wonder how someone once came to remember
The Empire of the East and the Empire of the West.
As an urn maybe delivered by chariot.

You could bring Germany back on a shield once
And France in a plume. England, I suppose,
Kept coming back a long time as a letter.

Once I saw Arthur dressed as the United States
Of America. Now I see the United States
Of America as Arthur in a flag-sealed domino.

And I would pray more good of Arthur
Than I can wholly believe. I would pray
An agreement with the United States of America

To equal Arthur's living as it equals his dying
At the red-taped grave in Woodmere
By the rain and oakleaves on the domino.

THOMAS MCGRATH (1916–1990)

REMEMBERING THAT ISLAND

Remembering that island lying in the rain
(Lost in the North Pacific, lost in time and the war)
With a terrible fatigue as of repeated dreams
Of running, climbing, fighting in the dark,
I feel the wind rising and the pitiless cold surf
Shaking the headlands of the black north.

And the ships come in again out of the fog—
As real as nightmare I hear the rattle of blocks
When the first boat comes down, the ghostly whisper of feet
At the barge pier—and wild with strain I wait
For the flags of my first war, the remembered faces,
And mine not among them to make the nightmare safe.

Then without words, with a heavy shuffling of gear,
The figures plod in the rain, in the seashore mud,
Speechless and tired; their faces, lined and hard,
I search for my comrades, and suddenly—there—there—
Harry, Charlie, and Bob, but their faces are worn, old,
And mine is among them. In a dream as real as war

I see the vast stinking Pacific suddenly awash
Once more with bodies, landings on all beaches,
The bodies of dead and living gone back to appointed places,
A ten year old resurrection,
And myself once more in the scourging wind, waiting, waiting.
While the rich oratory and the lying famous corrupt
Senators mine our lives for another war.

GWENDOLYN BROOKS (1917–2000)

Negro Hero

TO SUGGEST DORIE MILLER[6]

I had to kick their law into their teeth in order to save them.
However I have heard that sometimes you have to deal
Devilishly with drowning men in order to swim them to shore.
Or they will haul themselves and you to the trash and the fish beneath.
(When I think of this, I do not worry about a few
Chipped teeth.)

[6] Dorie Miller was a messman who manned a machine-gun during the attack on Pearl Harbor and brought down a number of Japanese planes. He was awarded the Navy Cross. He died two years later on an aircraft carrier.

It is good I gave glory, it is good I put gold on their name.
Or there would have been spikes in the afterward hands.
But let us speak only of my success and the pictures in the Caucasian
    dailies
As well as the Negro weeklies. For I am a gem.
(They are not concerned that it was hardly The Enemy my fight was
    against
But them.)

It was a tall time. And of course my blood was
Boiling about in my head and straining and howling and singing me on.
Of course I was rolled on wheels of my boy itch to get at the gun.
Of course all the delicate rehearsal shots of my childhood massed in
    mirage before me.
Of course I was child
And my first swallow of the liquor of battle bleeding black air dying and
    demon noise
Made me wild.

It was kinder than that, though, and I showed like a banner my kindness.
I loved. And a man will guard when he loves.
Their white-gowned democracy was my fair lady.
With her knife lying cold, straight, in the softness of her sweet-flowing
    sleeve.
But for the sake of the dear smiling mouth and the stuttered promise I
    toyed with my life.
I threw back!—I would not remember
Entirely the knife.

Still—am I good enough to die for them, is my blood bright enough to
    be spilled,
Was my constant back-question—are they clear
On this? Or do I intrude even now?
Am I clean enough to kill for them, do they wish me to kill
For them or is my place while death licks his lips and strides to them
In the galley still?

(In a southern city a white man said
Indeed, I'd rather be dead;

Indeed, I'd rather be shot in the head
Or ridden to waste on the back of a flood
Than saved by the drop of a black man's blood.)

Naturally, the important thing is, I helped to save them, them and a part
    of their democracy.
Even if I had to kick their law into their teeth in order to do that for
    them.
And I am feeling well and settled in myself because I believe it was a
    good job,
Despite this possible horror: that they might prefer the
Preservation of their law in all its sick dignity and their knives
To the continuation of their creed
And their lives.

ROBERT LOWELL (1917–1977)

MEMORIES OF WEST STREET AND LEPKE[7]

Only teaching on Tuesdays, book-worming
in pajamas fresh from the washer each morning,
I hog a whole house on Boston's
"hardly passionate Marlborough Street,"
where even the man
scavenging filth in the back alley trash cans,
has two children, a beach wagon, a helpmate,
and is a "young Republican."
I have a nine months' daughter,
young enough to be my granddaughter.
Like the sun she rises in her flame-flamingo infants' wear.

These are the tranquillized *Fifties*,
and I am forty. Ought I to regret my seedtime?
I was a fire-breathing Catholic CO.,

---

[7] Louis Buchalter (Lepke, "little Louis" in Yiddish, was an adopted name), was a notorious gangster, and after a long delay in prison occasioned by the unfulfilled promise that he would incriminate others, was executed for murder in 1944.

and made my manic statement,
telling off the state and president, and then
sat waiting sentence in the bull pen
beside a Negro boy with curlicues
of marijuana in his hair.

Given a year,
I walked on the roof of the West Street Jail, a short
enclosure like my school soccer court,
and saw the Hudson River once a day
through sooty clothesline entanglements
and bleaching khaki tenements.
Strolling, I yammered metaphysics with Abramowitz,
a jaundice-yellow ("it's really tan")
and fly-weight pacifist,
so vegetarian,
he wore rope shoes and preferred fallen fruit.
He tried to convert Bioff and Brown,
the Hollywood pimps, to his diet.
Hairy, muscular, suburban,
wearing chocolate double-breasted suits,
they blew their tops and beat him black and blue.

I was so out of things, I'd never heard
of the Jehovah's Witnesses.
"Are you a C.O.?" I asked a fellow jailbird.
"No," he answered, "I'm a J.W."
He taught me the "hospital tuck,"
and pointed out the T shirted back
of *Murder Incorporated's* Czar Lepke,
there piling towels on a rack,
or dawdling off to his little segregated cell full
of things forbidden the common man:
a portable radio, a dresser, two toy American
flags tied together with a ribbon of Easter palm.
Flabby, bald, lobotomized,
he drifted in a sheepish calm,

where no agonizing reappraisal
jarred his concentration on the electric chair—
hanging like an oasis in his air
of lost connections. . . .

HOWARD NEMEROV (1920–1991)

GRAND CENTRAL WITH SOLDIERS, IN EARLY MORNING

These secretly are going to some place,
Packing their belted, serviceable hearts.
It is the earnest wish of this command
That they may go in stealth and leave no trace,
In early morning before business starts.

A FABLE OF THE WAR

The full moon is partly hidden by cloud,
The snow that fell when we came off the boat
Has stopped by now, and it is turning colder.
I pace the platform under the blue lights,
Under a frame of glass and emptiness
In a station whose name I do not know.

Suddenly, passing the known and unknown
Bowed faces of my company, the sad
And potent outfit of the armed, I see
That we are dead. By stormless Acheron
We stand easy, and the occasional moon
Strikes terribly from steel and bone alike.

Our flesh, I see, was too corruptible
For the huge work of death. Only the blind
Crater of the eye can suffer well

The midnight cold of stations in no place,
And hold the tears of pity frozen that
They will implacably reflect on war.

But I have read that God let Solomon
Stand upright, although dead, until the temple
Should be raised up, that demons forced to the work
Might not revolt before the thing was done.
And the king stood, until a little worm
Had eaten through the stick he leaned upon.

So, gentlemen—by greatcoat, cartridge belt
And helmet held together for the time—
In honorably enduring here we seek
The second death. Until the worm shall bite
To betray us, lean each man on his gun
That the great work not falter but go on.

IFF[8]

1.

Hate Hitler? No, I spared him hardly a thought.
But Corporal Irmin, first, and later on
The O.C. (Flying), Wing Commander Briggs,
And the station CO. Group Captain Ormery—
Now there were men were objects fit to hate,
Hitler a moustache and a little curl
In the middle of his forehead, whereas these
Bastards were bastards in your daily life,
With Power in their pleasure, smile or frown.

2.

Not to forget my navigator Bert,
Who shyly explained to me that the Jews
Were ruining England and Hitler might be wrong

[8] Identification Friend or Foe, an electronic system developed for aircraft during World War II.

But he had the right idea . . . We were a crew,
And went on so, the one pair left alive
Of a dozen that chose each other flipping coins
At the OTU, but spoke no civil word
Thereafter, beyond the words that had to do
With the drill for going out and getting back.

3.

One night, with a dozen squadrons coming home
To Manston,[9] the tower gave us orbit and height
To wait our turn in their lofty waiting-room,
And on every circuit, when we crossed the Thames,
Our gunners in the estuary below
Loosed off a couple of dozen rounds on spec,
Defending the Commonwealth as detailed to do,
Their lazy lights so slow, then whipping past.
All the above were friends. And then the foe.

REDEPLOYMENT

They say the war is over. But water still
Comes bloody from the taps, and my pet cat
In his disorder vomits worms which crawl
Swiftly away. Maybe they leave the house.
These worms are white, and flecked with the cat's blood.

The war may be over. I know a man
Who keeps a pleasant souvenir, he keeps
A soldier's dead blue eyeballs that he found
Somewhere—hard as chalk, and blue as slate.
He clicks them in his pocket while he talks.

And now there are cockroaches in the house,
They get slightly drunk on DDT,
Are fast, hard, shifty—can be drowned but not

[9] An airfield in Kent, England, operated by the Royal Air Force during the war.

Without you hold them under quite some time.
People say the Mexican kind can fly.

The end of the war. I took it quietly
Enough. I tried to wash the dirt out of
My hair and from under my fingernails,
I dressed in clean white clothes and went to bed.
I heard the dust falling between the walls.

ELEANOR ROSS TAYLOR (B. 1920)

AFTER TWENTY YEARS

After twenty years in France
Do you dream in French my son? . . .
Home . . . ça existe encore.
Still, still exists Flagg Bros. store,
With new glass front, but behind
The dilapidated sheds
And packed road lined with maypops
Where you talked to the white horse.

Gloved, hatted, I kneel here
Where you by the sky-blue windows
Sang "Onward Christian Soldiers."
For I have needed pardon
Since the morning we found Dad
In the garage (It is hard
To be a father without
A son). I screamed, and without
A son to be a widow.
Shall I pray your pardon too?
Prince of Peace, absolve all warriors,
My warrior of the bow and arrow.
Your old girl married money.
She's grown stout. (*He* has ulcers.)

Last year they were in Nice
Not Normandy. . . .
My glove's rouge, with lipstick
Or with teeth. . . . Curse *men*, curse *free*—
God vault your freedom!

Oh the acres of undistinguished
Crosses make me sick.
Mother could mark Papa's grave
In the churchyard a mile from home,
By its firs and shaft. . . .
Your nothing grave . . .

Shame!
God I am of little understanding. . . .
But with God all things are possible. . . .
Give my son another life—
A Norwood ugliness, a bourgeois rot,
Dust and concrete, Falcons and Mustangs, not . . .

RICHARD WILBUR (B. 1921)

FIRST SNOW IN ALSACE[10]

The snow came down last night like moths
Burned on the moon; it fell till dawn,
Covered the town with simple cloths.

Absolute snow lies rumpled on
What shellbursts scattered and deranged,
Entangled railings, crevassed lawn.

As if it did not know they'd changed,
Snow smoothly clasps the roofs of homes
Fear-gutted, trustless and estranged.

---

[10] A province on the French-German border; the site of many battles.

The ration stacks are milky domes;
Across the ammunition pile
The snow has climbed in sparkling combs.

You think: beyond the town a mile
Or two, this snowfall fills the eyes
Of soldiers dead a little while.

Persons and persons in disguise,
Walking the new air white and fine,
Trade glances quick with shared surprise.

At children's windows, heaped, benign,
As always, winter shines the most,
And frost makes marvelous designs.

The night guard coming from his post,
Ten first-snows back in thought, walks slow
And warms him with a boyish boast:

He was the first to see the snow.

JAMES DICKEY (1923–1997)

THE FIREBOMBING

> Denke daran, dass nach den grossen Zerstörungen Jederman
> beweisen wird, dass er unschuldig war.[11]
>
> —Günter Eich
>
> Or hast thou an arm like God?
>
> —The Book of Job

Homeowners unite.

---

[11] "Consider, after the great destruction / Everyone will demonstrate that they were without guilt." Gunter Eich was a German poet (1907–1972).

All families lie together, though some are burned alive.
The others try to feel
For them. Some can, it is often said.

Starve and take off

Twenty years in the suburbs, and the palm trees willingly leap
Into the flashlights,
And there is beneath them also
A booted crackling of snailshells and coral sticks.
There are cowl flaps and the tilt cross of propellers,
The shovel-marked clouds' far sides against the moon,
The enemy filling up the hills
With ceremonial graves. At my somewhere among these,

Snap, a bulb is tricked on in the cockpit

And some technical-minded stranger with my hands
Is sitting in a glass treasure-hole of blue light,
Having potential fire under the undeodorized arms
Of his wings, on thin bomb-shackles,
The "tear-drop-shaped" 300-gallon drop-tanks
Filled with napalm and gasoline.

Thinking forward ten minutes
From that, there is also the burst straight out
Of the overcast into the moon; there is now
The moon-metal-shine of propellers, the quarter-
moonstone, aimed at the waves,
Stopped on the cumulus.

There is then this re-entry
Into cloud, for the engines to ponder their sound.
In white dark the aircraft shrinks; Japan

Dilates around it like a thought.
Coming out, the one who is here is over
Land, passing over the all-night grainfields,

In dark paint over
The woods with one silver side,
Rice-water calm at all levels
Of the terraced hill.
                            Enemy rivers and trees
Sliding off me like snakeskin,
Strips of vapor spooled from the wingtips
Going   invisible   passing   over   on.
Over   bridges   roads for nightwalkers
Sunday night in the enemy's country   absolute
Calm   the moon's face   coming   slowly
About
            the inland sea
Slants   is woven with wire thread
Levels out   holds together like a quilt
Off the starboard wing   cloud flickers
At my glassed-off forehead   the moon's now and again
Uninterrupted face going forward
Over the waves in a glide-path
Lost into land.

Going: going with it

Combat booze by my side in a cratered canteen,
Bourbon frighteningly mixed
With GI pineapple juice,
Dogs trembling under me for hundreds of miles, on many
Islands, sleep-smelling that ungodly mixture
Of napalm and high-octane fuel,
Good bourbon and GI juice.

Rivers circling behind me around
Come to the fore, and bring
A town with everyone darkened.
Five thousand people are sleeping off
An all-day American drone.
Twenty years in the suburbs have not shown me
Which ones were hit and which not.

Haul on the wheel   racking slowly
The aircraft blackly around
In a dark dream   that   this is
That is like flying inside someone's head

Think of this   think of this

I did not think of my house
But think of my house now

Where the lawn mower rests on its laurels
Where the diet exists
For my own good   where I try to drop
Twenty years, eating figs in the pantry
Blinded by each and all
Of the eye-catching cans that gladly have caught my wife's eye
Until I cannot say
Where the screwdriver is   where the children
Get off the bus   where the fly
Hones his front legs   where the hammock folds
Its erotic daydreams   where the Sunday
School text for the day has been put   where the fire
Wood is   where the payments
For everything under the sun
Pile peacefully up,

But in this half-paid-for pantry
Among the red lids that screw off
With an easy half-twist to the left
And the long drawers crammed with dim spoons,
I still have charge—secret charge—
Of the fire developed to cling
To everything: to golf carts and fingernail
Scissors as yet unborn   tennis shoes
Grocery baskets   toy fire engines
New Buicks stalled by the half-moon
Shining at midnight on crossroads   green paint
Of jolly garden tools   red Christmas ribbons:

Not atoms, these, but glue inspired
By love of country to burn,
The apotheosis of gelatin.

Behind me having risen the Southern Cross
Set up by chaplains in the Ryukyus—[12]
Orion, Scorpio, the immortal silver
Like the myths of king-
insects at swarming time—
One mosquito, dead drunk
On altitude, drones on, far under the engines,
And bites between
The oxygen mask and the eye.
The enemy-colored skin of families
Determines to hold its color
In sleep, as my hand turns whiter
Than ever, clutching the toggle—
The ship shakes   bucks
Fire hangs   not yet fire
In the air above Beppu[13]
For I am fulfilling

An "anti-morale" raid upon it.
All leashes of dogs
Break under the first bomb, around those
In bed, or late in the public baths: around those
Who inch forward on their hands
Into medicinal waters.
Their heads come up with a roar
Of Chicago fire:
Come up with the carp pond showing
The bathhouse upside down,
Standing stiller to show it more
As I sail artistically over
The resort town followed by farms,

---

[12] Islands off Japan; a battle site.
[13] A Japanese city.

Singing and twisting
All the handles in heaven   kicking
The small cattle off their feet
In a red costly blast
Flinging jelly over the walls
As in a chemical war-
Fare field demonstration.
With fire of mine like a cat

Holding onto another man's walls,
My hat should crawl on my head
In streetcars, thinking of it,
The fat on my body should pale.

Gun down
The engines, the eight blades sighing
For the moment when the roofs will connect
Their flames, and make a town burning with all
American fire.
                    Reflections of houses catch;
Fire shuttles from pond to pond
In every direction, till hundreds flash with one death.
With this in the dark of the mind,
Death will not be what it should;
Will not, even now, even when
My exhaled face in the mirror
Of bars, dilates in a cloud like Japan.
The death of children is ponds
Shutter-flashing; responding mirrors; it climbs
The terraces of hills
Smaller and smaller, a mote of red dust
At a hundred feet; at a hundred and one it goes out.
That is what should have got in
To my eye

And shown the insides of houses, the low tables
Catch fire from the floor mats,
Blaze up in gas around their heads
Like a dream of suddenly growing

Too intense for war. Ah, under one's dark arms
Something strange-scented falls—when those on earth
Die, there is not even sound;
One is cool and enthralled in the cockpit,
Turned blue by the power of beauty,
In a pale treasure-hole of soft light
Deep in aesthetic contemplation,
Seeing the ponds catch fire
And cast it through ring after ring
Of land: O death in the middle
Of acres of inch-deep water!   Useless

Firing   small arms
Speckles   from the river
Bank   one ninety-millimeter
Misses   far down   wrong petals   gone

It is this detachment
The honored aesthetic evil,
The greatest sense of power in one's life,
That must be shed in bars, or by whatever
Means, by starvation
Visions in well-stocked pantries:
The moment when the moon sails in between
The tail-booms   the rudders nod   I swing
Over   directly over the heart
The *heart* of the fire. A mosquito burns out on my cheek
With the cold of my face   there are the eyes
In blue light   bar light
All masked but them   the moon
Crossing from left to right   in the streams below
Oriental fish form quickly
In the chemical shine,
In their eyes one tiny seed
Of deranged, Old Testament light.

Letting go   letting go
The plane rises gently   dark forms
Glide off me   long water   pales

In safe zones   a new cry enters
The voice box of chained family dogs

We buck   leap over something
Not there   settle back
Leave it   leave it clinging and crying
It consumes them in a hot
Body-flash, old age or menopause
Of children, clings and burns
                              eating through
And when a reed mat catches fire
From me, it explodes through field after field
Bearing its sleeper   another

Bomb finds a home
And clings to it like a child. And so

Goodbye to the grassy mountains
To cloud streaming from the night engines
Flags   pennons   curved silks
Of air   myself streaming also
My body covered
With flags, the air of flags
Between the engines.
Forever I do sleep in that position,
Forever in a turn
For home that breaks out streaming banners
From my wingtips,
Wholly in position to admire.

O then I knock it off
And turn for home over the black complex thread worked through
The silver night-sea,
Following the huge, moon-washed steppingstones
Of the Ryukyus south,
The nightgrass of mountains billowing softly
In my rising heat.
                              Turn and tread down
The yellow stones of the islands

To where Okinawa[14] burns,
Pure gold, on the radar screen,
Beholding, beneath, the actual island form
In the vast water-silver poured just above solid ground,
An inch of water extending for thousands of miles
Above flat ploughland. Say "down," and it is done.

All this, and I am still hungry,
Still twenty years overweight, still unable
To get down there or see
What really happened.
                              But it may be that I could not,
If I tried, say to any
Who lived there, deep in my flames: say, in cold
Grinning sweat, as to another
Of these homeowners who are always curving
Near me down the different-grassed street: say
As though to the neighbor
I borrowed the hedge-clippers from
On the darker-grassed side of the two,
Come in, my house is yours, come in
If you can, if you
Can pass this unfired door. It is that I can imagine
At the threshold nothing
With its ears crackling off
Like powdery leaves,
Nothing with children of ashes, nothing not
Amiable, gentle, well-meaning,
A little nervous for no
Reason   a little worried   a little too loud
Or too easygoing   nothing I haven't lived with
For twenty years, still nothing not as
American as I am, and proud of it.

Absolution? Sentence? No matter;
The thing itself is in that.

[14] An island off of Japan, and a battle site.

JANE COOPER (B. 1924)

THE FAITHFUL

Once you said joking slyly, *If I'm killed*
I'll come to haunt your solemn bed,
I'll stand and glower at the head
And see if my place is empty still, or filled.

What was it woke me in the early darkness
Before the first bird's twittering?
—A shape dissolving and flittering
Unsteady as a flame in a drafty house.

It seemed a concentration of the dark burning
By the bedpost at my right hand
While to my left that no man's land
Of sheet stretched palely as a false morning. . . .

All day I have been sick and restless. This evening
Curtained, with all the lights on,
I start up—only to sit down.
Why should I grieve after ten years of grieving?

What if last night I was the one who lay dead
While the dead burned beside me
Trembling with passionate pity
At my blameless life and shaking its flamelike head?

ANTHONY HECHT (1923–2004)

STILL LIFE

Sleep-walking vapor, like a visitant ghost,
        Hovers above a lake
Of Tennysonian calm just before dawn.
Inverted trees and boulders waver and coast

In polished darkness. Glints of silver break
Among the liquid leafage, and then are gone.

Everything's doused and diamonded with wet.
        A cobweb, woven taut
On bending stanchion frames of tentpole grass,
Sags like a trampoline or firemen's net
With all the glitter and riches it has caught,
Each drop a paperweight of Steuben glass.

No birdsong yet, no cricket, nor does the trout
        Explode in water-scrolls
For a skimming fly. All that is yet to come.
Things are as still and motionless throughout
The universe as ancient Chinese bowls,
And nature is magnificently dumb.

Why does this so much stir me, like a code
        Or muffled intimation
Of purposes and preordained events?
It knows me, and I recognize its mode
Of cautionary, spring-tight hesitation,
This silence so impacted and intense.

As in a water-surface I behold
        The first, soft, peach decree
Of light, its pale, inaudible commands.
I stand beneath a pine-tree in the cold,
Just before dawn, somewhere in Germany,
A cold, wet, Garand rifle[15] in my hands.

---

[15] The M1 rifle, the main combat rifle of World War II and the Korean War.

ALAN DUGAN (1923–2003)

PORTRAIT FROM THE INFANTRY

He smelled bad and was red-eyed with the miseries
of being scared while sleepless when he said
this: "I want a private woman, peace and quiet,
and some green stuff in my pocket. Fuck
the rest." Pity the underwear and socks,
long burnt, of an accomplished murderer,
oh God, of germans and replacements, who
refused three stripes to keep his B.A.R.,[16]
who fought, fought not to fight some days
like any good small businessman of war,
and dug more holes than an outside dog
to modify some Freudian's thesis: "No
man can stand three hundred days
of fear of mutilation and death." What he
theorized was a joke: "To keep a tight
ass-hole, dry socks and a you-deep hole
with you at all times." Afterwards,
met in a sports shirt with a round wife, he was
the clean slave of a daughter, a power brake
and beer. To me, he seemed diminished
in his dream, or else enlarged, who knows?,
by its accomplishment: personal life
wrung from mass issues in a bloody time
and lived out hiddenly. Aside from sound
baseball talk, his only interesting remark
was, in pointing to his wife's belly, "If
he comes out left foot first" (the way
you Forward March!), "I am going to stuff
him back up." "Isn't he awful?" she said.

[16] Browning Automatic Rifle.

LUCIEN STRYK (B. 1924)

THE PIT

Twenty years. I still remember
The sun-blown stench, and the pit
At least two hundred yards from
The cove we'd anchored guns in.
They were blasting at the mountains,
The beach was nearly ours.

The smell kept leaking back.
I thought of garbage cans
Behind chopsuey restaurants
Of home, strangely appealing on
A summer's night, meaning another
Kind of life. Which made the difference.

When the three of us, youngest in
The crew, were handed poles and told
To get the deadmen underground
Or join them, we saw it a sullen
Sort of lark. And lashed to trees,
The snipers had us dancing.

Ducks for those vultures in the boughs,
Poles poking through the powder-
Bitten grass, we zigzagged
Toward the pit as into
The arse of death, the wittiest
Of us said but did not laugh.

At last we reached it, half full
Of sand and crawling. We clamped
Nose, mouth, wrenched netted helmets
To the chin, yet poles probed forward
Surgically, touching for spots
The maggots had not jelled.

Somehow we got the deadmen under,
Along with empty lobster tins,
Bottles, gear and ammo. Somehow
We plugged the pit and slipped back
To the guns. Then for days
We had to helmet bathe downwind.

I stuck my pole, clean end high,
Behind the foxhole, a kind of
Towelpeg and a something more.
I'd stare it out through jungle haze,
And wonder. Ask anyone who
Saw it: nobody won that war.

LOUIS SIMPSON (B. 1923)

CARENTAN O CARENTAN

Trees in the old days used to stand
And shape a shady lane
Where lovers wandered hand in hand
Who came from Carentan.[17]

This was the shining green canal
Where we came two by two
Walking at combat-interval.
Such trees we never knew.

The day was early June, the ground
Was soft and bright with dew.
Far away the guns did sound,
But here the sky was blue.

---

[17] A town on Normandy coast, between Omaha and Utah beaches, a site of fierce fighting and enormous Allied losses during the Invasion.

The sky was blue, but there a smoke
Hung still above the sea
Where the ships together spoke
To towns we could not see.

Could you have seen us through a glass
You would have said a walk
Of farmers out to turn the grass,
Each with his own hay-fork.

The watchers in their leopard suits
Waited till it was time,
And aimed between the belt and boot
And let the barrel climb.

I must lie down at once, there is
A hammer at my knee.
And call it death or cowardice,
Don't count again on me.

Everything's all right, Mother,
Everyone gets the same
At one time or another.
It's all in the game.

I never strolled, nor ever shall,
Down such a leafy lane.
I never drank in a canal,
Nor ever shall again.

There is a whistling in the leaves
And it is not the wind,
The twigs are falling from the knives
That cut men to the ground.

Tell me, Master-Sergeant,
The way to turn and shoot.
But the Sergeant's silent
That taught me how to do it.

O Captain, show us quickly
Our place upon the map.
But the Captain's sickly
And taking a long nap.

Lieutenant, what's my duty,
My place in the platoon?
He too's a sleeping beauty,
Charmed by that strange tune.

Carentan O Carentan
Before we met with you
We never yet had lost a man
Or known what death could do.

MEMORIES OF A LOST WAR

The guns know what is what, but underneath
In fearful file
We go around burst boots and packs and teeth
That seem to smile.

The scene jags like a strip of celluloid,
A mortar fires,
Cinzano falls, Michelin is destroyed,
The man of tires.

As darkness drifts like fog in from the sea
Somebody says
"We're digging in." Look well, for this may be
The last of days.

Hot lightnings stitch the blind eye of the moon,
The thunder's blunt.
We sleep. Our dreams pass in a faint platoon
Toward the front.

Sleep well, for you are young. Each tree and bush
Drips with sweet dew,

And earlier than morning June's cool hush
Will waken you.

The riflemen will wake and hold their breath.
Though they may bleed
They will be proud a while of something death
Still seems to need.

THE BATTLE

Helmet and rifle, pack and overcoat
Marched through a forest. Somewhere up ahead
Guns thudded. Like the circle of a throat
The night on every side was turning red.

They halted and they dug. They sank like moles
Into the clammy earth between the trees.
And soon the sentries, standing in their holes,
Felt the first snow. Their feet began to freeze.

At dawn the first shell landed with a crack.
Then shells and bullets swept the icy woods.
This lasted many days. The snow was black.
The corpses stiffened in their scarlet hoods.

Most clearly of that battle I remember
The tiredness in eyes, how hands looked thin
Around a cigarette, and the bright ember
Would pulse with all the life there was within.

W. S. MERWIN (B. 1927)

THE DACHAU SHOE

My cousin Gene (he's really only a Second cousin) has a shoe he picked up at Dachau.[18] It's a pretty worn-out shoe. It wasn't top quality in the first place, he explained. The sole is cracked clear across and has pulled loose from the upper on both sides, and the upper is split at the ball of the foot. There's no lace and there's no heel.

He explained he didn't steal it because it must have belonged to a Jew who was dead. He explained that he wanted some little thing. He explained that the Russians looted everything. They just took anything. He explained that it wasn't top quality to begin with. He explained that the guards or the kapos[19] would have taken it if it had been any good. He explained that he was lucky to have got anything. He explained that it wasn't wrong because the Germans were defeated. He explained that everybody was picking up something. A lot of guys wanted flags or daggers or medals or things like that, but that kind of thing didn't appeal to him so much. He kept it on the mantelpiece for a while but he explained that it wasn't a trophy.

He explained that it's no use being vindictive. He explained that he wasn't. Nobody's perfect. Actually we share a German grandfather. But he explained that this was the reason why we had to fight that war. What happened at Dachau was a crime that could not be allowed to pass. But he explained that we could not really do anything to stop it while the war was going on because we had to win the war first. He explained that we couldn't always do just what we would have liked to do. He explained that the Russians killed a lot of Jews too. After a couple of years he put the shoe away in a drawer. He explained that the dust collected in it.

Now he has it down in the cellar in a box. He explains that the central heating makes it crack worse. He'll show it to you, though, anytime you ask. He explains how it looks. He explains how it's hard to take it in, even for him. He explains how it was raining, and there weren't many things left when he got there. He explains how there wasn't anything of value and you didn't want to get caught taking anything of that kind, even if there

[18] A German concentration and extermination camp.
[19] Prisoners appointed to guard duty.

had been. He explains how everything inside smelled. He explains how it was just lying out in the mud, probably right where it had come off. He explains that he ought to keep it. A thing like that.

You really ought to go and see it. He'll show it to you. All you have to do is ask. It's not that it's really a very interesting shoe when you come right down to it but you learn a lot from his explanations.

JEROME ROTHENBERG (B. 1931)

DOS OYSLEYDIKN (THE EMPTYING)

at honey street in ostrova[20]
where did the honey people go?
empty   empty
miodowa[21] empty
empty bakery & empty road to warsaw
yellow wooden houses & houses plastered up with stucco
the shadow of an empty name still on their doors
shadai[22] & shadow shattering the mother tongue
the mother's tongue but empty
the way the streets are empty where we walk
pushing past crowds of children
old women airing themselves outside the city hall
old fanners riding empty carts down empty roads
who don't dispel but make an emptiness
a taste of empty honey
empty rolls you push your fingers through
empty sorrel soup dribbling from their empty mouths
defining some other poland
lost to us the way the moon
is lost to us
the empty clock tower measuring her light four ways

[20] A city in Estonia.
[21] A street name in Krakow and Warsaw.
[22] One of the epithets of God, implying the protector, in some rabbinical traditions.

sorrel in gardens mother of god at roadsides
in the reflection of the empty trains
only the cattle bellow in
like jews the dew-eyed wanderers
still present   still the flies
cover their eyeballs
the trains drive eastward, falling
down a hole (a holocaust) of empty houses
of empty ladders leaning against haystacks no one climbs
empty ostrova & empty ostrolenka[23]
old houses empty in the woods near vyzhkov
dachas the peasants would rent to you
& sleep in stables
the bialo[24] forest spreading to every side
retreating the closer we come to it to claim it
empty oaks & empty fir trees
a man in an empty ditch who reads a book
the way the jews once read
in the cold polish light   the fathers sat there too
the mothers posed at the woods' edge
the road led brightly to treblinka[25]
& other towns   beaches at brok
along the bug
marshes with cattails
cows tied to trees
past which their ghosts walk
their ghosts refuse to walk
tomorrow in empty fields of poland
still cold against their feet
an empty pump black water drips from
will form a hill of ice
the porters will dissolve with burning sticks
they will find a babe's face at the bottom
invisible & frozen imprinted in the rock

[23] A Polish city with many Jewish inhabitants before the war.
[24] A city in Poland.
[25] A German extermination camp.

LAWSON FUSAO INADA (B. 1938)

FROM LEGENDS FROM CAMP[26]

VI. THE LEGEND OF THE GREAT ESCAPE

The people were passive:
Even when a train paused
in the Great Plains, even
when soldiers were eating,
they didn't try to escape.

X. THE LEGEND OF THE MAGIC MARBLES

My uncle was going overseas.
He was heading to the European theater,
and we were all going to miss him.

He had been stationed by Cheyenne,
and when he came to say good-bye
he brought me a little bag of marbles.

But the best one, an agate, cracked.
It just broke, like bone, like flesh—
so my uncle comforted me with this story:

> "*When we get home to Fresno,*
> *I will take you into the basement*
> *and give you my box of magic marbles.*
>
> *These marbles are marbles—*
> *so they can break and crack and chip—*
> *but they are also magic*
>
> *so they can always be fixed:*
> *all you have to do is leave them*
> *overnight in a can of Crisco—*
>
> *next day they're good as new.*"

Uncle. Uncle. Uncle. What happened to *you*?

---

[26] The title refers to an internment camp for Americans of Japanese descent during the war.

XV. The Legend of the Full Moon over Amache

As it turned out,
Amache is said to have been named
for an Indian princess—

not a regular squaw—

who perished upstream,
in the draw,
of the Sand Creek Massacre.[27]

Her bones floated down
to where the camp was now.

The full moon?
It doesn't have anything to do
with this. It's just there,

illuminating, is all.

CHARLES SIMIC (B. 1938)

PRODIGY

I grew up bent over
a chessboard.

I loved the word *endgame*.

---

[27] The Sand Creek Massacre refers to the November 1864 attack on approximately 500 unsuspecting Indians, largely Cheyenne, of the Black Kettle tribe. The attack took place near Dawson's Creek, Colorado. Colonel John Chivington's 700 Colorado volunteers and Major Scot Anthony's 125 regular U.S. Army troops killed over 150 Indians, mostly women and children, badly mutilating many of the bodies. After the destruction of the buffalo herds, this group of Cheyenne, joined by some Arapaho, had been driven out of their usual territory by starvation; their leader, Black Kettle, was known throughout the region as peaceful. In good faith, he had placed his people under the protection of U.S. forces. The U.S. government later condemned Chivington's actions as "gross and wanton outrages."

All my cousins looked worried.

It was a small house
Near a Roman graveyard.
Planes and tanks
shook its windowpanes.

A retired professor of astronomy
taught me how to play.

That must have been in 1944.

In the set we were using,
the paint had almost chipped off
the black pieces.

The white King was missing
and had to be substituted for.

I'm told but do not believe
that that summer I witnessed
men hung from telephone poles.

I remember my mother
blindfolding me a lot.

She had a way of tucking my head
suddenly under her overcoat.

In chess, too, the professor told me,
the masters play blindfolded,
the great ones on several boards
at the same time.

JAMES TATE (B. 1943)

THE LOST PILOT

FOR MY FATHER, 1922–1944

Your face did not rot
like the others—the co-pilot,
for example, I saw him

yesterday. His face is corn-
mush: his wife and daughter,
the poor ignorant people, stare

as if he will compose soon.
He was more wronged than Job.
But your face did not rot

like the others—it grew dark,
and hard like ebony;
the features progressed in their

distinction. If I could cajole
you to come back for an evening,
down from your compulsive

orbiting, I would touch you,
read your face as Dallas,
your hoodlum gunner, now,

with the blistered eyes, reads
his braille editions. I would
touch your face as a disinterested

scholar touches an original page.
However frightening, I would
discover you, and I would not

turn you in; I would not make
you face your wife, or Dallas,
or the co-pilot, Jim. You

could return to your crazy
orbiting, and I would not try
to fully understand what

it means to you. All I know
is this: when I see you,
as I have seen you at least

once every year of my life,
spin across the wilds of the sky
like a tiny, African god,

I feel dead. I feel as if I were
the residue of a stranger's life,
that I should pursue you.

My head cocked toward the sky,
I cannot get off the ground,
and you, passing over again,

fast, perfect, and unwilling
to tell me that you are doing
well, or that it was mistake

that placed you in that world,
and me in this; or that misfortune
placed these worlds in us.

NORMAN DUBIE (B. 1945)

AUBADE OF THE SINGER AND SABOTEUR, MARIE TRISTE: 1941

In the twenties, I would visit Dachau often with my brother.
There was then an artists' colony outside the Ingolstadt Woods
And these estates had a meadow filled
With the hazy blood-campion, sumac and the delicate yellow cinquefoil.
At the left of the meadow there was a fast stream and pond, and
Along the stream, the six lodges and the oak Dachau Hall where
Meals were held and the evening concerts. In winter, the Hall
Was a hostel for hunters, and the violinists who were the first
Of the colony to arrive in spring would spend three days
Scouring the deer blood off the floors, tables, walls and sinks.
They would rub myrtle leaves into the wood to get out the stink!

The railway from Munich to Ingolstadt would deposit us by
The gold water-tower and my brother, Charles, and I would cut
Across two fields to the pastures behind Dachau Hall. Once,
Crossing these fields, Charles, who had been drinking warm beer
Since morning, stopped, and crouching low in the white chicory
And lupine found a single, reddish touch-me-not which is rare
Here in the mountains. A young surgeon, Charles assumed his
Condescending tone, and began by saying, "Now, little sister,

This flower has no perfume—what you smell is not your
Brother's breath either, but the yeast-sheds of the brewery just over
That hill. This uncommon flower can grow to an enormous height
If planted in water. It is a succulent annual. Its private
Appointments are oval and its nodding blossom takes its weight
From pods with crimson threadlike supports." With his bony fingers
He began to force open the flower. *I blushed.* He said, "It is
A devoted, sexual flower. Its tough, meatlike labia protrude
Until autumn and then shrivel; this adult flower
If disturbed explodes *into a small yellow rain like*
That fawn we watched urinating on the hawthorn just last August."

Charles was only two years younger but could be a wicked fellow.
Once, on our first day at the colony, at midnight, he was
Discovered nude and bathing in the pond with a cellist. She was
The only cellist, and for that week, Charles was their only doctor.
So neither was banished. But neither was spoken to except
For rehearsals and in illness. There is a short bridge passage
In a Scriabin sonata that reminds me of the bursting touch-me-nots,
That remind me, also, of Heisdt-Bridge *itself*, in Poland! We blew
It up in October. I had primed the packages of glycerin, kieselguhr,[28]
Woodmeal and chalk. We curbed the explosives with sulphur.
I sat in primrose and sorrel with the plunger-box and at four o'clock
Up went the munitions shipment from Munich to Warsaw. Those thin
Crimson supports of the flower tossed up like the sunburned arms
Of the pianist Mark Meichnik, arriving at his favorite E-flat
Major chord; and I guess that whenever a train or warehouse went
Four-ways-to-market right before my eyes, I thought
Of that large moment of Schumann's. The morning
After Heisdt-Bridge I was captured and Charles

Was shot.
I was at Dachau by the weekend. They have kept me in
A small cell. A young Lieutenant tortured me all that first night.
Knowing I was a singer they asked me to perform
For the Commandant early the next week.
By then I was able to stand again, but my Nazi inquisitor
Had for an hour touched live wires to me while holding
Me in a shallow ice bath. I had been
Made into a tenor voice! The Commandant's wife dismissed me
After just a few notes. As I was tortured I forced myself
To dwell on the adult life of the touch-me-not, that fawn in
Hawthorne and my brother's drunken anatomy lesson that showed
No skill at all there in the silver meadow. I was probably
Stupid not to have fallen unconscious. When I was
Ordered out of the parlor by the Nazi bitch, I did, for the first

[28] Diatomaceous earth used to absorb nitroglycerine in the manufacture of dynamite.

Time in two years, cry aloud. I think it was for my voice that
I cried so badly. The guards laughed, returning me to my cell.
My cell has a bench, a pail and a wire brush. Every two days
Without warning the hose comes alive with water, moving through
The space like a snake. Sometimes it wakes me about the face and legs.
I have lost so much weight that I can sleep comfortably
On the pine bench. I watch shadows in the cell become,
At night, the masquerade dance in the woodcut by Hans Burgkmair:[29]

Its bird shapes, that procession of *men* threading the dance,
And *Maximilian I* greeting them as they twist past the banquet tables.
My inquisitor, all that night in the chamber, commanding me
To sing, to sing!

When they fire the ovens out beside the pastures it is like
A giant catching his breath. And then there is the silence
Of the trucks with just their murmuring engines. My delusions:
A sound like my brother's cellist, at this early hour, opening
The morning with difficult arm exercises; he said that she would
Play for him naked and until he became jealous. Then I would
Say, "Oh, Charles!" He'd laugh.

My favorite pastime has become the imaginary destruction of flowers.
I hear their screams. They bleed onto the floor of my cell. I scrub
Afterwards sometimes for hours. I play the violin also. And I scrub
The wall where a *Bürgermeister* opened the artery of a doe that
He had shot just outside the window.
Later, the *Bürgermeister's* favorite butcher making venison flanks
Into roasts, how he sawed at the large femur of the deer
Like the cellist waking with her instrument, their right arms
Are beautiful with white muscles;
The butcher and the cellist died, here, admiring the noxious
Blue crystals on the floors of the gas-chamber: the way,

At first, they darken to indigo and like smoke
Climb over your ankles, reaching your waist—

[29] A German painter and designer of woodcuts (1473–1531).

You fall naked as into the field that is with a breeze turning
All its wildflowers, bladder-campion and myrtle, into
A melody of just three staves written for four voices:

Slaughter and music,
Two of the old miracles. They were not my choices.

MARY JO SALTER (B. 1954)

WELCOME TO HIROSHIMA

is what you first see, stepping off the train:
a billboard brought to you in living English
by Toshiba Electric. While a channel
silent in the TV of the brain

projects those flickering re-runs of a cloud
that brims its risen columnful like beer
and, spilling over, hangs its foamy head,
you feel a thirst for history: what year

it started to be safe to breathe the air,
and when to drink the blood and scum afloat
on the Ohta River. But no, the water's clear,
they pour it for your morning cup of tea

in one of the countless sunny coffee shops
whose plastic dioramas advertise
mutations of cuisine behind the glass:
a pancake sandwich; a pizza someone tops

with a maraschino cherry. Passing by
the Peace Park's floral hypocenter (where
how bravely, or with what mistaken cheer,
humanity erased its own erasure),

you enter the memorial museum
and through more glass are served, as on a dish
of blistered grass, three mannequins. Like gloves
a mother clips to coatsleeves, strings of flesh

hang from their fingertips; or as if tied
to recall a duty for us, *Reverence*
the dead whose mourners too shall soon be dead,
but all commemoration's swallowed up

in questions of bad taste, how re-created
horror mocks the grim original,
and thinking at last *They should have left it all*
you stop. This is the wristwatch of a child.

Jammed on the moment's impact, resolute
to communicate some message, although mute,
it gestures with its hands at eight-fifteen
and eight-fifteen and eight-fifteen again

while tables of statistics on the wall
update the news by calling on a roll
of tape, death gummed on death, and in the case
adjacent, an exhibit under glass

is glass itself: a shard the bomb slammed in
a woman's arm at eight-fifteen, but some
three decades on—as if to make it plain
hope's only as renewable as pain,

and as if all the unsung
debasements of the past may one day come
rising to the surface once again—
worked its filthy way out like a tongue.

LEE ANN RORIPAUGH (B. 1965)

HIROSHIMA MAIDEN

I.

My mother recognized
my feet and claimed me
at the hospital,
my face hot wax poured
into a Noh mask.
She used to chide me
for my pride
because I always
carried a parasol,
wasted money
on watermelons
to scrub my skin.
She's frightened
to look at me now
because I might see
myself in her eyes.

II.

Everybody stared
at Mrs. Roosevelt's
tea party, and I felt
a flash of shame
each time a reporter
snapped another picture.
After plastic surgery
at the American hospital
we looked like so many
rows of Q-Tips.
It was a relief not
to see each others
faces, and our hands
began to take on
their former girlish

gestures. We almost
felt pretty again,
until one girl died
on their table. She found
the opening where they
were sewing on a new
mouth, and flew away.

III.

The other hibakusha[30]
say I put on airs
since I came back.
I learned how to draw
on eyebrows, make
my skin all the same
color. They gave me
a wig made of real hair
that I brush down
a certain way to hide
my missing ear.
Mother tells me
not to listen,
they're only jealous,
and maybe now
I'll find a husband.
Maybe an ugly man,
though kind. But
I sour inside like
an unripe persimmon,
and every day become
stranger to myself
behind this other
person's face—a lie,
richly embroidered
by unfamiliar hands.

[30] Witnesses/survivors of the atomic bombing of Hiroshima and Nagasaki.

FROM *HEART MOUNTAIN*, 1943[31]

I. KIMIKO OZAWA

Oka-san keeps stuffing rags under
the barracks door, around cracks
in the window, to keep out smells
of snow, sage and cattle,
families pressed around us.
My feet, my mind, become numb
from standing in line all day—
lines to eat, shower, shit
in the dirty outdoor benjos.[32]
Evenings I sweep my anger
off the barracks floor,
but the next morning it's coated
with dust, corners filled again.
Shikata ga nai, my parents keep[33]
chanting. There is nothing
to be done. I watch
my father grow thin. Nights
he plays his shakuhachi flute,[34]
the sound not unlike the cries
outside the barracks. The wind,
he says, takes everything.
I think this must be true.
I have taken walks inside
the barbed-wire fences,
and all the words
are pulled from my mouth.
My brothers, too, scattered
like dust. Ken fights
in the all-Nisei[35] combat unit,

---

[31] An internment camp in Wyoming for Americans of Japanese descent.
[32] Latrines.
[33] A Japanese phrase meaning "it cannot be helped."
[34] Traditional end-blown Japanese flute, tuned to the pentatonic scale.
[35] A person born in America from parents who emigrated from Japan.

and Toji, who said No once,
No again, taken to Tule Lake.[36]
My scalp itches and flakes, my lips,
my hands, chapped and cracked.
Sometimes I use a drop of cooking oil
to keep from blowing away.

DIANE THIEL (B. 1967)

THE MINEFIELD

He was running with his friend from town to town.
They were somewhere between Prague and Dresden.
He was fourteen. His friend was faster
and knew a shortcut through the fields they could take.
He said there was lettuce growing in one of them,
and they hadn't eaten all day. His friend ran a few lengths ahead,
like a wild rabbit across the grass,
turned his head, looked back once,
and his body was scattered across the field.

My father told us this, one night,
and then continued eating dinner.

He brought them with him—the minefields.
He carried them underneath his good intentions.
He gave them to us—in the volume of his anger,
in the bruises we covered up with sleeves.
In the way he threw anything against the wall—
a radio, that wasn't even ours,
a melon, once, opened like a head.

---

[36] By not answering yes to two questions about loyalty to America one was sent to a segregation camp at Tule Lake in California.

In the way we still expect, years later and continents away,
that anything might explode at any time,
and we would have to run on alone
with a vision like that
only seconds behind.

THE KOREAN WAR

1950–1953

I think the first time they hit us was about eight o'clock at night. It was the damndest thing I ever saw—they came swarming over the hills making all kinds of noise, blowing bugles and rattling cans and shooting off flares and yelling their heads off in these high-pitched sing-song voices. They had no armor. No vehicles of any kind. . . . They were shooting burp guns and rifles but I'll tell you, they were lousy shots. What caused us the most trouble was grenades. And the fact that there were so goddamn many of them. Just wave after wave. You'd shoot down a whole line of Chinamen and another line would be right behind. They'd stop to pick up the weapons of the ones that had been shot, and then they'd come on like the first ones. We'd shoot them down, and there would be another line right behind them.

—George Zonge at Sachang, 1950, from Rudy Tomedi, *No Bugles, No Drums* (1993)

Coming less than a decade after the global engagement and all-out mobilization of World War II, and a little more than a decade before the war in Vietnam, the Korean War never occupied the national imagination as did either of those wars. This was true even though ultimately more than a million Americans, plus the troops of more than a dozen countries, served in Korea under the flag of the United Nations. According to recent counts, there were 37,000 Americans who lost their lives in that country, with twice that many wounded, even though the Korean War lasted a third of the time that the Vietnam War did.[1]

---

[1] The number of American fatalities inscribed on the Korean War Memorial in Washington D.C. is 54,268, a number roughly equal to the losses during the Vietnam War. Paul Edwards of the Center for the Study of the Korean War, Richard Kolb, editor of *VFW Magazine*, and Harry

The Korean War was conducted as a limited war; Harry Truman recalled Douglas MacArthur from active duty to stop him from carrying the war beyond the Yalu River or into China. American action seesawed between advance, when the North Koreans retreated because of over-stretched supply lines, and retreat, when policy determined that an American offensive would risk provoking a nuclear response from Russia or opening a land war with China. Cities and outposts were taken, retaken, and taken again. Truce negotiations began in 1951, but bogged down repeatedly. In 1953, the rush by the North Koreans to take the whole of the peninsula—the precipitating cause of the war—had been beaten back, and a ceasefire was signed at Panmunjom on July 27. By 1953, a war of attrition had left the Chinese and the North Koreans on one side of the Thirty-eighth Parallel, and the Americans and the South Koreans on the other side, very much where they had been before 1950. A peace treaty never followed the ceasefire of 1953.

This war anticipated much that would be told of the war in Vietnam. South Korea was an American client state in the game of global domination, and yet differences in language and culture prevented the successful blending of American and South Korean military and geopolitical goals. Most Americans soldiers had little interest in acquiring the ability to tell the difference between South Koreans and North Koreans, and when they could, saw little to respect in the ill-trained and undermotivated followers of the corrupt dictatorship of Syngman Rhee, who led our ostensible allies. Korean reunification remained a matter of indifference at home and to the soldier on the ground, where the issue appeared to have little visible connection to our own security.

While some literature of the Korean War trickled out until the 1960s, more was published in the 1980s and 1990s, when the Korean War had been reintroduced in the imagination as a complementary part of the experience in Vietnam. Reg Saner's "They Said" was written with his Korean War experience in mind, yet it was published in 1976, when much

---

Summers, Jr. (*Korean War Almanac*) all agree on a total of 103,284 Americans wounded in action; all three authorities, however, cite between 33,000 and 34,000 deaths as their total. The frequently cited figure of 54,000 is obtained by adding to the sum of fatalities all nonhostile deaths in the U.S. military anywhere in the world during the "conflict period," when in fact only 3,262 of those deaths occurred in Korea itself. This information is drawn from a paper Richard Kolb delivered in 2000 entitled "War in Memory, Popular Culture, and Folklore." W. D. Ehrhart drew my attention to Kolb's work.

poetry by Vietnam War soldier poets was appearing. In harmony with the spirit of these poets of a later war, Saner mocks the degradation of military language, as it blurs truth with euphemism by way of technology. After World War II, helped by writers like Joseph Heller, satire of the inadequacies of military language to cover the political or psychological reality on the ground had grown rapidly into a permanent feature of all war literature, including poetry.

For a member of a previous generation of soldiers like Hayden Carruth, the Korean battles folded into those of his own war, and his sense of war's perpetuity; for Thomas McGrath, the dead were indistinguishable from other Asian losses. Soldiers of World War II, the Korean War, and the Vietnam War alike begin to emphasize that casualties are not just physical injuries, but a mutilation of both flesh and spirit. Battles, too, more and more clearly recount not just individual soldierly accomplishment, but also horrifying occasions of impersonal mass death. Rolando Hinojosa comments dryly: "No one talks about the cold anymore, nor about the dead. / Theirs or ours, but mostly theirs. / Also, we never seem to run out of shells." American culture under Eisenhower now accepted the condition of permanent military alert that marks the garrison state: the Korean War was the first American war not to conclude in a large-scale disarmament and demobilization.

However bitterly American soldiers may have suffered wounds and deaths, in this and other twentieth-century limited wars, fatalities were borne disproportionately by the other side. Late twentieth-century poets write at length about mass graves, burial details, and terrifying wounds that, because of advances in medical technology, no longer lead inevitably to death. On an increasingly global and time-melting scale, American poets have been given somber cause to measure war's lasting physical, psychological, and environmental aftermath. Korean War soldier poets may have been encouraged by the example of the widely published and more numerous poets of the Vietnam War to bring the harsher details of the effects of war on a civilian population into their own poems. Their poems, too, testify to the numbing brutalization of the soldier, to their complicity in the prostitution of a peasant population's women, and to the destruction of an alien countryside still glimpsed by them as heartachingly beautiful.

THOMAS MCGRATH (1916–1990)

ODE FOR THE AMERICAN DEAD IN ASIA

1.

God love you now, if no one else will ever,
Corpse in the paddy, or dead on a high hill
In the fine and ruinous summer of a war
You never wanted. All your false flags were
Of bravery and ignorance, like grade school maps:
Colors of countries you would never see—
Until that weekend in eternity
When, laughing, well armed, perfectly ready to kill
The world and your brother, the safe commanders sent
You into your future. Oh, dead on a hill,
Dead in a paddy, leeched and tumbled to
A tomb of footnotes. We mourn a changeling: you:
Handselled to poverty and drummed to war
By distinguished masters whom you never knew.

2.

The bee that spins his metal from the sun,
The shy mole drifting like a miner ghost
Through midnight earth—all happy creatures run
As strict as trains on rails the circuits of
Blind instinct. Happy in your summer follies,
You mined a culture that was mined for war:
The state to mold you, church to bless, and always
The elders to confirm you in your ignorance.
No scholar put your thinking cap on nor
Warned that in dead seas fishes died in schools
Before inventing legs to walk the land. .
The rulers stuck a tennis racket in your hand,
An Ark against the flood. In time of change
Courage is not enough: the blind mole dies,
And you on your hill, who did not know the rules.

3.

Wet in the windy counties of the dawn
The lone crow skirls his draggled passage home:
And God (whose sparrows fall aslant his gaze,
Like grace or confetti) blinks and he is gone,
And you are gone. Your scarecrow valor grows
And rusts like early lilac while the rose
Blooms in Dakota and the stock exchange
Flowers. Roses, rents, all things conspire
To crown your death with wreaths of living fire.
And the public mourners come: the politic tear
Is cast in the Forum. But, in another year,
We will mourn you, whose fossil courage fills
The limestone histories: brave: ignorant: amazed:
Dead in the rice paddies, dead on the nameless hills.

WILLIAM MEREDITH (B. 1919)

A KOREAN WOMAN SEATED BY A WALL

Suffering has settled like a sly disguise
On her cheerful old face. If she dreams beyond
Rice and a roof, now toward the end of winter,
Is it of four sons gone, the cries she has heard,
A square farm in the south, soured by tents?
Some alien and untranslatable loss
Is a mask she smiles through at the weak sun
That is moving north to invade the city again.

A poet penetrates a dark disguise
After his own conception, little or large.
Crossing the scaleless asia of trouble
Where it seems no one could give himself away,
He gives himself away, he sets a scale.

Hunger and pain and death, the sorts of loss,
Dispute our comforts like peninsulas
Of no particular value, places to fight.
And what is it in suffering dismays us more:
The capriciousness with which it is dispensed
Or the unflinching way we see it home?

She may be dreaming of her wedding gift;
A celadon bowl of a good dynasty
With cloud and heron cut in its green paste,
It sleeps in a hollow bed of pale blue silk.
The rice it bought was eaten the second winter.
And by what happier stove is it unwrapped
In the evening now and passed around like a meat,
Making a foliage in the firelight?

She shifts the crate she sits on as the March
Wind mounts from the sea. The sun moves down the sky
Perceptibly, like the hand of a public clock,
In increments of darkness though ablaze.
Ah, now she looks at me. We are unmasked
And exchange what roles we guess at for an instant.
The questions Who comes next and Why not me
Rage at and founder my philosophy.
Guilt beyond my error and a grace past her grief
Alter the coins I tender cowardly,
Shiver the porcelain fable to green shards.

HAYDEN CARRUTH (B. 1921)

ON A CERTAIN ENGAGEMENT SOUTH OF SEOUL

A long time, many years, we've had these wars.
When they were opened, one can scarcely say.
We were high school students, no more than sophomores,

When Italy broke her peace on a dark day,
And that was not the beginning. The following years
Grew crowded with destruction and dismay.

When I was nineteen, once the surprising tears
Stood in my eyes and stung me, for I saw
A soldier in a newsreel clutch his ears

To hold his face together. Those that paw
The public's bones to eat the public's heart
Said far too much, of course. The sight, so raw

And unbelievable, of people blown apart
Was enough to change us without that bark and whine.
We grew disconsolate. Each had his chart

To mark on the kitchen wall the battle-line,
But many were out of date. The radio
Droned through the years, a faithful anodyne.

Yet the news of this slight encounter somewhere below
Seoul stirs my remembrance: we were a few,
Sprawled on the stiff grass of a small plateau,

Afraid. No one was dead. But we were new—
We did not know that probably none would die.
Slowly, then, all vision went askew.

My clothing was outlandish; earth and sky
Were metallic and horrible. We were unreal,
Strange bodies and alien minds; we could not cry

For even our eyes seemed to be made of steel;
Nor could we look at one another, for each
Was a sign of fear, and we could not conceal

Our hatred for our friends. There was no speech.
We sat alone, all of us, trying to wake
Some memory of the selves beyond our reach.

That place was conquered. The nations undertake
Another campaign now, in another land,
A stranger land perhaps. And we forsake

The miseries there that we can't understand
Just as we always have. Yet still my glimpse
Of a scene on the distant field can make my hand

Tremble again. How quiet we are. One limps,
One cannot walk at all, or one is all right,
But one has this experience that crimps

Forgetfulness, especially at night.
Is this a bond? Does this make us brothers?
Or does it bring our hatred back? I might

Have known, but now I do not know. Others
May know. I know when I walk out-of-doors
I have a sorrow not wholly mine, but another's.

KEITH WILSON (B. 1927)

THE CIRCLE

—U.S.S. VALLEY FORGE, 1950

Out of the stirrings of the Yellow Sea,
20 miles off from Inchon Channel[1]
we came to—blue *leis*
thrown on the water.

Sea, glassy. No wind.
I sat atop a 5″ director, the ship
steamed on, no planes in sight:
a pleasant gunwatch, little excitement,
lost in quiet.

---

[1] The site of a decisive invasion that cut off the North Korean army in the South in 1950.

The first I knew we
were among them, circles of men
bound in faded blue lifejackets,
lashed together

Most of the men leaned
back, heads bobbing against
kapok collars, mouths open,
tongues swollen

—hundreds of them.
We steamed by, group after group,
for all my watch. I searched for
any sign of motion, any gesture
of any hand, but soon I just
watched as

        bobbing gently, each circle
        undulated, moved independently;
        once or twice a hand did flop
        & I caught the man's face in
        my binoculars instantly,
        slowly let them drop

We sailed on. I suppose that's all
there is to say: wartime commitments
the necessity for being where you must
be & when
        they were dead, hundreds
of them, a troopship gone down somewhere
—Korean, uncounted.

        I remember one man, remember
        him clearly. God knows why
        but his ass was up instead
        of his head; no pants left,
        his buttocks glistened
        greyish white in the clear sun.
        the only one.

& we steamed on, routine patrol,
launched planes at 1800 for night
CAP, leaving the last of the circles
rocking gently in our darkening wake.

> . . . seid stolz: Ich trage die Fahne,
> seid ohne Sorge: Ich trage die Fahne,
> habt mich lieb: Ich trage die Fahne—

> . . . und die reglose Fahne hat unruhige
> Schatten. Sie träumt.[2]

WATERFRONT BARS

& how they look—from the sea
the neon glitter softens, grows
warm

                —a man can almost smell
beer, women

From Beppu,[3] on the Inland Sea,
the giant "Asahi" beersign stood
steady as any navigational light

                        drew, caught
attention: we, sailing by
returned to seadamp bunks
strong coffee

3 months on service duty ahead
north of the bombline &
then back we came, wondering

---

[2] ". . . be proud: I carry the flag, / do not be concerned: I carry the flag, / love me: I carry the flag— / . . . and the ungovernable flag has unquiet / shadows. It dreams." From the German of Rainer Maria Rilke, taken from passages in *The Lay of the Love and Death of Cornet Christoph Rilke*, a romantic tribute to young death and soldierly glory written in 1899, when Rilke was 24.
[3] A resort city in Japan.

—lights of Yokusuka, Sasebo
Yokohama.[4] We sailed to them
each in turn. Worlds brushed,
passed

      each in turn.

—leaving the darkness of
watches, silver turning of screws,
wake piled high behind
the blackened ship: little pieces
of a man, left here, there.

MEMORY OF A VICTORY

Off the Korean Coast, beyond Wonsan[5]
waiting for invasion soft winds blew
the scent of squid drying in the sun,
homely smells of rice paddies, cooking fires.

It was a picture world with low hills
much like New Mexico, except for water,
the strange smells. Little plumes of smoke.
Here & there, the glint of steel.

Under the waiting guns lay peachblossoms.
I could see them with my binoculars.
The planes still had not come, all eternity
waited beneath the sweep second hand.

Then the crackling radio commanded
"Fire!" and a distant world I could have loved
went up in shattering bursts, in greyblack explosions,
the strange trees that suddenly grew on the hillside.

---

[4] Yokusuka, Sasebo, and Yokahoma are all port cities in Japan.
[5] A city on the eastern coast of North Korea, the site of an Allied landing.

They fired their rifles, light howitzers
back. After a while we sent boats into the silence.

REG SANER (B. 1929)

THEY SAID

They said, "Listen class attention before sorting
your blocks put the red ones in the tray
and yellow in the bowl." So most got all but one
or two of them right and drank from paper cups
of pre-sweetened juice voting later to stuff
them nicely down the trash-clown on the way home.

They said, "Now color Holy Manger brown
the Virgin Mary blue the Christ child pink
and St. Joseph anything you like." So this one boy
colored him polka-dot but was allowed to try again
on a fresh sheet getting a green paper star on his
second St. Joseph he colored him pink a suitable choice.

They said, "Democracy is at the crossroads everyone
will be given a gun and a map in cases like this
there is no need to vote." Our group scored quite
well getting each of its villages right except
one but was allowed to try again on a fresh village
we colored it black and then wore our brass
stars of unit citation almost all the way home.

FLAG MEMOIR

The white crosses alter whenever I move. Row on row, they realign precisely, geometrically: perfect as close-order drill. While I look for the friend I don't find, the arms on the crosses shift, so as always to focus and open toward me. They do it by night too; faces and places I start awake from, as if hitting a trip wire. Back where the past is mined.

~

Once monsoons begin, the sky hangs dark and heavy as hides. Logs, burlap, rain. After the sixth straight 24-hours, anything wearable is sodden as bunkers and trench walls collapsing. Daytimes I choose some one patch of overcast to brighten on will power, while leather gear re-stitches itself with green mold. By week two, the only imaginable sound is rain letting up, and whenever I listen, I hear it.

~

"At ease, gentlemen. Let's keep it brief. This map gives our share of the ridge: markings in blue, our howitzers and 8-inch pieces. Lacking radios the enemy's greater numbers are noise: bugle signals, hand-sirens, even bells. We own the air. That means night attacks, with only their first two waves coming armed. Their third and fourth waves may carry scythes, hooks, farm tools, sticks. Their fifth waves carry nothing. Remind your men Eighth Army is in full support if needed. Later today my G4 will have details on the R&R's we're rewarding every five kills confirmed."

~

When it comes to a .50 caliber machine gun, single shots call for technique. And for tripod legs sandbagged against kick. They call for a boxed belt full of fat nails, and this flat trigger: the butterfly switch. But because any bullet that misses will crack the air overhead like a cattlewhip, my first shot could drop him from view and back under cover, leaving the eye unsure what's been hit. Here where everyone's next breath can depend on ballistics mixing with windage, my forefinger has traveled seven thousand miles by water to poise over this bit of gunmetal blue and fire at a difference in cloth. I wait till he sets down his ammo load; half standing, looking my way. Then soft as a penis kissing an apple, my finger gives one quick, accurate tap.

~

At Graves Registration two clerks young as I am act like old hands: "This is your first KIA, lieutenant?"
    "Yes."
    Whereupon, with almost a flourish, they unzip a dark rubber bag to show a slashed head like Barnett's, the country boy who'd bragged he screwed goats. North Carolina? Possibly Georgia. It's him, but I face the remains of his face by saying inwardly, again and again, "This isn't him,

he's not here. He's elsewhere." Then I sign two certifications small as cards, for sliding into the book of the dead. Outside a PFC pulls the pin on 3.2 beers we suck lather-warm from cans, talking Red Sox and Yankees under summer shreds of something once like an orchard.

~

"Despite problems last night, mainly we held. These map-changes update our positions. Division Rear is doubling artillery. During the break-through, Tyler kept his head and called in fire on his own bunkers. We killed ten to their one, but their later waves picked up rifles and handguns, advancing. Temporarily, Battalion Medical will regroup back to Wonju. Stop your men shooting rats by explaining that the fever spreads when vermin desert the carcass. With perimeters fluid, be sure all squads get late changes in password. Tyler knew none of our officers has ever been cap-tured. I'm putting his name in for a Silver Star. Now G4 has one or two changes on ammo and food."

~

Patrolling the river by night our cover is chestnut trees. Near the south bank we snort and choke as we drink from the stream, like hogs at trough. Luhan sits back on his haunches, dark hair dripping, the butt-plate of his rifle grinding on rock in the shallows. A moon, large and low, rises through leaves as one by one other faces tilt, look toward it, blinking streamwater off lashes. Stagner lifts his eyes, forehead still streaming: "Fuck the moon!" And watches the moon go up.

~

In Battalion HQ, from commo wire looped between tent poles, a skull swings as a joke, though nobody can say whose side it was on. Because of that gunk they soak into the army's tent canvas, daylight barely penetrates; yet the sergeant-major and I can see well enough to feel we're growing into our jobs. He gives me a grin like the pearl handles customizing his gun-metal hip as he twists the skull round to show off its eyes, green crabap-ples plugged into each socket.

~

"Word on the fever seems good. Eighth Army says close to a cure. Warn units that self-inflicted wounds equal refusal to serve. And appoint some-one from each crew to make sure men don't fill their canteens out of your water-cooled .30 calibers. Our flares last night lit up their dead by the hundreds along the major assault routes, though by daybreak the bodies were gone. With so much ammo showing corrosion, check boxes for date. Take names of men who pocket those leaflets offering soft terms for surrender. Remind each man that First Battalion has never abandoned its wounded. Later, possibly even today, a member of my staff will outline the new situation on water."

~

Fresh bursts. Against the night sky, more parachute flares ignite, float smoking down, oscillating like pendulums. As the stadium audience applauds like rain, rice farmers go poking along muddy ox-roads, into the usual drizzle. Far south of the MLR by now, traveling perhaps by dog.

And still on the 4th, every 4th of July, after the municipal sunset, after applause for each name on the committee, the skyrockets rise and die beautifully, the white-hot shrapnel spurts, furrows the air, each burst. Aerial salutes report to the eye as muzzle flash and sheared jaw, red teeth, clay dirt on the brains. Or maybe with one long zipper pull some corporal exactly my age throws open a dark rubber bag, there yet, in any such zipper I hear: a metallic hiss taking my breath, taking it back through tanks gutted and rusting like fire, through cratering in fields and roads, through stump forests reseeded in shoe mines that end legs at the ankle.

A stadium anthem can do it, or flag at a ballpark, its vague sidle, stirring in breeze over one or two rows of empty seats. The flag slowly dipping, lifting, over nobody there. Explaining. Trying to explain.

WILLIAM CHILDRESS (B. 1933)

TRYING TO REMEMBER PEOPLE I NEVER REALLY KNEW

There was that guy
on that hill in Korea.
Exploding gasoline made him
a thousand candles bright.
We guided the Samaritan copter
in by flashlight

to a rookery of rocks,
a huge, fluttering nightbird
aiming at darting fireflies,
and one great firefly
rolling in charred black screams.

There was the R.O.K.[6] soldier
lying in the paddy,
his lifted arms curved
as he stiffly embraced death,
a tiny dark tunnel over his heart.
Such a small door
for something as large as life
to escape through.

Later, between pages and chapters
of wars not yet written up
in Field Manuals or Orders of the Day,
there came shrieking down
from a blue Kentucky sky
a young paratrooper whom technology failed.
(I must correct two common errors:
they are never called *shroud lines*,
and paratroopers do not cry *Geronimo*.)

I wish I could say
that all three men fathered sons,
that some part of them still lived.
But maybe I don't, for the children's ages
would now be such as to make them
ready for training as hunters of men,
to stalk dark forests
where leaden rains fall with a precision
that can quench a hunter's fire.

---

[6] Republic of Korea.

ROLANDO HINOJOSA (B. 1929)

THE JANUARY–MAY 1951 SLAUGHTER

I'm sick. They didn't stop coming,
And we wouldn't stop firing.

At the beginning, in January,
It looked like the Chongchon[7] action for us again,
But we stopped them.
Brutally.

I passed on the beer ration again.
Drink? I don't even want to eat . . .
Our counter-offensive started on January 21;
    Happy Birthday, Rafe.

In February, it was just as bad. If possible: it was worse.
No one talks about the cold anymore, nor about the dead,
Theirs or ours, but mostly theirs.
Also, we never seem to run out of shells.

March, and Seoul's been retaken. We took our time.
I don't want to look at the Chinese dead.
There are hundreds of them out there. They died in the city,
They died in the fields and in the hillsides.
They died everywhere.

At one point,
It was artillery against artillery in the city.
It's early April.
I am not going to talk about this again, and so I will say it
This once:
    We fired twelve thousand rounds of 105 mm. in twenty-four hours
In support of the Second Div.
    I don't see how people can understand what

---

[7] A river in North Korea, the scene of an American retreat.

I am saying when I say
   12,000 rounds of 105s in 24 hours.

It means this:

Seventeen of us were wounded. Minor wounds they were,
And all wounds bleed, but we kept firing.
There was no pain . . . the blood caked and we kept up the fire.
We're animals,
But then, so are they.
At the aid station, Sonny Ruiz said it best:

"They came at the infantry down there like pigs in a chute,
   And we just cut their necks off from up here."

The officers are now ordering us to eat,
But we notice that their appetite hasn't improved either.

May, and I'm overdue for an R&R; I'm one of the medicals;
Personally, I think it's mental.

JACOB MOSQUEDA WRESTLES WITH THE ANGELS

Mosqueda doesn't believe it for one minute,
   but it's true;
And although he swears he'll never forget it,
   he will
As we all do, as we all should
   and do.

The scraps of flesh on Mosqueda's sleeve
Belonged to Hatalski or Frazier,
   one of the two;
And when they splashed there, Mosqueda screamed and fainted
And soiled his fatigues. And yet,
Unhurt and all,
He was carried off as if a casualty, and maybe he was . . .
But he'll forget it, in time;
In time we all do, and should.

On the other hand,
If Mosqueda had lost an arm or a leg or an eye, a nose or an ear,
He'd not forget it nor would others let him, but
One man's meat is not another's souvenir,
And so, Mosqueda will forget;
If not, he'll become a bore, and a bother, or a public nuisance.
But Mosqueda will forget;
His skin wasn't even pinked, let alone charred or burned
Or blasted into someone else's clothing
When the rocket burst. And,
When the rocket burst, Mosqueda was between the gun
And Joey Vielma, a casual visitor who came calling,
But this proves little except, perhaps, a law of probabilities.
The burst took off Hatalski's face
And Frazier's life as well; Joey Vielma caught it in the chest and face,
But Mosqueda was unhurt . . .

   He screamed anyway,
And the other gun crews froze for an instant.
Some came running in time
To retch and gag and vomit over the dead
As the fainting Mosqueda screamed and cried and sobbed
   And yet

He was unhurt
When the rocket burst.

As for me, my hand was nicked a bit, my eyes and face peppered,
When the sun glasses broke in half;
Later, in a stagger, I came upon the binocs
Some fifteen yards away.
But, as I've said, Mosqueda was unhurt, and,
Given time,
   he'll forget.

MYUNG MI KIM (B. 1957)

UNDER FLAG

Is distance. If she knows it

Casting and again casting into the pond to hook the same turtle

Beset by borders conquered, disfigured

One house can be seen

Then another thatched roof

On this side of the sea the rancor of their arrival
Where invasion occurs according to schedule

Evacuees, a singular wave set against stubbled bluffs

Rigor of those who carry households on their backs

Above: victims.
Below: Chonui, a typical Korean town. In the distance,
        a 155-mm shell has exploded.

Of elders who would have been sitting in the warmest part
of the house with comforters draped around their shoulders
peeling tangerines

Of an uncle with shrapnel burrowing into shinbone
for thirty years

A wave of much white cloth

Handful of millet, a pair of never worn shoes, one chicken
grabbed by the neck, ill-prepared for carrying,
carrying through

Not to have seen it yet inheriting it

Drilled at the core for mineral yield and this, once depleted,
never to be replaced

At dawn the next morning, firing his machine gun, Corporal Leonard H.
was shot and instantly killed while stopping the Reds' last attempts
to overrun and take the hilltop

The demoralized ROK troops disappeared but the handful of Ameri-
cans,
completely surrounded, held out for seven hours against continuous
attack, until all ammunition was exhausted

General D.'s skillful direction of the flight was fully as memorable
as his heroic personal participation with pistol and bazooka

Grumman F9F
Bell H-130s
Shooting Stars
Flying Cheetahs

They could handle them if they would only use the weapons we have
given them properly, said Colonel Wright

Lockheed F-04 Starfire
Lockheed F-803
Bell H-13 Sioux
Bell H-13Ds

More kept coming. More fell

Is distance. If she could know it

Citizens to the streets marching

Their demands lettered in blood

The leader counters them

With gas meant to thwart any crowd's ambition

And they must scatter, white cloths over their faces

Every month on the 15th, there is an air raid drill sometime during
the day, lasting approximately 15 minutes. When the siren goes off,

everyone must get off the streets. An all clear siren marks the
end of the drill.

And how long practice how long drill to subvert what borders are

What must we call each other if we meet there

Brother sister neighbor lover   go unsaid what we are

Tens of thousands of names

Go unsaid the family name

Sun, an affliction hitting white

Retinue of figures dwindling to size

The eye won't be appeased

His name stitched on his school uniform, flame

Flame around what will fall as ash

Kerosene soaked skin housing what will burn

Fierce tenement of protest

Faces spread in a field

On the breeze what might be azaleas in full bloom

Composed of many lengths of bone

SUJI KWOCK KIM (B. 1968)

The Chasm

(AUGUST, 1950)

In the dream vultures circle above my mother's cousin.
Eye the gash blown in his belly

by Soviet T-34 tanks or U.S. rocket-launchers
shooting at each other blind across the Naktong River—

a million refugees caught in the crossfire,
crossing far as the eye can see.

Vultures smell the kill.
My mother screams when one drops

on his chest, thrashing for foothold,
his small body shaking beneath its wings,

talons ripping away strips
of flesh like bandages.

She beats it with her walking stick
until it flies hissing to another corpse.

Then another one lands, then another, then another,
her beating the stick until they fly away too,

not for good, swarming again and again to his half-gnawed body,
wave after wave.

Her mother shouts at her to *leave him*.
Digs her nails into her arm and drags her on.

My mother can't see his face anymore
for their jaws, chewing on twisted entrails,

insides pulled out like ropes unlashed from the mast of the spine,
all the bleeding sinews and nerves, strange jellies,

all the hieroglyphs of generation.
Why won't they speak.

———————————

I know you were real, even if I can only see you
in dreams, I see

we'll never meet.
It's humiliating to wake up

alive, fifty years later, when I couldn't have saved you.
I couldn't have saved a dog.

For the birds change their faces
and wear the faces of soldiers.

FRAGMENTS OF THE FORGOTTEN WAR

FOR MY FATHER

You whom I could not protect,

                    when will I forget you:
when will I forget the Northern soldiers who took you away for
    questioning,
so we never saw you again?

———————————

We three sons fled south in January 1951

                        without you, with a million others
on Shinjangno, the old Imperial Highway between P'yongyang and
    Seoul—
I felt artillery crash miles away in the soles of my feet, the ground shud-
    dering.
I heard the drone and snarl of engines as B-29 bombers swarmed toward
    us

like a war in heaven but not heaven,
                              a war between gods who weren't gods,
now missiles whistling on their search-and-destroy,
now the endless columns of refugees screaming in terror,
now delayed-fuse demolition bombs exploding all around us,
blowing craters larger than houses,
                              now firing white phosphorus flares
                              3000 feet high,
while we knelt like beggars before the blasts,
                              using the dead as shields, corpse-
                              greaved,
covering our faces from the blizzard of shrapnel,
blizzard of limbs and flaming skin,
                              of all who left this world in a grave of
                              smoke.
I'll never forget the smell of burning flesh.
I'll never forget the stench of open sores, pus, gangrene;
                              the smell of people rotting
                              who hadn't died yet:

or the cries of the wounded moaning without morphine,
a boy sinking his teeth into his arm
                              to take his mind off the gash that
                              ripped his stomach,
biting down and down until you saw bone glinting through
                              like teeth in a mass grave.

————————————

At night we fought for the few standing barns, shacks, outhouses.
Without fuel we burned shit for heat
                              until the light from our fires
                              drew bombers.
We caught fever and frostbite from walking hundreds of miles
through snow,
                              walking through Taejon, the Chollas,
                              Taegu, Chinju.
When food ran out we ate cattle feed,
                              ate bark, ate lice from our own
                              bodies

until our gums bled,

>> until we could only shit water by the time
>> we got to Pusan.

What I wouldn't give to bring back that miserable village I hated as a
boy.

Sometimes in my dreams you hoot like a soul-owl,
What have you done with your life,

>> *who will you become, who, who,*
>> *who?*

I can only speak to you in broken things,
I can only speak in bullets, grenade-shards, mortar casings and ROKA
barricades:

I know I'm orphaned,
I know you suffered, but I'll never know how.
I think of the loneliness of the dying,

>> the bodies I saw along the way,
>> rotting separately:

I think of that boy biting his arm

>> who didn't live through the night,
wild dogs gnawing at his skull in the morning, his whole face an "exit
wound":

I think of a carcass foaming with maggots, the bone black with hatching
flies.

THE VIETNAM WAR

1964–1975

> Then-Senator Lyndon Johnson publicly stated, "I am against send-
> ing American GIs into the mud and muck of Indochina on a blood-
> letting spree to perpetuate colonialism and white man's exploitation
> of Asia." In 1964, [Acting] President Johnson campaigned success-
> fully for election against Barry Goldwater on a promise to keep
> American GIs out of Vietnam. Four years later, while Lyndon John-
> son was still president, nearly half a million American GIs were
> fighting in the mud and muck of Indochina, and the blood-letting
> spree would eventually claim the lives of 1.7 million Vietnamese,
> wounding 3.2 million more, and leaving 12 million homeless.
>
> —W. D. Ehrhart, "Learning the Hard Way," from *In the Shadow of
> Vietnam: Essays, 1977–1991*

Unlike the GI Joe of World War II, whose average age was twenty-six, the
average age of the American grunt in Vietnam was nineteen-and-a-half;
he also faced a far greater likelihood of seeing combat. Of the 58,000
American dead whose names spread across the black granite of the Viet-
nam Veterans Memorial, many fell in a ground war whose major purpose
was to draw out North Vietnamese and southern Viet Cong forces into
territory where they could be punished by superior American air and
artillery. Yet in spite of mass casualties on their side, the Vietnamese pre-
vailed. Facing the political and military weakness of the South Vietnamese
government, our "domino" in the lineup of noncommunist states, Amer-
ican forces were compelled to withdraw in favor of the North Vietnamese.
This happened even after the Americans tried various formulas of direct
and indirect intervention and pacification and of different applications of
men and materiel. After a thirty-year-long war with the French, and after
more than ten years of struggle with an American government blinded by

its belief in a monolithic communist conspiracy, the south lost to the North Vietnamese, and Vietnam became a unified and independent state.

With the exception of the Civil War, no other war divided the American public so virulently and for so long a time—and yet the division that these war poems reflect is not one of politics, or of a division between support or lack of support for the war. In fact, no sophisticated or interesting prowar poetry has yet emerged from this period. Even the division in the poems between home front and battlefield ultimately gave way to a consensus of hearts and minds about stopping a war seen by nearly all those who chose to write poems as senseless and immoral. Some of the differences between those who went to war and those who stayed at home protesting intervention melts away when we consider how many older veterans of previous wars joined the dissenters. And yet the civilians who protested the war were usually of one generation, and the soldiers of another; then, too, a bitterness still smacking of class war continues to smolder in the relation between those of draft age who had managed to evade the war, and those who served and felt the consequences of their service.

The poetry of the Vietnam War flourished as an antiwar poetry. In a vital and egalitarian cornucopia of styles and voices, the poems were anti-imperialist, and they rejected Clausewitz's well-known formulation of war as an extension of diplomacy by other means. Moving away from conventional patriotism, the loyalty narrowed instead to the platoon, or broadened to an inclusive and internationalist outlook. While the political dissenters among the poets of an older generation may well have represented a greater variety of aesthetic traditions, the young soldier poets of this war were open to another sense of what poetry could or should do, and in fact widened the subject matter of the war poem beyond the practice of either World War I or World War II. Less reluctant to use the first person singular or plural, the Vietnam War poets made unapologetic and fresh use of the stance of the witness. They used a more vernacular language, stole liberally from prose genres, and in their own terse versions of modernism, emphasized techniques borrowed from the cinema, adding montage and jump-cuts, often wryly reflecting on how pop culture, notably the macho of Hollywood film, makes the heroic stale. Reality is blunted and peculiarly distorted in wars in which soldiers wearing headsets fire their weapons at unseen enemies, to the accompaniment of rock or rhythm 'n' blues.

The American poems of the two world wars were largely in harmony with English predecessors. While this is not true of mavericks like E. E. Cummings and Carl Sandburg, in World War I, American poets like Archibald MacLeish, Sara Teasdale, and Malcolm Cowley questioned militarism in competent if unoriginal rhyme, meter, and diction. In World War II, style became more varied—it moved from Lincoln Kirstein's deliberately bumptious and dark comic rhyme to the smooth elegance and satiric finish of Howard Nemerov's and Louis Simpson's rhyme and meter. But the soldier poetry of the Korean and Vietnam wars sounds different. In a disregard of the monuments of high culture that were more prominently and familiarly important to both World War I and World War II poets, the later poets claim kinship along lines that, whether rightly or wrongly, tended to reject the prosody that seemed part of a complicit assent to the systems of authority that had led America into a flagrantly unjust war. As American political and military ascendancy came to grief, the cultural forms that appeared to support those ascendancies were questioned both inside and outside the United States. Younger poets came to write their war poems in full belief—whether rightly or wrongly—that a direct, colloquial American language plunged the speaker closer to reality.

The response to the Vietnam War occurred in dominantly free verse, first-person narrative. Pervading many of the war poems was the same outpouring of interest in sexual and personal candor, in generational rebellion, and in the overthrow of social conventions that had characterized the sixties and that had resulted in the slogan "the personal is the political." But the pain and outrage of the soldier poets, their sense of betrayal, brought a moral urgency to their criticism of the debacle of American involvement in Vietnam, giving their poems a different edge. A verbal saltiness, a canny, ironic politics, and a core of sympathy for the enemy also undercut what might have been the narcissism of a simple insistence on first-person expressivity.

Most importantly, for the first time, these war poets represented themselves as soldiers who are simultaneously both victim and victimizer. In World War II, Randall Jarrell's poems speak within the shelter of the third person, even as Jarell moved to accept a general condemnation of the corrupted direction of the civilization of which he was also a self-acknowledged and often deeply admiring part. But in spite of the Allied bombing of civilians, World War II ultimately remained justified, if queasily so, to Jarrell. The confessional "we" of Vietnam War soldier-poets, however, differs significantly from Jarrell's forgiving "they." By the time that James Dickey accepts self-accusation in "The Firebombing," the weight of personal responsibility had to be acknowledged in any poem published in the near shadow of the American experience in Vietnam.

In Vietnam War poetry, there are descriptions of graphic war wounds in fellow soldiers, and there are explicit poems about genital injury and fear of emasculation. The poems also render as brutal and exploitative, as well as occasionally affectionate—even if self-deluded—the relations between soldier and civilian. Many poems about men and women fill in the blank that so often covers up the role of women in war. An infrequent theme earlier, racial and ethnic dissonance crops up in Vietnam War poetry, as contemporary turbulence over the denial of civil rights to blacks became a part of the baggage of black soldiers. Older poets such as Allen Ginsberg as well as younger poets like D. F. Brown make a note of the debasement of public language itself, using a fertile subversion of media-speak and technospeak. In older warrior poems, a company of men took comfort in miming the bonds of family unity: a leader—a Washington or Lincoln—became a substitute father. Failing confidence in leaders, soldiers turn to one another, a chain of dependent brothers facing death. But in the poetry of the Vietnam War, even this pattern of loyalty, while not disappearing, undergoes revision.

ROBERT LOWELL (1917–1977)

THE MARCH 1[1]

(FOR DWIGHT MACDONALD)[2]

Under the too white marmoreal Lincoln Memorial,
the too tall marmoreal Washington Obelisk,
gazing into the too long reflecting pool,
the reddish trees, the withering autumn sky,
the remorseless, amplified harangues for peace—
lovely to lock arms, to march absurdly locked
(unlocking to keep my wet glasses from slipping)
to see the cigarette match quaking in my fingers,
then to step off like green Union Army recruits
for the first Bull Run,[3] sped by photographers,
the notables, the girls . . . fear, glory, chaos, rout . . .
our green army staggered out on the miles-long green fields,
met by the other army, the Martian, the ape, the hero,
his new-fangled rifle, his green new steel helmet.

THE MARCH 2

Where two or three were flung together, or fifty,
mostly white-haired, or bald, or women . . . sadly
unfit to follow their dream, I sat in the sunset
shade of our Bastille, the Pentagon,
nursing leg- and arch-cramps, my cowardly,
foolhardy heart; and heard, alas, more speeches,
though the words took heart now to show how weak
we were, and right. An MP sergeant kept
repeating, "March slowly through them. Don't even brush

---

[1] The title refers to the 1967 march on the Pentagon, a historic antiwar demonstration.
[2] Dwight Macdonald, a brilliant political and literary journalist, accompanied Lowell on the Pentagon march.
[3] A disaster for the Union Army during the Civil War, where the attackers were mowed down by withering fire.

anyone sitting down." They tiptoed through us
in single file, and then their second wave
trampled us flat and back. Health to those who held,
health to the green steel head . . . to your kind hands
that helped me stagger to my feet, and flee.

HAYDEN CARRUTH (B. 1921)

ON BEING ASKED TO WRITE A POEM AGAINST THE WAR IN VIETNAM

Well I have and in fact
more than one and I'll
tell you this too

I wrote one against
Algeria that nightmare
and another against

Korea and another
against the one
I was in

and I don't remember
how many against
the three

when I was a boy
Abyssinia[4] Spain and
Harlan County

and not one
breath was restored
to one

[4] The Italian invasion of Ethiopia.

shattered throat
mans womans or childs
not one not

one
but death went on and on
never looking aside

except now and then like a child
with a furtive half-smile
to make sure I was noticing.

RICHARD HUGO (1923–1982)

ON HEARING A NEW ESCALATION

From time one I've been reading slaughter,
seeing the same bewildered face of a child
staring at nothing beside his dead mother
in Egypt, the pyramid blueprints approved,
the phrases of national purpose streaming
from the mouth of some automated sphinx.
Day on day, the same photographed suffering,
the bitterness, the opportune hate handed down
from Xerxes to Nixon, a line strong
as transatlantic cable and stale ideals.
Killing's still in though glory is out of style.
And what does it come to, this blood cold
in the streets and a history book printed
and bound with such cost saving American
methods, the names and dates are soon bones?
Beware certain words: Enemy. Liberty. Freedom.
Believe those sounds and you're aiming a bomb.

DENISE LEVERTOV (1923–1997)

WEEPING WOMAN

She is weeping for her lost right arm.
She cannot write the alphabet any more
on the kindergarten blackboard.

She is weeping for her lost right arm.
She cannot hold her baby and caress it at the same time
ever again.

She is weeping for her lost right arm.
The stump aches, and her side.

She is weeping for her lost right arm.
The left alone cannot use a rifle
to help shoot down the attacking plane.

In the wide sides over the Delta
her right hand that is not there
writes indelibly,
             "Cruel America,
when you mutilate our land and bodies,
it is your own soul you destroy,
not ours."

AT THE JUSTICE DEPARTMENT

NOVEMBER 15, 1969

Brown gas-fog, white
beneath the street lamps.
Cut off on three sides, all space filled
with our bodies.
      Bodies that stumble
in brown airlessness, whitened
in light, a mildew glare,
      that stumble

hand in hand, blinded, retching.
Wanting it, wanting
to be here, the body believing it's
dying in its nausea, my head
clear in its despair, a kind of joy,
knowing this is by no means death,
is trivial, an incident, a
fragile instant. Wanting it, wanting
        with all my hunger this anguish,
        this knowing in the body
the grim odds we're
up against, wanting it real.
Up that bank where gas
curled in the ivy, dragging each other
up, strangers, brothers
and sisters. Nothing
will do but
to taste the bitter
taste. No life
other, apart from.

PHILIP APPLEMAN (B. 1926)

PEACE WITH HONOR

> Solitudinem faciunt,
> pacem appellant.[5]

1

The outer provinces are never secure:
our Legions hold the camps, their orders
do not embrace the minds
and hearts of barbarians. So, when the late-
late news reported the outlandish

---

[5] "They made a wasteland and called it a peace," from a speech by Calgacus, a Caledonian tribal leader, describing the Roman Army's practice before the defeat by Agricola. In Tacitus *Agricola* 30.

screams in that distant temple,
the great bronze Victory toppled,
red stains in the sea, corpses
stranded by the ebb tide—all of that,
and only four hundred
armed men at the garrison—why,
of course it had to come, the massacre,
the plundering.

2

It was the decade's scandal at home,
the humiliation, the Eagles gone.
Senators put on grim faces
and gossiped over Bloody
Marys—what laureled head would roll for this?
Reports from the field
were cabled not to the Emperor but
to the Joint Chiefs, to filter
through at last, edited
and heavy with conclusions: the traitor,
they revealed, was not in uniform,
the treason was our own permissiveness;
in sterner times our Fathers would not
have suffered such dishonor.
We nodded: yes, they knew,
the Chiefs, what ancient virtue was.
The twilight shudders of matrons
seasoned our resolution. Somber, we took
a fourth martini, wandered to the couches,
the tables rich with peacocks' tongues,
and nodded,
nodded, waiting.

3

They sent our toughest
veterans, the Ninth Legion, the Fourteenth,
the Hundred-and-First, their orders un-
ambiguous: teach the barbarians respect.

Our marshals chose the spot: a steep defile
covering the rear, our regular troops drawn close,
light-armed auxiliaries at their flanks,
cavalry massed on the wings.
The enemy seethed everywhere, like a field
of wind-blown grasses.
There were the usual
harangues, the native leaders boasting
their vast numbers, screaming
freedom or death;
our generals, with that subtle sneer
they learn at the Academy,
pointing only to the Eagles on their tall shafts—
and every man remembered
the shame of Eagles fallen, comrades' bones
unburied: there was that curious thing,
men in bronze and steel, weeping.
And then the charge, the clash of arms,
cavalry with lances fixed, the glorious
victory: a hundred thousand tons of TNT
vaporized their villages, their forests were
defoliated, farmland poisoned forever,
the ditches full of screaming children,
target-practice for our infantry.
The land, once green and graceful,
running with pleasant streams in the rich brown earth,
was charred and gutted—not even a bird
would sing there again.

4

A glorious victory, of course,
but in a larger sense, a mandatory act
of justice: the general peace
was kept, the larger order held; peasants
for a thousand leagues around
are working their mules again.
Our prisoners and Eagles all returned,
we dine at the rich tables,

thinking of the Sunday games,
thinking of anything but rebellion—thinking
the honor of Empire
is saved.

ROBERT BLY (B. 1926)

COUNTING SMALL-BONED BODIES

Let's count the bodies over again.

If we could only make the bodies smaller,
The size of skulls,
We could make a whole plain white with skulls in the moonlight!

If we could only make the bodies smaller,
Maybe we could get
A whole year's kill in front of us on a desk!

If we could only make the bodies smaller,
We could fit
A body into a finger-ring, for a keepsake forever.

ALLEN GINSBERG (1927–1997)

FROM IRON HORSE

Who's the enemy, year after year?
     War after war, who's the enemy?
What's the weapon, battle after battle?
What's the news, defeat after defeat?
What's the picture, decade after decade?
          Television shows blood,
               print broken arms burning skin photographs,
                    wounded bodies revealed on the screen
Cut Sound out of television you won't tell who's Victim

Cut Language off the Visual you'll never know
                Who's Aggressor—
                    cut commentary from Newscast
                    you'll see a mass of madmen at murder.
Chicago train soldiers chatted over beer
        They, too, vowed to fight the Cottenpickin Communists
                and give their own bodies to the fray.
        Where've they learnt the lesson? Grammarschool
                taught 'em Newspaper Language?
        D'they buy it at Safeway with Reader's Digest?

"Reducing the Unreal to Unreality, and causing the one
real Self to shine, the Guru . . ."
        1966 trains were crowded with soldiers.
        ". . . the Divine Eye, the eye that is pure Consciousness
which has no visions. Nothing that is seen is real."
                Passing tollgate,
                        regatta of yachts on river hazed
                bend at Reading, giant smokestacks, watertowers
                        feed elevators—

"Seeing objects and conceiving God in them are mental processes,
        but
that is not seeing God, because He is within.
        "Who am I? . . . You're in truth a pure spirit but you identify it with
a body . . ."
                The war is Appearances, this poetry Appearances
                        . . . measured thru Newspapers
                All Phantoms of Sound
                        All landscapes have become Phantom—
                giant New York ahead'll perish with my mind.
                        "understand that the Self is not a Void"
not this, not that,
                Not my *anger*, not War Vietnam
                Maha Yoga[6] a phantom
                        Blue car swerves close to the bus

[6] A meditation practice concerned with world peace as well as inner peace.

     —not the Self.
   Ramana Maharshi,[7] whittle myself a walkingstick,
     waterspray irrigating the fields
        That's not the Self—
    hard-on spring in loins
      rocking in highway chair,
        poignant flesh spasm not it Self,
          body's speaking there,
          & feeling, that's not Self
      Who says No, says Yes—not Self.
Phelps Dodge's giant white building
       highway side, not Self.
   Who? Who? both asleep & awake
       closes his eyes?
       Who opens his eyes to Sweden?
   You happy, Lady, writing yr
      checks on Howard Johnson's counter?
   Mind wanders. Sleep, cough & sweat . . .
          Mannahatta's
tunnel-door cobbled for traffic,
      trucks into that mouth
        MAKE NO IMAGE
Mohammedans say
    Jews have no painting
      Buddha's Nameless
        Alone is Alone,
   all screaming of soldiers
        crying on wars
     speech politics massing armies
        is false-feigning show—
Calm senses, seek self, forget
    thine own adjurations
       Who are you?
     to mass world armies in planet war?
McGraw-Hill building green grown old, car fumes &
   Manhattan tattered, summer heat,
      sweltering noon's odd patina

[7] A mystic (1879–1950), writer in Tamil and famous spiritual teacher.

on city walls,
Greyhound exhaust terminal,
trip begun,

taxi-honk toward East River where
Peter waits working

W. S. MERWIN (B. 1927)

THE ASIANS DYING

When the forests have been destroyed their darkness remains
The ash the great walker follows the possessors
Forever
Nothing they will come to is real
Nor for long
Over the watercourses
Like ducks in the time of ducks
The ghosts of the villages trail in the sky
Making a new twilight
Rain falls into the open eyes of the dead
Again again with its pointless sound
When the moon finds them they are the color of everything

The nights disappear like bruises but nothing is healed
The dead go away like bruises
The blood vanishes into the poisoned farmlands
Pain the horizon
Remains
Overhead the seasons rock
They are paper bells
Calling to nothing living

The possessors move everywhere under Death their star
Like columns of smoke they advance into the shadows
Like thin flames with no light
They with no past
And fire their only future

GEORGE STARBUCK (1931–1996)

OF LATE

"Stephen Smith, University of Iowa sophomore, burned what
        he said was his draft card"
and Norman Morrison, Quaker, of Baltimore Maryland,
        burned what he said was himself.
You, Robert McNamara, burned what you said was a concen-
        tration of the Enemy Aggressor.
No news medium troubled to put it in quotes.

And Norman Morrison, Quaker, of Baltimore Maryland,
        burned what he said was himself.
He said it with simple materials such as would be found in
        your kitchen.
In your office you were informed.
Reporters got cracking frantically on the mental disturbance
        angle.
So far nothing turns up.

Norman Morrison, Quaker, of Baltimore Maryland, burned,
        and while burning, screamed.
No tip-off. No release.
Nothing to quote, to manage to put in quotes.
Pity the unaccustomed hesitance of the newspaper editorialists.
Pity the press photographers, not called.

Norman Morrison, Quaker, of Baltimore Maryland, burned
        and was burned and said
all that there is to say in that language.
Twice what is said in yours.
It is a strange sect, Mr. McNamara, under advice to try
the whole of a thought in silence, and to oneself.

WALTER MCDONALD (B. 1934)

HAULING OVER WOLF CREEK PASS IN WINTER

If I make it over the pass
I park the rig, crawl back to the bunk
and try to sleep, the pigs swaying
like a steep grade, like the last curve
Johnson took too fast and burned.
But that was summer. His fire
spread to the next county.

It doesn't worry me.
I take the east climb no sweat
and the rest is a long coasting
down to the pens in Pagosa Springs.
It's the wolves I wait for.
We never see them any other way,
not in this business.
Sometimes five, six hauls before
propped on one arm, smoking,
I see them slink from the dark pines
toward the truck. They drive the pigs
crazy, squealing
as if a legion of demons had them.
Later, when I start up and go,
the pigs keep plunging,
trying to drive us over the cliff.

I let them squeal, their pig hearts
exploding like grenades.
The wolves are dark and silent.
Kneeling, I watch them split up
like sappers, some in the tree lines,
some gliding from shadow to shadow,
red eyes flashing in moonlight,
some farther off, guarding the flanks.
Each time, they know they have me.

I take my time, knowing I can crawl
over the seat, light up,
sip from the steaming thermos.
I crank the diesel,
release the air brakes
like a rocket launcher.
Wolves run in circles. I hit the lights.
Wolves plunge through deep snow
to the trees, the whole pack starving.
Revving up, the truck rolls down the highway
faster, the last flight out of Da Nang.
I shove into third gear, fourth,
the herd of pigs screaming, the load
lurching and banging on every turn,
almost delivered, almost airborne.

JIM NYE (B. 1939)

DEAD WEIGHT

Brown took 5 rounds from an AK-47,
    Tore his skinny body to pieces
We wrapped him in a poncho
    Tied him up tight.
But the canopy was 120 feet high—
    No place for a chopper to land.
    Jordan knew him from home
Wouldn't let anyone carry him.
    It was 16 klicks[10] to a clearing
Up the ridge line.
    We carried Jordan's ruck, weapon and gear
He carried Brown
    It took a very long time—
Stopping for Jordan to rest.
    But we made it.

[10] Kilometers.

The choppers picked up Brown,
    Jordan sat exhausted,
Looked at me and said,
    "I'm finally done with that
Son of a bitch,
    Don't have to carry him no more."

DAVID HUDDLE (B. 1942)

WORK

I am a white, Episcopal-raised, almost
college-educated, North American male.
Sergeant Tri, my interpreter, is engrossed
in questioning our detainee, a small,
bad-smelling man in rags who claims to be
a farmer. I am filling in the blanks
of a form, writing down what Sergeant Tri
tells me. This is dull. Suddenly Tri yanks

our detainee to his feet, slaps him twice
across the bridge of his nose. The farmer
whimpers. Tri says the farmer has lied and waits
for orders. Where I grew up my father
waits at the door while my mother finishes
packing his lunch. I must tell Tri what next.

HAIRCUT

Open shop on the strip: Vietnamese barber
standing up is not quite as tall as GI
sitting down, but very serious, scampers
around, snips those scissors, raises them high

---

[8] A resort town in South Vietnam, an R&R center during the war.
[9] Base camp of the Twenty-fifth Infantry Division, famous for its tunnel complex.

over GI's head as if GI had hair
longer than a quarter of an inch to start
with and this was a *salon* in Paris
instead of a shack with no walls and a dirt

floor. At the end he carefully clips hairs
from GI's nose, inserts two small hollow
bamboo sticks in GI's ears, twists them on each
side to ream out the wax, then twangs the sticks. Holds
GI's head, limbers the neck, pops it, scares
GI. Could have died then. 25 p. please.

VERMONT

I'm forty-six. I was twenty-three then.
I'm here with what I've dreamed or remembered.
In the Grand Hotel in Vung Tau[8] one weekend
I spent some time with the most delicate
sixteen-year-old girl who ever delivered
casual heartbreak to a moon-eyed GI.
I am trying to make it balance, but I
can't. Believe me, I've weighed it out:

rising that morning up to the cool air where
the green land moved in its own dream down there,
and I was seeing, the whole flight back to Cu Chi,[9]
a girl turning her elegant face away
after I'd said all I had to say.
This was in Vietnam. Who didn't love me.

SHARON OLDS (B. 1942)

MAY 1968

When the Dean said we could not cross campus
until the students gave up the buildings,

we lay down, in the street,
we said the cops will enter this gate
over us. Lying back on the cobbles,
I saw the buildings of New York City
from dirt level, they soared up
and stopped, chopped off—above them, the sky,
the night air over the island.
The mounted police moved, near us,
while we sang, and then I began to count,
12, 13, 14, 15,
I counted again, 15, 16, one
month since the day on that deserted beach,
17, 18, my mouth fell open,
my hair on the street,
if my period did not come tonight
I was pregnant. I could see the sole of a cop's
shoe, the gelding's belly, its genitals—
if they took me to Women's Detention and did
the exam on me, the speculum,
the fingers—I gazed into the horse's tail
like a comet-train. All week, I had
thought about getting arrested, half-longed
to give myself away. On the tar—
one brain in my head, another,
in the making, near the base of my tail—
I looked at the steel arc of the horse's
shoe, the curve of its belly, the cop's
nightstick, the buildings streaming up
away from the earth. I knew I should get up
and leave, but I lay there looking at the space
above us, until it turned deep blue and then
ashy, colorless, *Give me this one*
night, I thought, *and I'll give this child*
the rest of my life, the horses' heads,
this time, drooping, dipping, until
they slept in a circle around my body and my daughter.

DOUG ANDERSON (B. 1943)

INFANTRY ASSAULT

The way he made that corpse dance
by emptying one magazine after another into it
and the way the corpse's face began to peel off
like a mask because the skull had been shattered, brains
spilled out, but he couldn't stop killing that corpse,
wanted to make damn sure, I thought maybe
he was killing all the ones he'd missed, and

the way they dragged that guy out of the stream,
cut him to pieces, the stream running red
with all the bodies in it, and the way the captain
didn't try to stop them, his silence saying *No Prisoners* and

the way when all the Cong were dead, lined up in rows,
thirty-nine in all, our boys went to work on all the pigs
and chickens in the village until
there was no place that was not red, and

finally, how the thatch was lit, the village burned
and how afterwards we were quiet riding back
on the tracks, watching the ancestral serpent rise
over the village in black coils, and
how our bones knew what we'd done.

PAPASAN

In the monsoon when the heat dropped to ninety
we shivered in our ponchos, sand in our hair,
grit in our teeth, weapons jammed.
We dug ourselves in
in what we thought was an abandoned village
at the base of a mountain
and were startled to see him by the water buffalo,
three-strand beard moving in the wind.

He was eighty (his I.D. said),
wrestling a wooden plow all day
in paddies ruined by a swollen river,
a job for an absent son.
When he saw we planned to stay the night,
he stripped and squatted in the ditch to bathe,
scowled at us who stared at him
in this small privacy.
A Vietnamese would have known to turn his eyes away.

PURIFICATION

In Taiwan, a child washes me in a tub
as if I were hers.
At fifteen she has tried to conceal
her age with makeup, says her name is *Cher*.
Across the room,
her dresser has become an altar.
Looming largest,
photos of her three children, one black,
one with green eyes, one she still nurses,
then a row of red votive candles, and in front,
a Buddha, a Christ, a Mary.
She holds my face to her breasts, rocks me.
There is blood still under my fingernails
from the last man who died in my arms.
I press her nipple in my lips,
feel a warm stream of sweetness.
I want to be this child's child.
I will sleep for the first time in days.

JOHN BALABAN (B. 1943)

THOUGHTS BEFORE DAWN

FOR MARY BUI THI KHUY, 1944–1969

The bare oaks rock, and snowcrust tumbles down.
The creaking eave woke me thinking of you
crushed by a truck thirteen years ago
when the drunk ARVN lost the wheel.

We brought to better care the nearly lost,
the boy burned by white phosphorus, chin
glued to his chest; the scalped girl;
the triple amputee from the road-mined bus;
the kid without a jaw; the one with no nose.
You never wept in front of them, but waited
until the gurney rolled them into surgery.
I guess that's what amazed me most.
Why didn't you fall apart or quit?

Once, we flew two patched kids home,
getting in by Army chopper,
a Huey Black Cat that skimmed the sea.
When the gunner opened up on a whale
you closed your eyes and covered your ears
and your small body shook in your silk *ao dai*.

Oh, Mary. In this arctic night, I lie in bed
and rehearse your smile, bright white teeth,
the funny way you rode your Honda 50: perched
so straight, silky hair bunned up in a brim hat,
front brim blown back, and dark glasses.
Brave woman, I hope you never saw the truck.

APRIL 30, 1975

FOR BUI NGOC HUONG

The evening Nixon called his last troops off,
the church bells tolled across our states.
We leaned on farmhouse porch pilings, our eyes
wandering the lightning bug meadow thick with mist,
and counted tinny peals clanking out
through oaks around the church belltower.
You asked, "Is it peace, or only a bell ringing?"

This night the war has finally ended.
My wife and I sit on a littered park bench
sorting out our shared and separate lives
in the dark, in silence, before a quiet pond
where ducks tug slimy papers and bits of soggy bread.
City lights have reddened the bellies of fumed clouds
like trip flares scorching skies over a city at war.

In whooshing traffic at the park's lit edge,
red brake lights streak to sudden halts:
a ski-masked man staggers through lanes,
maced by a girl he tried to mug.
As he crashes to curb under mercury lamps,
a man snakes towards him, wetting his lips,
twirling the root of his tongue like a dial.

Some kids have burnt a bum on Brooklyn Bridge.
Screaming out of sleep, he flares the causeway.
The war returns like figures in a dream.
In Vietnam, pagodas chime their bells.
"A Clear Mind spreads like the wind.
By the Lo waterfalls, free and high,
you wash away the dust of life."

HORACE COLEMAN (B. 1943)

OK CORRAL EAST

BROTHERS IN THE NAM

Sgt. Christopher and I are
in Khanh Hoi down by the docks
in the Blues Bar where the women
are brown and there is no Saigon Tea
making our nightly HIT—'Hore Inspection Tour
watching the black   digging night sights
    soul sounds   getting tight

the grunts in the corner raise undisturbed hell
the timid white MP has his freckles pale
as he walks past the high dude
in the doorway in his lavender jump-suit
to remind the mama-san quietly of curfew
        he chokes on the weed smoke
        he sees nothing his color here
and he fingers his army rosary   his .45

but this is not Cleveland or Chicago
he can't cringe any one here and our
gazes like brown punji stakes impale him

we have all killed something recently
we know who owns the night
and carry darkness with us

BASIL T. PAQUET (B. 1944)

BASKET CASE

I waited eighteen years to become a man.
My first woman was a whore off Tu Do street,
But I wish I never felt the first wild

Gliding lust, because the rage and thrust
Of a mine caught me hip high.
I felt the rip at the walls of my thighs,
A thousand metal scythes cut me open,
My little fish shot twenty yards
Into a swamp canal.
I fathered only this—the genderless bitterness
Of two stumps, and an unwanted pity
That births the faces of all
Who will see me till I die deliriously
From the spreading sepsis that was once my balls.

It Is Monsoon at Last

The black peak at Xuan Loc[11]
pulls a red apron of light
up from the east.
105s and 155s are walking shells
toward us from Bear Cat
down some trail
washing a trail in fire.

An eagle flight snakes west toward Lai Khe,
a demonstration of lights
flashing green and red across a sky still black above.
Our boots rattle off the boardwalk
Cha-Chat-Cha-Chat
the sound spills across the helipad
out towards the forest
out towards the dawn;
it chases devil dusters
out to the jungle.

The boardwalk bends
with our ungainly walk
litter handles creak

[11] Near Saigon, a battle in the final North Vietnam Army offensive in 1975.

with the heavy weight of the dead,
the dull whoosh and thud of B-40s
sounds south along the berm
the quick flat answer of 16s follows.

Gunships are going up
sucking devil dusters into the air.
We can see them through the morgue door
against the red froth clouds
hanging over Xuan Loc.
We lift the boy into a death bag.
We lift the boy into the racks.
We are building a bunker of dead.
We are stacking the dead for protection.

This dead boy is on my hands
My thighs are wet with the vomit of death
His blood is on my mouth
My mouth My mouth tastes his blood.

The gunships are firing over the Dong Nai
throwing fire into the river
clouds are coming in from the sea
I can smell the rain, see it
over Xuan Loc, over me
it is monsoon at last.

GREG KUZMA (B. 1944)

PEACE, SO THAT

every stinking son of a bitch
can come home
to his lawn mower and rice paddy,
every punished son of a bitch
can return to his father's bedside,
every child of every bastard

every child of every hero of peace
of war
can talk it over with the man he blames,
every woman, mother, wife, daughter,
will rise in our arms like the tide,
every bomb be water
every bullet be smashed into frying pans,
every knife sharpened again
to cut fruit in thin slices,
every word flung out like a bullet
in anger
come back to putrefy the tongue,
every man who has sat silent
beware of his silence,
every rising of the blood
make love to a woman, a man,
every killer have only mirrors
to shoot at,
every child a thumb to suck,
every house its chance
to sink to the earth's calling,
every dead shall have no good reasons.

And we be a long time at this.

FRANK STEWART (B. 1946)

BLACK WINTER

> . . . for a coming time . . . the boys have
> memories.
> —Jeffers

1

The time between us stretches out
like a winter, lingering farther from the heart,
heavy as fourteen thousand miles of jet and rails.

Looking out, I can't tell whether the glass is crusted
with frost or if the land is beyond it, a white
face of resistance. The train from Malmo thrashes
the butcher-cold sleepers, drives me through the
gut of frozen landscape like a knife. Deep fog
so early. Us. Where can we meet anyone now except
on the edge of ice, anywhere so long as it isn't a jungle.

2

They said that Stockholm would make mortician
slabs of us American boys, cold and rootless. In
Montreal the summer before, underground
looking east and north, I met Charles X with you.
"Bright California black boy. He'll get everything right
in Sweden." And at first he was a fad in Lund, you
said, easy to get dates, domestic jobs like we all
needed. Then the exile's disease, common guilts,
assault, journalist's ink. Lost the same as if
in a jungle, you said. Everyday the papers full
of butchery. "Oriental rubbish swept into a
pile by black & white GIs." But here she's sweet,
he'd say. "She's Swedish pastry. No war and sweet
times." Someone else's car, six months into exile, a
yellow piece of dress, black billows, and just
small, American, Black rubbish on the ice.

3

First night we sat and watched the Swedish hospital bum,
bullhorn, glare of fire, lights, long engines—
imagining a jungle we'd both escaped beyond Honolulu.
"Exiles should stay out of the sun," you said laughing,
our breasts cold and tight so far north even self-
preservation froze. "Along the circle, the Lapps dance
and chant stories through half a year of night, not
for entertainment but to keep from going crazy in the
darkness." The survivors here are fractured like cold
glass, bits of ghost in ice and heavy smoke. Wet, black
winter's going out. No one talks of escape.

4

Out by the reef a low fire is burning on the sea,
and in the silent dark a color like old roses
is shining on the swells. When they'd burn off
the cover in those green jungles, the suffocating
small hills would crouch there beyond the flames
like these waves. Ten years beyond the war on this
wharf, I can justify almost nothing so simply as this
fire. The smell of petroleum burning and brine slams
me like a fist that strikes on a cold morning
and strikes again, insists and strikes until there's only
blood and burning through the nostrils. A black
mirror: "One should watch and not speak. And patriotism
has run the world through so many blood-lakes: and
we always fall in . . ."

5

Near the far horizon the fire is out. The stars
blink on again through heavy smoke. The Pacific sea
extends again into space. And who did we leave
in the north like ice, and who did we leave there
in the south, scattered on the land like coal?

DALE RITTERBUSCH (B. 1946)

CHOPPERS

Always the sound of choppers,
Chinooks, Cobras, Hueys,
a sensual drone of smooth, flashing blades
cutting through air,
churning acrid, Asian heat.

The sound mnemonically beats its way into the night
cutting through darkness like a bayonet

through the top of a C-ration can,
through a block of C-4.

It stays through the spring offensive,
through all the gardening years,
afternoons spent watching the light,
spent listening to the sky.

Years later, women who saw children
killed by the Khmer Rouge, saw heads of children
bashed against trees, became blind
though nothing was wrong with their eyes. And no one
hearing the sound of choppers
fails to look up to search the sky.

Half-deaf from mortar rounds
exploding too close to the bunker,
and artillery firing H&I[12] throughout the night,
ears still pick up the sounds
of rotor blades long before they appear
over trees, above the roof-line.
The heart beats with synchronicity:

Over the paddy a chopper calls out
to the hamlet, Do not run! *Those who run*
will be shot as VC. They run anyway,
stumbling as water sucks at their feet.
It is the line of the rounds as they skip
across the paddy running up their backs—
not the darkening water—that stays,
stays through those afternoons watching the light,
listening to the sky;

---

[12] W. D. Ehrhart notes, from correspondence with the editor: "H & I is short for Harassment and Interdiction Fire, artillery fired at random onto supposed suspected enemy concentrations, meetings, strongpoints, supply lines, and other targets of opportunity. In theory, it was designed to keep the VC/NVA [Viet Cong and North Vietnamese Army] off balance; in practice, it mostly killed and terrorized civilians."

it is the water buffalo blinking its eyes
as the wash from the blades drives down dust,
and water rides out in hideous waves
as if the paddy were beaten by rain.

GERALD MCCARTHY (B. 1947)

THE HOODED LEGION

> Let us put up a monument to the lie.
> —Joseph Brodsky

There are no words here
to witness why we fought,
who sent us or what we hoped to gain.

There is only the rain
as it streaks the black stone,
these memories of rain
that come back to us—
a hooded legion reflected in a wall.

Tonight we wander weaponless and cold
along this shore of the Potomac
like other soldiers who camped here
looking out over smoldering fires into the night.

*   *   *

What did we dream of
the summer before we went away?
What leaf did not go silver
in the last light?
What hand did not turn us aside?

YUSEF KOMUNYAKAA (B. 1947)

STARLIGHT SCOPE MYOPIA

Gray-blue shadows lift
shadows onto an oxcart.

Making night work for us,
the starlight scope brings
men into killing range.

The river under Vi Bridge
takes the heart away

like the Water God
riding his dragon.
Smoke-colored

Viet Cong
move under our eyelids,

lords over loneliness
winding like coral vine through
sandalwood & lotus,

inside our lowered heads
years after this scene

ends, The brain closes
down. What looks like
one step into the trees,

they're lifting crates of ammo
& sacks of rice, swaying

under their shared weight.
Caught in the infrared,
what are they saying?

Are they talking about women
or calling the Americans

beaucoup dien cai dau?[13]
One of them is laughing.
You want to place a finger

to his lips & say "shhhh."
You try reading ghost talk

on their lips. They say
"up-up we go," lifting as one.
This one, old, bowlegged,

you feel you could reach out
& take him into your arms. You

peer down the sights of your M-16,
seeing the full moon
loaded on an oxcart.

Tu Do Street

Music divides the evening.
I close my eyes & can see
men drawing lines in the dust.
America pushes through the membrane
of mist & smoke, & I'm a small boy
again in Bogalusa. *White Only*
signs & Hank Snow. But tonight
I walk into a place where bar girls
fade like tropical birds. When
I order a beer, the mama-san
behind the counter acts as if she
can't understand, while her eyes

---

[13] Pidgin for "plenty crazy."

skirt each white face, as Hank Williams
calls from the psychedelic jukebox.
We have played Judas where
only machine-gun fire brings us
together. Down the street
black GIs hold to their turf also.
An off-limits sign pulls me
deeper into alleys, as I look
for a softness behind these voices
wounded by their beauty & war.
Back in the bush at Dak To
& Khe Sanh, we fought
the brothers of these women
we now run to hold in our arms.
There's more than a nation
inside us, as black & white
soldiers touch the same lovers
minutes apart, tasting
each other's breath,
without knowing these rooms
run into each other like tunnels
leading to the underworld.

Bui Doi, Dust of Life[14]

You drifted from across the sea
under a carmine moon,
framed now in my doorway
by what I tried to forget.
Curly-headed & dark-skinned,
you couldn't escape
eyes taking you apart.
Come here, son, let's see
if they castrated you.

---

[14] Original title contains "Dui Boi," an incorrect transcription of the Vietnamese words *bui doi*, translated correctly by the poet as "dust of life."

Those nights I held your mother
against me like a half-broken
shield. The wind's refrain
etched my smile into your face—
is that how you found me?
You were born disappearing.
You followed me, blameless
as a blackbird in Hue
singing from gutted jade.

Son, you were born with dust
on your eyelids, but you bloomed up
in a trench where stones were
stacked to hold you down.
With only your mother's name,
you've inherited the inchworm's
foot of earth. *Bui doi.*
I blow the dust off my hands
but it flies back in my face.

FACING IT

My black face fades,
hiding inside the black granite.
I said I wouldn't,
dammit: No tears.
I'm stone. I'm flesh.
My clouded reflection eyes me
like a bird of prey, the profile of night
slanted against morning. I turn
this way—the stone lets me go.
I turn that way—I'm inside
the Vietnam Veterans Memorial
again, depending on the light
to make a difference.
I go down the 58,022 names,
half-expecting to find

my own in letters like smoke.
I touch the name Andrew Johnson;
I see the booby trap's white flash.
Names shimmer on a woman's blouse
but when she walks away
the names stay on the wall.
Brushstrokes flash, a red bird's
wings cutting across my stare.
The sky. A plane in the sky.
A white vet's image floats
closer to me, then his pale eyes
look through mine. I'm a window.
He's lost his right arm
inside the stone. In the black mirror
a woman's trying to erase names:
No, she's brushing a boy's hair.

D. F. BROWN (B. 1948)

WHEN I AM 19 I WAS A MEDIC

All day I always want to know
the angle, the safest approach.
I want to know the right time
to go in. Who is in front
of me, who is behind.
When the last shots were fired,
what azimuth will get me out,
the nearest landing zone.

Each night I lay out all my stuff:
morphine, bandages at my shoulder,
just below, parallel, my rifle.
I sleep strapped to a .45,
bleached into my fear.
I do this under the biggest tree,

some nights I dig
in saying my wife's name
over and over.

I can tell true stories
from the jungle. I never mention
the fun, our sense of humor
embarrasses me. Something
warped it out of place
and bent I drag it along—
keeping track of time spent,
measure what I think we have left.

Now they tell me something else—
I've heard it all before
sliding through the grass
to get here.

DAVID CONNOLLY (B. 1949)

THE LITTLE MAN

All of a sudden I see him standing there, just like that, like he dropped out of the sky. He's inside the perimeter we threw together when we were ambushed, this stringy, little brown rice-propelled killing machine, floppy hat, black shirt and shorts, his folding stock AK held close to him in his left hand. He's facing away from me, aiming at my brothers' backs, so I can't see his face. I notice the cover of his spider hole as he kicks it away; his head swivels. He's lining up his run through our hasty defensive position and his targets on the way out. The brothers are all facing outboard, away from him, intent on the jungle, the fire coming from it and their own outgoing.

I can't shoot him. My Mattie Mattel is gone, blown from my grasp and into little pieces earlier this evening by a B-40 rocket that broke my arm. I can't even get up to find a weapon. The first fusillade of this contact, a flurry of antitank rockets, has left me flat on my back twenty feet from the track I was standing on, as it merrily cooks. My guts, poking through the hole in my pants, shine wetly in the MO gas[15] and magnesium illumination; they sparkle as if they're iced.

I strain to reach the medic to tell him about the little man. He can't hear me. There's too much gunfire around us and he's too busy with the guy he's working on who's really chopped up. The medic's arm, all I can really see of him, shiny and black with blood, filling the fetid air between us with its biting scent, reaches over and pushes me back down.

So I begin to scream, "Get him! Get him, that bastard right there! Jesus, somebody get him!" Across twenty years I scream and no one seems to hear, not the medic, not the brothers who are about to die, not even the little man himself.

I bring myself back to now by screaming, gagging on the choke of cordite and coppery blood, and find my wife has heard. From a chair across the room, she says, "Dave, it's OK."

But you see it will never be OK. That little man will make his run in my head as I helplessly watch and neither time nor her tears will make him stop. It is not my fault I couldn't stop him. I know that. I've always known that.

But now she thinks it's her fault because she can't.

W. D. EHRHART (B. 1948)

BEAUTIFUL WRECKAGE

What if I didn't shoot the old lady
running away from our patrol,
or the old man in the back of the head,
or the boy in the marketplace?

---

[15] Author's Note: "MO Gas is Military Octane Gasoline. When I first got to Vietnam, our armored personnel carriers, M113s, were powered by gas. Later, they refitted them to run on diesel so they wouldn't blow up when their gas tanks were hit. Mattie Mattel was what we called the M16 rifle, which was at best, low-bid contract crap compared to the Automat Kalashnikov Type 47, the AK-47, our opponent's weapon, which was probably the best weapon ever devised for close combat."

Or what if the boy—but he didn't
have a grenade, and the woman in Hue
didn't lie in the rain in a mortar pit
with seven Marines just for food,

Gaffney didn't get hit in the knee,
Ames didn't die in the river, Ski
didn't die in a medevac chopper
between Con Thien and Da Nang.

In Vietnamese, Con Thien means
place of angels. What if it really was
instead of the place of rotting sandbags,
incoming heavy artillery, rats and mud.

What if the angels were Ames and Ski,
or the lady, the man, and the boy,
and they lifted Gaffney out of the mud
and healed his shattered knee?

What if none of it happened the way I said?
Would it all be a lie?
Would the wreckage be suddenly beautiful?
Would the dead rise up and walk?

How It All Comes Back

The bullet entered between the eyes,
a hole like a punctuation mark
from an AK-47 or M-16,
white at the edges but glistening black,
a tunnel straight to the brain.
That's what I saw when I picked her up

before crushed veins reopened, blood
began to cover my shirt, reflex
covered the hole with my hand,
and I started calling for help.

It was only a child's fall on a rock;
it only took three stitches to close,
but I couldn't look at my daughter
for months without seeing that hole:
I'd seen holes like that before,
but never on someone alive.

FINDING MY OLD BATTALION COMMAND POST

What we came here to find
was never ours. After the miles
we've traveled, after the years
we've dreamed if only we could touch
the wound again, we could be whole,
no small wonder to discover
only a lethal past between us,
what we thought a brotherhood
only a mutual recollection of fear.

Something was lost, but it wasn't ours,
and if not here, we'd only have lost it
somewhere else. The young always do.
That is why we remember the young
who die too soon to lose
anything but their lives.
That is why we envy them.
They will always believe the world
is simple, and they only die once.

This is not what I intended,
but it won't stay down: nobody
wants a fool for a lover, a fool
for a father, a foolish friend.
Nobody wants excuses. Still,
there are stars that burn with no light;
there are things too evil for words,
too evil for silence.
Even a fool needs a friend.

But only the dead are permanent,
so we've come to this place to find—
what? Lost innocence? Our true selves?
What we think we were before we learned
to recognize incoming enemy mortars
in our sleep? What you've found is just
how frail I am. Now you think I can't
be trusted to my buttons. Grunt to grunt,
you say, it's all that matters.

Never mind particulars. This is just
between the two of us: "Heave ho,
into the lake you go with all
the other alewife scuz and foamy
harbor scum. But isn't it a pity."
Yes, a pity, though I've long since learned
that losses are the way things are.
And look, I've found a village where I once
thought nothing green would ever grow.

BRUCE WEIGL (B. 1949)

WHAT SAVES US

We are wrapped around each other
in the back of my father's car parked
in the empty lot of the high school
of our failures, sweat on her neck
like oil. The next morning I would leave
for the war and I thought I had something
coming for that, I thought to myself
that I would not die never having
been inside her body. I lifted
her skirt above her waist like an umbrella
blown inside out by the storm. I pulled
her cotton panties up as high
as she could stand. I was on fire. Heaven

was in sight. We were drowning
on our tongues and I tried
to tear my pants off when she stopped
so suddenly we were surrounded
only by my shuddering
and by the school bells
grinding in the empty halls.
She reached to find something,
a silver crucifix on a silver chain,
the tiny savior's head
hanging, and stakes through his hands and his feet.
She put it around my neck and held me
so long my heart's black wings were calmed.
We are not always right
about what we think will save us.
I thought that dragging the angel down that night
would save me, but I carried the crucifix in my pocket
and rubbed it on my face and lips
nights the rockets roared in.
People die sometimes so near you,
you feel them struggling to cross over,
the deep untangling, of one body from another.

Burning Shit at An Khe

Into that pit
    I had to climb down
With a rake and matches; eventually,
    You had to do something
Because it just kept piling up
    And it wasn't our country, it wasn't
Our air thick with the sick smoke
    So another soldier and I
Lifted the shelter off its blocks
    To expose the homemade toilets:
Fifty-five-gallon drums cut in half
    With crude wood seats that splintered.

We soaked the piles in fuel oil
    And lit the stuff
And tried to keep the fire burning.
    To take my first turn
I paid some kid
    A care package of booze from home.
I'd walked past the burning once
    And gagged the whole heart of myself—
It smelled like the world
    Was on fire,
But when my turn came again
    There was no one
So I stuffed cotton up my nose
    And marched up that hill. We poured
And poured until it burned and black
    Smoke curdled
But the fire went out.
    Heavy artillery
Hammered the evening away in the distance,
    Vietnamese laundry women watched
From a safe place, laughing.
    I'd grunted out eight months
Of jungle and thought I had a grip on things
    But we flipped the coin and I lost
And climbed down into my fellow soldiers'
    Shit and began to sink and didn't stop
Until I was deep to my knees. Liftships
    Cut the air above me, the hacking
Blast of their blades
    Ripped dust in swirls so every time
I tried to light a match
    It died
And it all came down on me, the stink
    And the heat and the worthlessness
Until I slipped and climbed
    Out of that hole and ran
Past the olive drab
    Tents and tracks and clothes and everything

Green as far from the shit
    As the fading light allowed.
Only now I can't fly.
    I lay down in it
And finger paint the words of who I am
    Across my chest
Until I'm covered and there's only one smell,
    One word.

THE LAST LIE

Some guy in the miserable convoy
Raised up in the back of our open truck
And threw a can of c-rations at a child
Who called into the rumble for food.
He didn't toss the can, he wound up and hung it
On the child's forehead and she was stunned
Backwards into the dust of our trucks.

Across the sudden angle of the road's curving
I could still see her when she rose
Waving one hand across her swollen, bleeding head,
Wildly swinging her other hand
At the children who mobbed her,
Who tried to take her food.

I grit my teeth to myself to remember that girl
Smiling as she fought off her brothers and sisters.
She laughed
As if she thought it were a joke
And the guy with me laughed
And fingered the edge of another can
Like it was the seam of a baseball
Until his rage ripped
Again into the faces of children
Who called to us for food.

RAY A. YOUNG BEAR (B. 1950)

Wa ta se Na ka mo ni, *Vietnam Memorial*

Last night when the yellow moon
of November broke through the last line
of turbulent Midwestern clouds,
a lone frog, the same one
who probably announced
the premature spring floods,
attempted to sing.
Veterans' Day, and it was
sore-throat weather.
In reality the invisible musician
reminded me of my own doubt.
The knowledge that my grandfathers
were singers as well as composers—
one of whom felt the simple utterance
of a vowel made for the start
of a melody—did not produce
the necessary memory or feeling
to make a Wadasa Nakamoon,
Veterans' Song.
All I could think of
was the absence of my name
on a distant black rock.
Without this monument
I felt I would not be here.
For a moment, I questioned
why I had to immerse myself
in country, controversy and guilt,
but I wanted to honor them.
Surely, the song they presently
listened to along with my grandfathers
was the ethereal kind which did not stop.

BARBARA TRAN (B. 1965?)

THE WOMEN NEXT DOOR

Whenever Mother was out at the market
or inside praying, we'd sneak up to the railing.
I could never tell if the women in the courtyard
were trying to break away, but their cries
always seemed pained and they were always
on the bottom, as if hiding their bodies
under the large, pale American men.

The women knew my brothers
and I often crouched at the railing,
peering farther over the edge
with each cry, on to the open courtyard.
Once, I met Hien's eyes. She withdrew
under the body above her, quickly as a reflex,
her hair snaking under the dingy sheet.
She stayed quiet for minutes after our eyes met.
I was frozen in that spot, watching
the soldier fight her harder and harder.
The cot rocked and creaked, the women
around, joining in its cries. Slowly,
I backed up against the wall, stood,
ran away.

My brothers and I wanted to know
what these soldiers were paying for.
We saw them, the younger ones
line up at the front door on certain days,
money in hand. The older ones
were surer, patting all the men
in the village on the head, no matter
what their age. They'd boom
their greetings and swing a girl
or two into their chests before the door
closed and we couldn't see anymore.

Then we'd run up to the terrace
on the 2nd floor, just as the men
emerged into the courtyard, drink
in hand, woman leading them to a bed.

BAO-LONG CHU (B. 1965?)

MOTHER'S PEARLS

Broken shadow gestured winter
trees in Maine, black on white
I thought of my mother's pearls,
ebony seeds, old as the sea
They lie
suspended from her white ao dai
   The color of mourning
   or of mornings in 1975
   unbroken, silent
   after a rain of bombs
   except for the tears of women
   crying for broken temples against green
   sky; fallen idols
   with carved breasts,
   jade, I think, in the black earth,
   in the twisted vines

Last summer, in Washington
I saw the black wall
My shadow reflected
the names of faceless men.
I traced the ruins
carved in stone but did not find
Mother's name
or the names of other women
who stood against the wall of a temple
garden, parting leaves, weeping

napalm tears
   Sandalwood incense
   sweet crooked smoke
they drove all things
out of mind.
And the pearls
forty seeds, black and unruly,
I thought they were beautiful against
my mother's carved breasts.

They lie now,
I think, on a sloping knoll
farther than Maine
or Washington.

EL SALVADOR, BOSNIA, KOSOVO,

AFGHANISTAN, AND THE PERSIAN GULF

As applied to the United States, small wars are operations under-
taken under executive authority, wherein military force is combined
with diplomatic pressure in the internal or external affairs of
another state whose government is unstable, inadequate or unsatis-
factory for the preservation of life and of such interests as are deter-
mined by the foreign policy of our Nation. . . . In small wars diplo-
macy has not ceased to function and the State Department exercises
a constant and controlling influence over the military opera-
tions. . . . In small wars, tolerance, sympathy and kindness should be
the keynote to our relationship with the mass of the population.

—U.S. Marine Corps, *Small Wars Manual*, 1940, quoted by Max
Boot, *The Savage Wars of Peace* (2002)

Since the beginning of its history, the United States of America has inter-
vened with armed troops in countries all over the globe, both openly and
covertly, in the interest of either creating or sustaining a position of global
power. Yet as Max Boot recognizes in the title of his recent book, the "small
war," or war waged during a general peace, does not lack a penetrating
ferocity. The number of American soldiers killed in the current Iraqi con-
flict already surpasses all the other small wars put together, and whether

---

[1] Up to the present moment, the count for civilian losses for the second Iraq War varies consid-
erably. An estimate published in October 2004 in the British medical journal *The Lancet* gives
the figure of 100,000 civilian deaths. A London-based group of scholars called Iraq Body
Count gives a more comprehensively researched figure of as many as 30,051 Iraqi dead since
the American-led invasion. Iraq Body Count derives its figures from 10,000 media reports,
cross-referenced for accuracy (Sabrina Tavernise, *New York Times*, October 26, 2005).

the number of Iraqi civilians killed in the invasion and occupation of Iraq exceeds 100,000 or not, the definition of a small war has been outrun, and the need for diplomacy is no less urgent.[1]

In the late twentieth and early twenty-first centuries, reaction in poetry to these engagements over far-flung territory, in medium or low intensity conflict, has been prolific; yet while formal diversity continues to multiply, and changes of emphasis are discernible, the general content of ideas in antiwar poetry remains a familiar opposition. While some poets affirm and others reject the high romanticism of Percy Bysshe Shelley's vision of poets as the "unacknowledged legislators of the world," poets and critics of poetry alike appear as oppressed and torn by the complexity of modern war and geopolitics as any other thinking groups. Caught in the painful dilemmas of contemporary citizenship, contemporary poems articulate neither a realistic rejection of war altogether, nor do they offer faith—no doubt for sound historical reasons—in a compelling or even credible version of America's constabulary role in the preservation of world order.

The two Gulf Wars produced thousands of antiwar poems, some hopeful, some apocalyptic, and most marked by a desire only to reverse a specific war policy. In their sometimes numbing flood, the poems represent an art whose individual potency is not yet quite visible or measurable. Any selection from this outpouring must necessarily be provisional and incomplete; while war continues, any selection is merely an interim progress report. The principles of choice, however, remain the same: directing an editor toward newer voices and current experience of war, and toward those poets we have already learned to listen to for something worth hearing.

The current antiwar poems are, by self-definition, clearly opposed to the traditional themes of the war lyric. In them, the old familiar stiffeners of right action—pride, courage, loyalty, and endurance—still glimmer, but in new, not entirely visible realignments. These recent poems, wary of cultural arrogance, feel no need to exalt our sense of nation or mission. While some poems may engage in what resembles classic lamentation for the fallen war dead, they do not in glad triumph affirm the validity of sacrifice, or call for vengeance or retaliation. Nor do they recognize the traditional boundaries of wartime: beyond sketching a new intensity or escalation of war power, the poems seem all middle-time, with no discernible sense of anything but endlessly opening hostilities, within a mounting proliferation of new weaponry. David Rieff recently cited statistics that illustrate the inevitably savage collisions between military and civilian in modern warfare: in World War I, 10 percent of the fatalities were civilian and 90 percent were military; in World War II, fatalities were roughly even between civilian and military; and in post–World War II conflicts, fatalities and injuries are now 90 percent civilian. Surely this imbalance is even more in evidence in the counterinsurgency that defines our current war.

If there is a central theme, it is that waging war, or the outbreak of state violence, is perpetual: people of all countries, all ages, suffer bitterly in war, with little glory and with little advancement of any just cause. In changing times, fearfully, we only see and write how, in Ralph Waldo Emerson's words, "Things are in the saddle / and ride mankind." If their speech cannot be made to represent hope, at least the poems show a commitment to an uncertain but stubborn honesty, which may in the end be as good as hope.

CAROLYN FORCHÉ (B. 1950)

THE COLONEL

What you have heard is true. I was in his house. His wife carried a tray of coffee and sugar. His daughter filed her nails, his son went out for the night. There were daily papers, pet dogs, a pistol on the cushion beside him. The moon swung bare on its black cord over the house. On the television was a cop show. It was in English. Broken bottles were embedded in the walls around the house to scoop the kneecaps from a man's legs or cut his hands to lace. On the windows there were gratings like those in liquor stores. We had dinner, rack of lamb, good wine, a gold bell was on the table for calling the maid. The maid brought green mangoes, salt, a type of bread. I was asked how I enjoyed the country. There was a brief commercial in Spanish. His wife took everything away. There was some talk then of how difficult it had become to govern. The parrot said hello on the terrace. The colonel told it to shut up, and pushed himself from the table. My friend said to me with his eyes: say nothing. The colonel returned with a sack used to bring groceries home. He spilled many human ears on the table. They were like dried peach halves. There is no other way to say this. He took one of them in his hands, shook it in our faces, dropped it into a water glass. It came alive there. I am tired of fooling around he said. As for the rights of anyone, tell your people they can go fuck themselves. He swept the ears to the floor with his arm and held the last of his wine in the air. Something for your poetry, no? he said. Some of the ears on the floor caught this scrap of his voice. Some of the ears on the floor were pressed to the ground.

May 1978

WENDY ROSE (B. 1948)

THE DAY THEY CLEANED UP THE BORDER:
EL SALVADOR, FEBRUARY 1981

> Government soldiers killed my children. I saw it. Then I saw the
> head of a baby floating in the water.
>
> —survivor, El Salvador, 1981

How comforting
the clarity
of water,
flute music
in a rush
or startling hush,
crackle of grass
like seeds
in a gourd
and the soothing whisper
of the reeds.
I prayed
the whole night
to be taken
to my past
for the pounding of rifles
comes again and again
morning by morning
til my two babies lay
with names stolen away
in their beds
and on the ground
where they played.
So many gone
and I prayed
to be taken
for the lizards
to notice and begin
eating at my feet,
work their way up

til even my heart
is nibbled away.
I have come
so many mornings
to the stream,
so many times prayed
in the glistening mist
and now drink oceans
to drown myself
from the mountains
of memory.

But look—that little melon rind
or round gourd, brown and white
in the water where I
could pluck it out
and use it dry, slipping
past me in the ripples
and turning
til its tiny mouth
still suckling
points at me.

JOSEPH BRODSKY (1940–1996)

BOSNIA TUNE

As you sip your brand of scotch,
crush a roach or scratch your crotch
as your hand adjusts your tie,
people die.

In the towns with funny names
hit by bullets, caught in flames,
by and large, not knowing why,
people die.

In small places you don't know
of, yet big for having no
chance to scream or say goodbye,
people die.

People die as you elect
new apostles of neglect,
self-restraint, etc.—whereby
people die.

Too far off to practise love
for thy neighbour/brother Slav,
where our cherubs dread to fly,
people die.

As you watch the athletes score,
check your latest statement, or
kissing your child a lullaby,
people die.

Time, whose sharp, blood-thirsty quill
parts the killed from those who kill,
will pronounce the latter tribe
as your type.

JOHN MATHIAS (B. 1941)

BOGOMIL IN LANGUEDOC[1]

One stone at Domazan is enough.
In southern France among
the Catharist sarcophagi beyond
a village full of tiled roofs.

He is the warrior of Radimlja and he
has come this far. He raises both his arms.
He spreads wide both enormous hands.
Although he is entirely silent here,

his mason, up from Tuscany and
proselytizing songs along the hot Apennine,
spouted bits he'd learned from
Interrogatio Johannis[2] to his missionary

friend who left the book at Carcassonne.
When all matter is to be destroyed,
the stone warrior here at Domazan
will give the sign. He will finally

drop his arms. And where he stood
the hole in space will spread until
all nothing speaks in tongues to no one.
May he, then, forever raise his hands.

[1] When John Matthias visited refugee camps in Bosnia in 1993, he was struck by the history of the Bogomils, the erection of whose symbolic statues the poem notes. The Bogomils were an ascetic Muslim sect, which had originated in Bosnia, and which had splintered off from the dualistic Christian heresy of Manichaeanism. Bogomils forswore alcohol and meat and dismissed the hierarchy of priests, believing in the holiness of the nonmaterial world. Eventually, Bogomilism developed into the Catharist movement, spreading widely in the thirteenth century in France into Languedoc, the center of Occitan civilization in Provence. "Bogomil" means "dear to God"; the ascendancy of the Bogomils, through the Cathars, led to their massacre and persecution by the Inquisition, a history parallel to the religious persecution then rampant in Bosnia, the effects of which Mathias was witnessing
[2] The *interrogatio iohannes*, or the *Questions of John*, is the secret book of the Bogomil/Cathars, found in the archives of the Inquisition of the thirteenth century. A copy of this apocryphal text now resides in a museum of the Inquisition in Carcassonne, in southern France. It contains remnants of the Cathar/Bogomil ritual used to instruct adepts.

DALE RITTERBUSCH (B. 1946)

A THOUSAND CRANES

You wonder why it never changes
when change is the basis of everything—
cranes move across the sky, but it is not
the same sky tomorrow, although
the image, hand shading the eyes, stays
and stays until the next time
when the present moment
eclipses some old remembrance.
But this is too abstract, you cannot see
the cranes from what I've said—
you may remember the first time you watched
a pair hunting in the shallows for fish,
the sharp, quick stab into the muck,
and the fish wriggling in its beak;
you watched until they rose above
the brackish water into the orange light
of dusk—that is what you remember;
it is yours, nothing I say will change that
nor will my memory of their flight
across the sun, their voices calling,
be altered by your wise remembrance.
But today, when I listen to a woman
say nothing is happening in Kosovo,
the Kosovars are making it up,
the men separated, beaten, taken away,
this is all a lie, nothing is happening,
no one is dying—no one ever dies—
I note how F-16's rise like cranes across the screen,
but the metaphor will not hold—
it is the memory of seeing war again
that passes across the sky.
It is good that you and I see things
differently—maybe the cranes weren't even cranes,
herons perhaps? Great blue herons
or something else entirely.

It is good that you and I remember
separately, as one war melds
into the next; it is good
that nothing changes.

ADRIAN OKTENBERG (B. 1947)

IT WAS AN OPEN-AIR MARKET

It was an open-air market   in full swing   midday February 1994
The stalls were nearly bare   a few cabbages   garlic
UN lunch packets   humanitarian aid   macaroni and rice
Old clothes   small sizes only   utensils
plastic for blasted windows   very rare and dear
Nevertheless it was crowded   deutsche marks only accepted
noisy with bargaining   The city under siege   for some time
People learned to take some risks
Besides, they had to live   When the shell screamed in
limbs, a severed head, flew   bodies   broken equipment
          bloody tissue   sirens
Rescue workers ran   calling to each other
working fast   Sixty-eight were killed   in a moment
many wounded   The UN called a conference   The "contact group"
                                                            of five
met five times   This was after   the shelling of the bakery line
the shelling of the water line   and Sniper Alley
A "*pin-prick*" air-strike   was called
down on a single Serbian gun   in the mountains above the city
Now the main Sarajevo market   is in an alley six feet wide

DALE JACOBSON (B. 1950)

NIGHT VISION OF THE GULF WAR

1.

They came to rearrange the dust and shadows.
They were right because it felt good.
They released the power of seven
Hiroshima bombs, 88,500 tons,
to alter the attitude of bridges
modify the roads and their vistas,
amend the attitude of buildings. . . .

Some 200,000 buried alive—no one
cared to keep count, or could.
Through the billowing smoke, the clouds of earth,
the light from the flames shifted,
the shadows shifted and the dust.
Everything shifted.

2.

In the capital of the empire the trees
dormant in their winter sturdiness
waited in their branches for their green
elaboration toward the sky.

If the stars were the nation's pity
they would be dark and hard
like the dense core of the gold ball
the Commander-in-Chief, "the Great Ass-Kicker,"
shot around the green while
on the desert the soldiers died.

It was a festival of death, yellow ribbons
everywhere, the color of pale distance by moonlight,
or the water-logged blade of a fallen windmill—
or the color of poison—easy hatred, easy love,
the sentimental crime: the citizens, so angry lost or afraid
in their own country, they revelled in bombing another—
power in their name, though they themselves had none.

The million-dollar missiles rose over the sea,
and the swift jets. The pilots said:
"We own the night."

3.

More likely the night now owns us . . .

It is a country larger than the nation,
more ancient than history,
and flies no flag.

In Iraq the night is owned by the corrupted water.

It rises like a poisonous mist around the Iraqi children,
hurries them away—55,000—
perhaps another 170,000 within the year.

The night belongs to the rising and falling of the wind,
its additions and subtractions
through which their deaths move, unnoticed.

No stealth bomber is as stealthy as the night
that comes home.

4.

Near Fort Ransom, North Dakota
is perhaps the oldest pyramid in the world.

No one knows who built it.

The Fort is long gone.

The rains that fall on the absent Fort,
and on the pyramid, arrive
out of the horizon where the waters climb
tiny ladders and everything is flat.

The droplets spin through
the immense shadow of the clouds.

WENDY BATTIN (B. 1953)

MONDRIAN'S FOREST

IN MEMORY OF GREG LEVEY, D. FEBRUARY 18, 1991

1. FEBRUARY 19, 1991

Every car drones a radio,
every shop keeps the TV on.

The smart bombs are thinking their way
into Baghdad, on video grids, in primary colors,

and yesterday in the middle of Amherst, a man
drenched himself in gasoline and lit a match.

Next to the body bagged on the Commons,
"Peace" on a sheet of cardboard, and his

driver's license, safe, and the old oaks
safe, only the grass charred.

Already the papers have found
neighbors willing to say that he'd *seemed depressed*,

someone to call him *isolated*.
Nine Cambodian Buddhists come

down from Leverett in their saffron robes
to pray. Two Veterans of Foreign Wars

heckle over the chants and the slow
gong, a circle of voices on the block of lawn.

2. TREES ON THE GEIN, WITH RISING MOON (1908)

When Mondrian began
his world held rivers and trees, but not

the water's compliance and not
the ash's stillness, for he was in them.

He stood five trees against a red sky;
floated five more

in the mirror of the red river,
all ten wringing their black trunks

into green.
The trees on the water are breaking up,

breaking up, and still remain
trees in the center of their dissolution.

The trees on the bank flame up inside
their heavy outlines:

imagine a death in a man that pushes
first here then there at the lively

pliable skin. The limbs
distend, too full of ripening.

Thick oils eddy and ripple, a slick
on the turbulence of things.

3. BODHI

Today on the woods trail by Amethyst Brook,
I prayed, *Kuan Yin*. Kuan Yin, enthroned

in the Asian Museum, enormous in limestone.
"she who hears the cries of the world,"

her spine sheer as a bluff, and both hands open.
I couldn't say if the polished eyes

were open or lidded. *In the new representation,
reason takes first place*, wrote Mondrian,

his labor then to save the trees from the wind,
to rescue his clean strict sight from the eyes

in his head, that saw only through blood.
I'm not one for praying, but somehow the ice

breaking up, the meltwater surge
of the brook gouged her name from my throat,

the way it gouges the bank out from under the trees
and digs bare the root-weave. Not she

who answers the cries, Kuan Yin. Not she who consoles.
Her body is still, is stone:

She who will not kindle and blaze
when she hears a man burn.

KRISTI GARBOUSHIAN (B. 1968)

FROM *THE RIBBON ON HELL'S TREE*

X

. . . unexploded ordinance carries instructions:

Reduce to the lowest common denominator.
What goes into one   goes into all.

So much for friendly fire—Commentator,
please flash the cards for the cameras.

The world needs to know how division is done.
In Iraq the land mines nap like sand dollars.

This is for us, this ambush,
not a hoax

this time,   these slumbering mines
in the sandstorm.

An American female from a National Guard unit
accidentally disturbs one from its sleep,
making it   her own.

Her mine is singular & claims the earth.
It absorbs her warmth,
self-destructs on release of her weight,
plots to take her leg,
takes it,
yanks her intestine,

makes of itself
a suicide mission   embedding
shrapnel in a shoulder—

It is her last bad date.

Composting flesh, this bulb of flesh,
"*idea*":
passing from hand to hand
as someone once said,
"There can be no economy where there is no efficiency."

Life wells efficiently
to the corporeal surface
when leaving:

her intestines piled like coiled
rope on her stomach
beneath the blanket,
her leg gone,
please save my leg
please tell my dad I love him
but we don't know who
she is.   with my   hand

on   her forehead.   i brush
the.   hair back from.   her eyelids.
with my.   hand on.   her arm i.
place it.   back under.   the blank-
et. *etc.*

My hand, on fire for hours.

In Kuwait   we have
a field memorial for our dead,
the chaplain calming
our riot of flight.

Sand in our boots.—
exquisite:

we have a show of beautiful, bad
taste as in O Chaplain, my chaplain!

The prayers are said
& the heart feels itself enlarged.

My hand, on fire for hours.

J. D. MCCLATCHY (B. 1945)

JIHAD

A contrail's white scimitar unsheathes
Above the tufts of anti-aircraft fire.
Before the mullah's drill on righteousness,
Practice rocks are hurled at chicken-wire

Dummies of tanks with silhouetted infidels
Defending the nothing both sides fight over

In God's name, a last idolatry
Of boundaries. The sirens sound: take cover.

He has forced the night and day, the sun and moon,
Into your service. By His leave, the stars
Will shine to light the path that He has set

You to walk upon. His mercy will let
You slay who would blaspheme or from afar
Defile His lands. Glory is yours, oh soon.

Of the heart. Of the tongue. Of the sword. The holy war
Is waged against the self at first, to raze
The ziggurat of sin we climb upon
To view ourselves, and next against that glaze

The enemies of faith will use to disguise
Their words. Only then, and at the caliph's nod,
Are believers called to drown in blood the people
Of an earlier book. There is no god but God.

He knows the day of death and sees how men
Will hide. Who breaks His covenant is cursed.
Who slights His revelations will live in fire.

He has cast aside the schemer and the liar
Who mistake their emptiness of heart for a thirst
That, to slake, the steams of justice descend.

Ski-masked on videotape, the skinny martyr
Reads his manifesto. He's stilted, nervous.
An hour later, he's dropped at the market town,
Pays his fare, and climbs aboard the bus.

Strapped to his chest is the death of thirty-four
—Plus his own—"civilians" on their way
To buy or sell what goods they claim are theirs,
Unlike our fates, which are not ours to say.

Under the shade of swords lies paradise.
Whom you love are saved with you, their souls
In His hand. And who would want to return to life

Except to be killed again? Who can thrive
On the poverty of this world, its husks and holes?
His wisdom watches for each sacrifice.

GALWAY KINNELL (B. 1927)

WHEN THE TOWERS FELL

From our high window we saw the towers
with their bands and blocks of light
brighten against a fading sunset,
saw them at any hour glitter and live
as if the spirits inside them sat up all night
calculating profit and loss, saw them reach up
and steep their tops in the first yellow
of sunrise, grew so used to them
often we didn't see them, and now,
not seeing them, we see them.

The banker is talking to London.
Humberto is delivering breakfast sandwiches.
The trader is already working the phone.
The mail sorter has started sorting the mail.

> *. . . povres et riches*
Sages et folz, prestres et laiz
Nobles, villains, larges et chiches
Petiz et grans et beaulx et laiz . . . [3]

---

[3] ". . . poor and rich / Wise and foolish, priests and laymen, / Noblemen, serfs, generous and mean, / Short and tall and handsome and homely . . ." From Francois Villon, "The Testament."

The plane screamed low down lower Fifth Avenue,
lifted at the Arch, someone said, shaking the dog walkers
in Washington Square Park, drove for the north tower,
struck with a heavy thud, released a huge bright gush
of blackened fire, and vanished, leaving a hole
the size and shape a cartoon plane might make
if it had passed harmlessly through and were flying away now,
on the far side, back into the realm of the imaginary.

Some with torn clothing, some bloodied,
some limping at top speed like children in a three-legged race,
some half dragged,
some intact in neat suits and dresses,
they walk in silence up the avenues,
all dusted to a ghostly whiteness,
all but their eyes, which are rubbed red as the eyes of a Zahoris,
who can see the dead under the ground.

Some died while calling home to say they were O.K.
Some died after over an hour spent learning they would die.
Some died so abruptly they may have seen death from within it.
Some broke windows and leaned out and waited for rescue.
Some were asphyxiated.
Some burned, their very faces caught fire.
Some fell, letting gravity speed them through their long moment.
Some leapt hand in hand, the elasticity in their last bits of love time let-
    ting—I wish I could say—their vertical streaks down the sky happen
    more lightly.

At the high window, where I've often stood
to escape a nightmare, I meet
the single, unblinking eye
that lights the all-night lifting
and sifting for bodies, for pieces of bodies,
for anything that is not nothing,
in the search that always goes on
somewhere, now in New York and Kabul.

On a street corner she holds up a picture—
of a man who is smiling. In the gray air
of today few pass. Sorry sorry sorry.
She startles. Suppose, down the street, that headlong lope . . .
Or over there, that hair so black it's purple . . .
And yet, suppose some evening I forgot
The fare and transfer, yet got by that way
Without recall,—lost yet poised in traffic.
Then I might find your eyes . . .[4]

It could happen. Sorry sorry good luck thank you.
On this side it is "amnesia"—forgetting the way home—;
on the other, "invisibleness"—never entirely returning.
Hard to see clearly in the metallic mist,
or through the sheet of supposed reality
cast over our world, bourne that no creature born
pokes its way back through, and no love can tear.

The towers burn and fall, burn and fall—
in a distant shot, like smokestacks spewing oily earth remnants.
Schwarze Milch der Frühe wir trinken sie abends
wir trinken sie mittags und morgens wir trinken sie nachts
wir trinken und trinken[5]
Here is not a comparison but a corollary,
not a likeness but a common lineage
in the twentieth-century history of violent death—
black men in the South castrated and hanged from trees,
soldiers advancing in mud at 90,000 dead per mile,
train upon train headed eastward of boxcars shoved full to the corners
    with Jews and Gypsies to be enslaved or gassed,
state murder of twenty, thirty, forty million of its own,
atomic blasts wiping cities off the earth, fire bombings the same,
death marches, starvations, assassinations, disappearances,

---

[4] From Hart Crane, "For the Marriage of Faustus and Helena."
[5] "Black milk of daybreak we drink it at evening / we drink it at midday and morning we drink
it at night / we drink it and drink it." From the German of Paul Celan, "Todesfuge."

entire countries turned into rubble, minefields, mass graves.
Seeing the towers vomit these omens, that the last century dumped into
    this one, for us to dispose of, we know
they are our futures, that is our own black milk crossing the sky: *wir
    schaufeln ein Grab in den Lüften da liegt man nicht eng*[6]

Burst jet fuel, incinerated aluminum, steel fume, volatized marble,
    exploded granite, pulverized wallboard, berserked plastic, mashed
    concrete, gasified mercury, scoria, vapor
of the vaporized—draped over our island up to streets regimented into
    numbers and letters,
breathed across the great bridges to Brooklyn and the waiting sea:
astringent, sticky, miasmic, empyreumatic,
air too foul to take in, but we take it in,
too gruesome for seekers of lost beloveds
to breathe, but they breathe it and you breathe it.

A photograph of a woman hangs
from his neck. He doesn't look up.
He stares down at the sidewalk of flagstone slabs
laid down in Whitman's century, gutter edges
iron wheels rasped long ago to a melted roundedness:
conscious mind envying the stones.
Nie stają się, są,
Nic nad to, myślalem,
zbrzydziwszy sobie
wszystko co staje się.[7]

And I sat down by the waters of the Hudson,
by the North Cove Yacht Harbor, and thought
of what those on the high floors must have suffered: knowing
they would burn alive, and then, burning alive.
Could there be a mechanism of death

---

[6] "We're digging a grave in the sky there'll be plenty of room to lie down there." From "Todesfuge."
[7] "They do not become; they are. / Nothing but that, I thought. / Now loathing within myself / Everything that becomes." From the Russian of Aleksander Wat, "Songs of a Wanderer."

so mutilating to existence, that no one
gets over it ever, not even the dead?
And then I saw before me, in steel letters welded
to the steel railing posts, Walt Whitman's words
written when America plunged into war with itself:
City of the world! . . .
Proud and passionate city—mettlesome, mad, extravagant city![8]
Words of a time of illusions. And then I remembered
others of his words after the war was over and Lincoln dead:
I saw the debris and debris of all the slain soldiers of the war,
But I saw they were not as was thought,
They themselves were fully at rest—they suffer'd not,
The living remain'd and suffer'd, the mother suffer'd,
And the wife and the child and the musing comrade suffer'd . . . [9]

In our minds the glassy blocks
succumb over and over into themselves,
slam down floor by floor into themselves.
They blow up as if in reverse, explode
downward and outward, billowing
through the streets, engulfing the fleeing.

Each tower as it falls concentrates
into itself, as if transforming itself
infinitely slowly into a black hole

infinitesimally small: mass
without space, where each light,
each life, put out, lies down within us.

---

[8] From Walt Whitman, "City of Ships."
[9] From Walt Whitman, "When Lilacs Last in the Dooryard Bloom'd."

ADRIENNE RICH (B. 1929)

THE SCHOOL AMONG THE RUINS

Beirut. Baghdad. Sarajevo. Bethlehem. Kabul. Not of
course here.

1.

Teaching the first lesson and the last
—great falling light of summer will you last
longer than schooltime?

When children flow
in columns at the doors
BOYS GIRLS and the busy teachers

open or close high windows
with hooked poles drawing darkgreen shades

closets unlocked, locked
questions unasked, asked, when

love of the fresh impeccable
sharp-pencilled yes
order without cruelty

a street on earth neither heaven nor hell
busy with commerce and worship
young teachers walking to school

fresh bread and early-open foodstalls

2.

When the offensive rocks the sky when nightglare
misconstrues day and night when lived-in

rooms from the upper city
tumble cratering lower streets

cornices of olden ornament human debris
when fear vacuums out the streets

When the whole town flinches
blood on the undersole thickening to glass

Whoever crosses hunched knees bent a contested zone
knows why she does this suicidal thing

School's now in session day and night
children sleep
in the classrooms teachers rolled close

3.

How the good teacher loved
his school the students
the lunchroom with fresh sandwiches

lemonade and milk
the classroom glass cages
of moss and turtles
teaching responsibility

A morning breaks without bread or fresh-poured milk
parents or lesson-plans
diarrhea first question of the day
children shivering it's September
Second question: where is my mother?

4.

One: I don't know where your mother
is Two: I don't know
why they are trying to hurt us
Three: or the latitude and longitude
of their hatred Four: I don't know if we
hate them as much I think there's more toilet paper
in the supply closet I'm going to break it open

Today this is your lesson:
write as clearly as you can
your name home street and number
down on this page
No you can't go home yet
but you aren't lost
this is our school

I'm not sure what we'll eat
we'll look for healthy roots and greens
searching for water though the pipes are broken

5.

There's a young cat sticking
her head through window bars
she's hungry like us

but can feed on mice
her bronze erupting fur
speaks of a life already wild

her golden eyes
don't give quarter She'll teach us Let's call her
Sister
when we get milk we'll give her some

6.

I've told you, let's try to sleep in this funny camp
All night pitiless pilotless things go shrieking
above us to somewhere

Don't let your faces turn to stone
Don't stop asking me why
Let's pay attention to our cat she needs us

Maybe tomorrow the bakers can fix their ovens

7.

"We sang them to naps told stories made
shadow-animals with our hands

washed human debris off boots and coats
sat learning by heart the names
some were too young to write
some had forgotten how"

TONY HOAGLAND (B. 1953)

THE KIND OF SHADOW THAT CALLS OUT FATE

Early in the day reports said our planes
had bombed a wedding in a distant country—

We could tell it had really happened
from the way the spokespersons on TV hesitated

before denying it—from the way they cleared their throats
and said it was pending investigation.

You know those crazy natives and their customs,
well, apparently it was their way of celebration
to shoot their rifles into the air

and jets showed up soon afterwards—forty dead,
and some of them horses.

Hearing about it over and over through the week
hearing the descriptions repeated over and over

of the colorful wedding clothes made brighter by the blood
the groans coming from the dying bride,

the bad news surrounded our house, like something rotten:
We sensed we couldn't get away with this one.

It was exactly the sort of thing which in a Greek play
would initiate a sequence of events

that turns inexorably back to bite
the hand that set it into motion

—and we knew we also were part of the plot.
We sat there in the audience as we have so often

as at a scene where the king drops his crown
which rolls across the floor and falls offstage

while he scrambles after it
—and thoughtfully, the queen watches.

C.K. WILLIAMS (B. 1936)

SHRAPNEL

1.

Seven-hundred tons per inch, I read, is the force in a bomb or shell in
the microsecond after its detonation,
and two-thousand feet per second is the speed at which the shrapnel,
the materials with which the ordnance
is packed, plus its burst steel casing, "stretched, thinned, and
sharpened" by the tremendous heat and energy,
are propelled outwards in an arc until they strike an object and either
ricochet or become embedded in it.

In the case of insufficiently resistant materials, the shards of
shrapnel can cause "significant damage;"
in human tissue, for instance, rupturing flesh and blood vessels and
shattering and splintering bone.

Should no essential organs be involved, the trauma may be termed
"superficial," as by the chief nurse,
a nun, in Ian McEwan's *Atonement*, part of which takes place in a
hospital receiving wounded from Dunkirk.

It's what she says when a soldier cries, "Fuck!" as her apprentice, the
heroine, a young writer-to-be,
probes a wound with her forceps to extract one of many jagged frag-
    ments
of metal from a soldier's legs.
"Fuck!" was not to be countenanced back then. "How dare you speak
    that
way?" scolds the imperious sister,
"Your injuries are superficial, so consider yourself lucky and show
some courage worthy of your uniform."

The man stays still after that, though "he sweated and . . . his knuckles
turned white round the iron bedhead."
"Only seven to go," the inexperienced nurse chirps, but the largest
chunk, which she's saved for last, resists;
at one point it catches, protruding from the flesh—("He bucked on the
bed and hissed through his teeth")—
and not until her third resolute tug does the whole "gory, four-inch
stiletto of irregular steel" come clear.

2.

"Shrapnel throughout the body," is how a ten-year old killed in a
recent artillery offensive is described.
"Shrapnel throughout the body:" the phrase is repeated along with the
name of each deceased child
in the bulletin released as propaganda by our adversaries, at whose
operatives the barrage was directed.
There are photos as well—one shows a father rushing through the street,
his face torn with a last frantic hope,

his son in his arms, rag-limp, chest and abdomen speckled with deep,
dark gashes and smears of blood.
Propaganda's function, of course, is exaggeration: the facts are there,

though, the child is there . . . or not there.
    . . . As the shrapnel is no longer there in the leg of the soldier: the girl
holds it up for him to see, the man quips,
"Run him under the tap, Nurse, I'll take him home," then, " . . . he
    turned
to the pillow and began to sob."

Technically, I read, what's been called shrapnel here would have once
been defined as "splinters" or "fragments."
"Shrapnel" referred then only to a spherical shell, named after its
inventor, Lieutenant Henry Shrapnel.
First used in 1804, it was " . . . guaranteed to cause heavy casualties . . .
    the
best mankiller the army possessed."
Shrapnel was later awarded a generous stipend in recognition of his
contribution "to the state of the art."

Where was I? The nun, the nurse; the nurse leaves the room, throws up;
the fictional soldier, the real child . . .
The father . . . What becomes of the father? He skids from the screen,
    from
the page, from the mind . . .
Shrapnel's device was superseded by higher-powered, more efficient
projectiles, obsolete now in their turn.
One war passes into the next. One wound is the next and the next.
Something howls. Something cries.

ELEANOR WILNER (B. 1937)

FOUND IN THE FREE LIBRARY

> Write as if you lived in an occupied country.
> —Edwin Rolfe

And we were made afraid, and being afraid
we made him bigger than he was, a little man
and ignorant, wrapped like a vase of glass

in bubble wrap all his life, who never felt
a single lurch or bump, carried over
the rough surface of other lives like
the spoiled children of the sultans of old
in sedan chairs, on the backs of slaves,
the gold curtains on the chair
pulled shut against the dust and shit
of the road on which the people walked,
over whose heads, he rode, no more aware
than a wave that rattles pebbles on a beach.

And being afraid we forgot to notice
who pulled his golden strings, how
their banks overflowed while
the public coffers emptied, how
they stole our pensions, poured their smoke
into our lungs, how they beat our ploughshares
into swords, sold power to the lords of oil,
closed their fists to crush the children
of Iraq, took the future from our failing grasp
into their hoards, ignored our votes,
broke our treaties with the world,
and when our hungry children cried,
the doctors drugged them so they wouldn't fuss,
and prisons swelled enormously to hold
the desperate sons and daughters of the poor.
To us, they just said war, and war, and war.

For when they saw we were afraid,
how knowingly they played on every fear—
so conned, we scarcely saw their scorn,
hardly noticed as they took our funds, our rights,
and tapped our phones, turned back our clocks,
and then, to quell dissent, they sent. . . .
(but here the document is torn)

BRIAN TURNER (B. 1967)

HERE, BULLET

If a body is what you want,
then here is bone and gristle and flesh.
Here is the clavicle-snapped wish,
the aorta's opened valves, the leap
thought makes at the synaptic gap.
Here is the adrenaline rush you crave,
that inexorable flight, that insane puncture
into heat and blood. And I dare you to finish
what you've started. Because here, Bullet,
here is where I complete the word you bring
hissing through the air, here is where I moan
the barrel's cold esophagus, triggering
my tongue's explosives for the rifling I have
inside of me, each twist of the round
spun deeper, because here, Bullet,
here is where the world ends, every time.

BIOGRAPHIES IN BRIEF

THOMAS BAILEY ALDRICH (1836–1907)
Ferris Greenslet quotes Aldrich on himself: "Though I am not genuine Boston, I am Boston-plated." This quip referred to the prominent influence of Boston writers on him, and to his sense of his own Brahmin identity. His poem "Unguarded Gates" bespeaks the fear of immigrant hordes shared by many blue-bloods of his time. Aldrich was born in Portsmouth, New Hampshire. Publishing his early poems in the 1850s, Aldrich lived in New York during the Civil War.

DOUG ANDERSON (B. 1943)
Originally from Memphis, Tennessee, Anderson served as a medical corpsman with Third Battalion First Marines in Vietnam during 1967 and 1968. After the war, he worked as a carpenter, marble-mill laborer, bartender, actor, cabdriver, and computer operator before returning to graduate school and an academic career. He teaches at the University of Connecticut at Storrs. Anderson has written plays, fiction, and film scripts; *The Moon Reflected in Fire* (1994) was his first collection of poems. Part of a second wave of poets from this war, he explores the experience of being a foot soldier in the Vietnam war to the experience of being a soldier in other wars, from Homer's Iliad to the Peninsular campaign of Francisco Goya's witness.

PHILIP APPLEMAN (B. 1926)
In 1944–1945, Philip Appleman became an aviation cadet in the U.S. Army Air Corps and served as a physical training instructor. He is the author of six books of poetry and three novels. *New and Selected Poems: 1956–1996* appeared in 1996. Appleman is a Distinguished Professor of English at Indiana University.

JOHN BALABAN (B. 1943)
In 1967, John Balaban joined the International Voluntary Services and went to Vietnam as a conscientious objector. For a few months, Balaban taught at a uni-

versity in the Mekong Delta, then during the Tet Offensive of 1968, he found himself taking a machine gun to protect Air Force surgeons operating in a regional hospital, then scrambling though fire as a medical orderly for casualties, before being himself wounded. Possessed of a growing conviction that as an IVS member he was inadvertently boosting a propaganda war favoring American intervention, Balaban went home to convalesce, only to return to Saigon six weeks after leaving Vietnam. This time, staying for a year, he was a part of the Committee of Responsibility to Save War-Burned and War-Injured Children. Balaban made many subsequent trips to Vietnam during the war years and after. Then fluent in Vietnamese, he collected *ca dao* (traditional oral poems) and taught at Hue University. John Balaban has published many books of poetry, as well as a memoir, *Remembering Heaven's Face* (2002). He is Poet-in-Residence and professor of English at North Carolina State University.

JOEL BARLOW (1754–1812)

Patriot, diplomat, poet, and pamphleteer, Joel Barlow was born and raised as a farm boy in Redding, Connecticut. In 1774, he went to Yale; in 1776, he marched to war with General Washington, where he fought and retreated at the Battle of Long Island. He rejoined the Revolutionary War in 1780, serving as a chaplain. In 1787, he published the first version of *The Columbiad*, which he titled *The Vision of Columbus*. *The Columbiad*, revised in 1807 to include a more deist point of view, was subscribed to by notables including Thomas Jefferson, George Washington, and Benjamin Franklin, none of whom professed to have read the book. Barlow's prose in *Advice to the Privileged Orders* remains a classic treatise in political thinking. Appointed a minister to France in 1811 because of his long residence in France and diplomatic experience, he was sent abroad to conclude a treaty with Napoleon on matters concerning American naval rights, a central issue in the War of 1812. Caught up in Napoleon's retreat during the disastrous Russian campaign, Barlow died of pneumonia in the Polish village of Zarnowiecz. His last poem, "Advice to a Raven in Russia," was written shortly before his death.

WENDY BATTIN (B. 1953)

Wendy Battin teaches poetry at the Massachusetts Institute of Technology. She is the director of CAPA, the Contemporary American Poetry Archive, on the Web. Her collection of poems, *Little Apocalypse*, appeared in 1997.

ALEXANDER BERGMAN (1912–1940)

Alexander F. Bergman was born in Brooklyn. He graduated from an agricultural high school in Elmhurst, Long Island, and became a bookkeeper for the Consolidated Edison Company. From 1938 until his death in 1940 at age 28, he was completely bedridden with tuberculosis; during this time, he wrote most of the poetry contained in his posthumous collection *They Look Like Men*. His boyhood friend Eugene Loveman was later killed while serving as part of the Abraham Lincoln Brigade.

AMBROSE BIERCE (1842–1914?)

Ambrose Bierce was born in Meigs County, Ohio. After a year in a military academy, his wartime career began at the age of eighteen, with the Ninth Indiana Volunteers in 1861. His Civil War story "Chickamauga" draws from his experience at this battle, in which 34,000 men were killed. A skilled field mapmaker, he risked his life twice to rescue comrades under fire, ultimately receiving fifteen commendations for bravery under fire. Participating in some of the bloodiest battles of the war, he was seriously wounded at Kenesaw Mountain. In 1913, Bierce went to Mexico to meet Pancho Villa, the leader of the Mexican revolution. Though the details of his death are unknown, historians surmise he died in the siege of Ojinaga, in January, 1914. In a farewell letter he wrote: "If you hear of my being stood up against a Mexican stone wall and shot to rags, please know that I think it a pretty good way to depart this life."

ELIZABETH BISHOP (1911–1979)

A great traveler, Elizabeth Bishop was born in Worcester, Massachusetts, lived in Canada during her childhood, and as an adult, resided in Brazil for many years. Her World War II experience was limited to a few days grinding lenses in a Key West naval yard. In the sixties, as she watched from a window, pistol hidden for security, she witnessed an armed takeover by Brazilian revolutionaries in Rio de Janeiro. Throughout her life she had an active, if skeptical and curious, eye for military dress and ritual.

ROBERT BLY (B. 1926)

Robert Bly's poetry, heavily influenced by the magic realism of South American poets like Neruda, and by European poets like Georg Trakl and Federico Garcia Lorca, was also central in the movement toward the Deep Image, where primal figures are seen as filtered through the depths of the psyche. He was born in Madison, Minnesota, and served in the Navy during World War II. In 1966, he founded American Writers against the Vietnam War. Bly remains active in contemporary peace movements, publishing in 2004 a collection of poetry and prose entitled *The Insanity of Empire: A Book of Poems Against the Iraq War.*

LOUISE BOGAN (1897–1970)

Born in Livermore Falls, Maine, Louise Bogan began publishing her poems in 1923. Her first marriage, at nineteen, to a professional Army man ended in divorce in 1919. She spent World War I, in which her brother died, in Portland. The poetry editor and reviewer at *The New Yorker* from 1931 to 1969, she also served as consultant to the Library of Congress (1945–1946), always writing formidably as both a poet and a critic. Bogan declares that her only defenses are her realism and her wit. Of both she had a copious supply.

JOSEPH BRODSKY (1940–1996)
A protégé of Anna Akhmatova, Joseph Brodsky was born in Leningrad at the onset of World War II. Despite his erratic exposure to educational institutions, Brodsky cobbled together a thorough literary knowledge of Russian, Polish, and English. Sentenced to hard labor in Archangelsk for his defiance of Soviet orthodoxy, he was released in 1965 and ultimately exiled to the United States. There he wrote trenchant essays on American and English poets in an English both inventive and original. In 1987, he was awarded a Nobel Prize. Having experienced totalitarianism, Brodsky preserved a vigilant antagonism toward what he perceived as political injustice.

GWENDOLYN BROOKS (1917–2000)
Her poetry was always interested in the everyday lives of Afro-Americans, but her tight, explosive poems defy stereotype. Born in Topeka, Kansas, Gwendolyn Brooks spent most of her life in the Midwest, even though she won awards for her poetry nationally, being granted fifty-one honorary degrees over the course of a lifetime. It is characteristic of her cool gaze that her portraits of wartime soldiering balance a respect for black accomplishment—an accomplishment gained in the teeth of racism—against an evident distaste for heroic bombast.

D. F. BROWN (B. 1948)
D. F. Brown served in the U.S. Army as a medic from 1968 through 1977, and in 1969 and 1970, served in Vietnam as a member of the First/Fourteenth Infantry Battalion, Fourth Infantry Division. He earned an M.A. at San Francisco State, and published a book of poems about his experience in Vietnam entitled *Returning Fire*. Brown's poems are notable for cinematic montage and experimental line breaks; these techniques use time and tense distortion to get at the fractured quality of combat experience as the senses render it.

WILLIAM CULLEN BRYANT (1794–1878)
Regarded by his nineteenth-century century contemporaries as one of their brightest stars, Bryant was born in Cummington, Massachusetts. "Thanatopsis" is still probably his best-known poem. In 1832, Bryant's first collection, *Poems*, sold out nearly the whole of its first edition within six weeks. In 1827, he started work at the New York Evening Post, and by 1829 became its editor-in-chief, a

post he held until his death. Bryant was a strong abolitionist. Walt Whitman referred to him as a "bard of the river and wood, ever conveying a taste of the open air, with scents as from hayfields, grapes, birch-borders . . . through all . . . touching the highest universal truths, enthusiasms, duties."

HAYDEN CARRUTH (B. 1921)

Born in Waterbury, Connecticut, Hayden Carruth served in the Army Air Force in Italy, in the public relations office of a bomber group. *The Voice That Is Great Within Us*, the anthology he edited of selections from American poetry, is a classic of its kind. A dry fatalism pervades his antiwar poems. In 1996, *Scrambled Eggs and Whiskey* received the National Book Award.

WILLIAM CHILDRESS (B. 1933)

William Childress came from a family of sharecroppers and migrant cotton pickers. Joining the army in 1951 at the age of eighteen, he was sent to Korea the following year, serving as a demolitions expert and secret courier. Eventually, he published two books of poetry during the 1960s and 1970s, later combined as *Burning the Years* and *Lobo: Poems 1962–1975*. While the bulk of his war poems mirror his experience in Korea, publishing in the wake of the Vietnam War allowed him to benefit from the politics of later wars. Childress's poems see his war partly from his own historical experience and partly filtered through subsequent thinking about war.

BAO-LONG CHU (B. 1965?)

Bao-Long Chu is currently the Program Director for Writers in the Schools, a nonprofit organization operating in schools and community settings in Houston. His poems have appeared in *The Asian Pacific American Journal* and *The Viet Nam Forum*.

JOHN CIARDI (1916–1986)

Editor, translator, lecturer, teacher, critic, and poet, John Ciardi was born in Medford, Massachusetts. A graduate of Tufts University in 1938, Ciardi served in the Army Air Force from 1942 through 1945. Many poems reflect his wartime experience: he was an aerial gunner on a B-29, saw combat in the Pacific, and came home as a medaled war hero. He was the poetry editor at the Saturday Review from 1956 through 1972, and his program for National Public Radio, "Words in Your Ear," was broadcast widely.

HORACE COLEMAN (B. 1943)

Serving in the U.S. Army Air Corps, Horace Coleman was a weapons director/interceptor controller, or air traffic controller. He considers himself a member of the Class of 1967, having been stationed in Vietnam from 1967 to 1968. He has taught at Ohio State University and been a writer-in-the-schools and a technical writer. Coleman's *In the Grass* was published by Vietnam Generation/Burning Cities Press.

DAVID CONNOLLY (B. 1949)

David Connolly served in the U.S. Army from 1967 to 1971, and in 1968 and 1969 was an infantryman assigned to the Eleventh Armored Cavalry Regiment at Blackhorse Forward near Xuan Loc. Still a proud member of Vietnam Veterans Against the War, Connolly is the Slam Master of the Southie Slam, as well as both managing editor and poetry editor of the *South Boston Literary Gazette*. He lives in South Boston, where he was born and raised.

JANE COOPER (B. 1924)

Suffering all her life from primary immune deficiency, Jane Cooper was born in Atlantic City, New Jersey. In the summer of 1947, she left to tour a Europe still picking up the pieces of the recent war. She visited a ravaged St. Malo, then went to study at Oxford. She tells of these years of writing and study in her 1974 memoir piece "Nothing Has Been Used in the Manufacture of This Poetry That Could Have Been Used in the Manufacture of Bread." Her title echoes a sign seen in the window of a postwar Parisian bakery. Cooper's poems follow families and relationships, yet never lose sight of the larger communities that also define us. Well aware of the power of the artist, in her acceptance speech for nomination as the New York State Poet of 1996–1997, she noted that "a people deprived of the arts will not know its own worth."

MALCOLM COWLEY (1898–1989)

His birthplace was Pittsburgh, but Cowley thought of himself as a native of Belsano, Pennsylvania, where his family spent summers. He enrolled at Harvard in 1915, but by the summer of 1917, Cowley was driving a five-ton munitions truck as a volunteer for the American Field Service, supplying front lines in France. From 1948 to 1985, he worked for Viking Press, and was instrumental in getting writers like Jack Kerouac published. *Blue Juniata: A Life* contains his collected poems. Besides literary history and criticism, he wrote several memoirs, the best-known of these being *Exiles Return: A Literary Odyssey of the Twenties.*

STEPHEN CRANE (1871–1900)

Born in Newark, New Jersey, Stephen Crane's writing career began when he picked up the family business. Crane began working at his brother Townley's news bureau at the age of sixteen. By the age of twenty-two, he had written *The Red Badge of Courage*, and at twenty-three, the poems collected in *The Black*

Rider. Crane's imagining the experience of battle came first in his life; then came his reporting of it. Writing in what has been called the Golden Age of journalism, before modern standards of verifiability or of fixed codes of military censorship, Crane made use of the blurring divide between fact and fiction to experiment with tone and point of view, as well as with modernist irony, fragmentation, and expressionist imagery. In 1900, Crane witnessed the Spanish-American War, writing fifty war dispatches for *The New York Journal* and *The New York World.* 1900 saw the publication of *Wounds in the Rain,* containing short stories and sketches about the war. Contracting tuberculosis, Crane died at Badenweiler in Germany at the age of twenty-nine.

E. E. CUMMINGS (1894–1962)

Born in Cambridge, Massachusetts, Edward Estlin Cummings attended Harvard University. In 1917, he joined the Norton-Harjes Ambulance Service, and was detained in France for the better part of three months in a prison camp, incarcerated unjustly on a charge of treasonable correspondence. Released from this camp by the unceasing efforts of friends and family, he then served in the United States Army in 1918 and 1919. *The Enormous Room* (1922), the book he wrote about his experience of detention, is considered a classic prison document. A notable poet of the modernist movement, Cummings conducted endless, restless experiments with typography, playing outrageously and triumphantly with the vernacular and with fragmenting syntax and imagery. A two-volume edition of his *Complete Poems* was published in 1981.

JOHN WILLIAM DE FOREST (1826–1906)

J. W. De Forest is known primarily for *Miss Ravenel's Conversion* (1867), a novel about the Civil War, which was praised for the realism of its style. Writing in both prose and poetry, De Forest based his work on his four-year term as a soldier, most of it as a captain, in the Civil War; his pieces in *The Atlantic Monthly* were graphic accounts of the war he had seen first hand. De Forest fought in Louisiana and with General Philip Sheridan in the valley of the Shenandoah. From 1865 until 1868, he remained in the army, an adjutant general of the veteran reserve corps, and then served as chief of a district in the Freedman's Bureau. He was born in Humphreysville (now Seymour), Connecticut, and educated informally abroad.

JAMES DICKEY (1923–1997)

James Dickey's first book, *Into the Stone, and Other Poems,* published in 1960, showed Dickey as a survivor of violence and death. An interest in war as the testing of masculine character, combined with a horror of it—and with perhaps even a relish for that horror—is a major force in his work. Nevertheless, his description of firebombing in the poem of that title, "The Firebombing," soberly queries the ethics of aerial bombardment. He was born in Atlanta, Georgia, and graduated *magna cum laude* from Vanderbilt University in Tennessee. From there he went into the U.S. Army Air Force during World War II, becoming a pilot. During the Korean War, he served as a training officer. His writing included novels, collections of shrewd and lively critical prose, and the screenplay for *Deliverance*. In 1993, he published his World War II novel, *To the White Sea*.

EMILY DICKINSON (1830–1886)

Emily Dickinson published no more than eight of the nearly 1,800 poems she was eventually to write during her lifetime. Almost half of her poetry was written from 1861 to 1865. Deeply reclusive, Dickinson lived out the Civil War years in her home in Amherst, Massachusetts, only aware of the consequences of the conflagration that was sweeping her country as the deaths of neighbors and Amherst college boys were reported to her by family and friends. On December 31, 1861, after hearing of the death of two sons of Mrs. Adams, the wife of the president of Amherst College, she wrote: "Another one died in October—from fever caught in the camp. Mrs. Adams herself has not risen from her bed since then. 'Happy new year' step softly over such doors as these! 'Dead! Both her boys!' . . . Christ be merciful! Frazer Stearns is just leaving Annapolis. His father has gone to see him today. I hope that ruddy face won't be brought home frozen. Poor little widow's boy, riding tonight in the mad wind, back to the village burying-ground where he never dreamed of sleeping! Ah! The dreamless sleep!"

H.D. [HILDA DOOLITTLE] (1886–1961)

A part of the High Modernist revolution of the twentieth century, H. D. met Ezra Pound in Pennsylvania during their adolescence; Pound was the first to recognize her talent. The poet William Carlos Williams wrote of the young H.D. that she had "a provocative indifference to rule and order which I liked. She dressed indifferently, almost sloppily and looked to a young man, not inviting—she had none of that—but irritating, with a smile." Installed in Europe in 1911, H. D. was first associated with imagism. Married briefly to Richard Aldington, she spent World War I in England, enduring the hardships and chaos of those war years. After moving to Switzerland, she began the longer narrative poems on which her reputation currently rests. Returning to London in 1939, she remained there for six years, enduring the Blitz. This experience is recorded in *The Walls Do Not Fall* (1944).

NORMAN DUBIE (B. 1945)

The son of a congregational minister and a hospital nurse, Norman Dubie was born in Barre, Vermont. As a college student, Norman listened to his father in the pulpit, protesting American involvement in Vietnam. His poem "Aubade of the Singer and Saboteur, Marie Triste" came into being when Dubie discovered that the concentration camp Dachau had formerly been a retreat of both hunters and musicians and composers. He comments on this poem: "Though people have spoken of Marie Triste from time to time in reviews as a historical being, I must say that I know her as simply an invention of the poem. Through-out history, music has always made slaughter easy—old men and our military are piping it hot into the ears of soldiers in Iraq today and not just to make them brave, but to make them vicious." In 2001, *The Mercy Seat: Collected and New Poems 1967–2001* won the PEN USA prize for poetry. Dubie has been a serious student of Buddhism for decades. He teaches at Arizona State University.

ALAN DUGAN (1923–2003)
Coming to writing—or at least to publishing—somewhat late, Dugan, who was born in Brooklyn, New York, started out as a left-wing antifascist, entering the Army Air Force during World War II. He worked in an advertising agency, at a staple factory, and a payroll office. When George Starbuck, then an editor at Lit-tle Brown, went to meet the unknown poet whom Dudley Fitts had awarded the 1961 Yale Younger Poets Prize, Starbuck found him at a table full of plastic mod-els of body parts being manufactured for medical use: that was then Dugan's job. Many publications followed, as well as long years of teaching and being a primary part of the artists' community at the Fine Arts Work Center in Provincetown, Massachusetts.

PAUL LAURENCE DUNBAR (1872–1906)
Born in Dayton, Ohio, to parents who had been slaves in Kentucky, Dunbar was the only black student in his school. Too poor to go to college, and barred by his race from the journalistic career that his writing talent might have pointed him toward, Dunbar self-published, eventually getting poems picked up by the *New York Times.* Feted by William Dean Howells, Dunbar had to strike a balance between playing to the white reading public's preference for his dialect poems, and his own passionate desire to be part of mainstream American literature. Dunbar was both a poet and a novelist, writing much about the Civil War, including the role of black soldiers in it and the consequences of the subsequent Jim Crow laws. His use of both vernacular and standard English has helped to create a black poetic diction; his strong sense of narrative color and of charac-ter are part of what J. Saunders Redding has called his "fierce, secret energies," or the powers "directed towards breaking down the vast wall of emotional and intellectual misunderstanding with which he, as a poet, was immured."

RICHARD EBERHART (1904–2005)
A master of formal verse, Eberhart was born in Austin, Minnesota, and gradu-ated from Dartmouth in 1926. By 1927, he had published eight poems in *Poetry.*

At the height of the Depression years, Eberhart could find work only in a slaughterhouse, which he called "a vision of hell." In World War II, from 1942 to 1946, he served in the U.S. Navy as an aerial gunnery instructor, attaining the rank of lieutenant commander. His war poem "The Fury of Aerial Bombardment," along with "The Groundhog," are probably Eberhart's best-known poems. After a fling in the business world, he settled into a steady succession of teaching positions, culminating in his final post as the poet-in-residence at Dartmouth.

W. D. EHRHART (B. 1948)

W. D. Ehrhart enlisted in the U.S. Marine Corps at the age of seventeen, turning down four college acceptances to do so. He fought in Vietnam and was awarded a Purple Heart for wounds received in action in Hue during the 1968 Tet Offensive. His first published poetry appeared in the 1972 anthology *Winning Hearts and Minds: War Poems by Vietnam Veterans*. He is the author of *Vietnam-Perkasie: A Combat Marine Memoir*, which details his anguished evolution toward an antiwar perspective. He has published *Beautiful Wreckage: New and Selected Poems* in addition to twelve other books, and has edited or coedited four anthologies of Vietnam and Korean War literature. Through tireless industry and a discerning eye for good work, Ehrhart has been largely responsible for kindling interest in post–World War II war poetry.

THOMAS STEARNS ELIOT (1888–1965)

With his long poem *The Waste Land* (1920), T. S. Eliot, born in St. Louis, Missouri, ushered in the modernist American poetry of the twentieth century. *The Waste Land*, too long and complicated to extract from safely, is now considered a portrait of the world as it had been left by World War I. Other impressive achievements followed, including *Four Quartets*, which appeared from 1940 to 1943, and Eliot's verse dramas *Murder in the Cathedral* (1935) and *The Cocktail Party* (1950). No one interested in the peak accomplishments of American poetry can ignore Eliot's sonorous cadences, coupled with his jagged sound, flashing symbols, and richly colored diction. Eliot's poetry, along with that of Wallace Stevens and Ezra Pound, first became famous for its meditative depth and difficulty of access, but Eliot also wrote teasing, funny poems, among them the sequence set to music that after his death became the theatrical production *Cats*. Living in London as an expatriate for most of his life, he lived through both world wars, acting as an air-raid warden during the Blitz.

RALPH WALDO EMERSON (1803–1882)

Born in Boston, Massachusetts, the leading writer of the New England Transcendentalist movement, Ralph Waldo Emerson is better known for his essays than his poems. For him, at bottom, all political questions become ethical questions. The Unitarian minister William Ellery Channing initially guided the evolution of Emerson's thinking, but ultimately Emerson wrote his own distinctive version of the self's necessary striving. After resigning his Unitarian pulpit, traveling to Europe, and returning to deliver controversial addresses at Harvard, Emerson began protesting the treatment of Native Americans in 1831. His "Ode, Inscribed to W. H. Channing" incorporates Emerson's growing passion for the abolitionist cause, as well as his antimaterialism, his mistrust of the territorial expansionism of the proslavery forces in the United States to extend slavery in the West, and his opposition to the provisions of the Fugitive Slave Act.

LOUISE ERDRICH (B. 1954)

A member of the Turtle Mountain band of the Chippewas, Louise Erdrich was born in Wahpeton, North Dakota. The author of ten novels and a memoir about early motherhood, she is best known for her fiction, but like other Indian novelists, she has published many poems as well. *Original Fire: Selected and New Poems* appeared in 2003.

MARTIN ESPADA (B. 1957)

Born to Puerto Rican parents in Brooklyn, Martin Espada has published seven collections of poetry. *Alabanza: New and Selected Poems* was published in 2003. His professional life has been split three ways, between writing and editing, teaching, and serving as a tenant lawyer and supervisor of a legal services program. Full of restless inquiry into the history of Spanish-speaking minorities in America both present and past, Espada's poems look at his own Puerto Rican background, but also set that heritage within a broader coverage of the Latino and Latina experience in America.

CAROLYN FORCHÉ (B. 1950)

Poet, translator, editor, and international rights activist, Carolyn Forche began publishing poetry in the 1970s. Born into a working-class family in Detroit, Forche's fascination with and love for the character of her Slovakian grandmother provided the impetus for a lifelong interest in other languages and cultures. As a student protester against the Vietnam War, Forche was deeply affected by the suicide of a lover and fellow protester. In 1977, she went to Spain to meet the poet Claribel Alegria. Subsequently, Alegria's nephew Leonel Gomez Vides persuaded her to visit El Salvador and to involve herself in its political struggles. For the next two years, Forche worked intermittently with the Salvadoran resistance movement.

PHILIP FRENEAU (1752–1832)

Known to historians as the "Poet of the American Revolution," Philip Freneau was born in New York City to an affluent family. Tutored in Latin and Greek, Freneau was educated at Princeton, where he took part in pre-Revolutionary politics. Freneau's poems were accomplished in the forms of his day, and ranged with some real success over a canny variety of subjects. Yet little marks his work with the incisive originality achieved by American writers in the following century, as they set about peeling American culture away from its British origins.

ROBERT FROST (1874–1963)

Born in San Francisco, where he lived until the age of eleven, Robert Frost then moved to a Massachusetts mill town—hardly the rural New England Frost liked to claim as his heritage and experience. Setting his face in apparent opposition to the High Modernism of the early twentieth century, it has taken the work of decades of scholars for Frost's traditional meters and prosody, and his apparently folksy idiom, to have their dark and nuanced underside exposed. Frost's first public recognition came in England, where his first two books were published in 1913 and 1914 respectively. The outbreak of World War I forced his return to the United States. Lacking the difficult access of poems like Pound's *Cantos* or T. S. Eliot's *Four Quartets*, Frost's openly narrative poetry acquired a wide popularity that it has never lost.

KRISTI GARBOUSHIAN (B. 1968)

Kristi Garboushian grew up in San Jose, California. After high school, she entered active duty in the U.S. Army, serving from 1987 to 1991. Garboushian was trained at Fort Gordon, Georgia. After asking what specialty a woman was least likely to request, and being told combat signaler, she immediately signed up as a "wire dog," and was trained in field communications and FM radio systems. Garboushian was shipped to the Persian Gulf in December 1990. During the next six months, she was stationed in Saudi Arabia; she then entered Iraq and convoyed north through that country into Kuwait during the ground war. She received her M.F.A. in 2002, from Arizona State University. "The Ribbon on Hell's Tree" stems from a journal kept in the war zone; the present poem was written over the next five years. In 1998, she received the Associated Writing Programs Introductory Award for poetry.

ALLEN GINSBERG (1926–1997)

Initially associated with the Beat revolution, Allen Ginsberg, born in Newark, New Jersey, also drew the roots of his nonmetrical poetry from the broader modernist tradition of William Carlos Williams, an early mentor. While *Howl and Other Poems* (1956) brought him instant attention and huge followings in San Francisco and New York, Ginsberg went on to publish poems and prose in the mood of the radical revisionism of the 1960s, embracing aesthetic, sexual, and political freedom from orthodox restraint. All these preoccupations melded in long, looping lines or in short, excitable whoops, a style designed to be close to the spontaneity of a living speech. Through an intricate line of male lovers, he also liked to think of himself as connected sexually all the way back to Walt Whitman.

RAYNA GREEN (B. 1942)

A Cherokee Indian from Oklahoma, Rayna Green earned a Ph.D. in folklore from Indiana University. Her primary interest is in Native American scientific and technical development. Herself widely anthologized, she has edited *That's What She Said: Contemporary Poetry and Fiction by Native American Women*, published by Indiana University Press in 1984.

CHARLOTTE L. FORTEN GRIMKE (1837–1914)

A member of the black aristocracy of Philadelphia, Charlotte Forten Grimke was educated at home. Settling in Salem, Massachusetts in 1853, she began writing her *Journals* and working as an antislavery activist, meeting and being befriended by all of the leading orators, writers, and statesmen involved in the abolitionist cause. Her poems and essays appeared frequently in black periodicals. During the Civil War, she taught freed slaves in a school on St. Helena Island in South Carolina, transcribing their hymns and shouts and describing her experiences during this time. Grimke eventually moved to Washington, D.C., where she married the Reverend Francis James Grimke in 1878. Their life together was devoted to forwarding racial equality.

JOY HARJO (B. 1951)

Joy Harjo celebrates her Muskogee Creek heritage, plying loose, evocative rhythms that evoke the aural nature of her sources. Born in Tulsa, Oklahoma, her poems reflect the mixed distresses of contemporary Native American life and deal with the bitterness of the determined erasure of Native American customs and community by the dominant culture. However, while her heritage is sturdily Native American, her poems also mirror contemporary issues for feminist and minority groups both national and global. Besides writing poetry, she plays the saxophone in her group Poetic Justice.

ANTHONY HECHT (1923–2004)

A native New Yorker, Anthony Hecht graduated from Bard College in 1944 and immediately entered the U.S. Army. He served in Europe and Japan, calling the memory of his wartime years "grotesque beyond anything I could possibly write." His intricate poems accomplish both urbanity and elegance of tone and diction, as well as meditative depth.

ERNEST HEMINGWAY (1899–1961)

A clear symbol of international modernism, Ernest Hemingway's books made it onto the pile burnt by the Nazis in Berlin as "decadent literature." While his World War I novel *A Farewell to Arms* (1929) defined the war experience of an American generation, Hemingway also kept notebook jottings that effectively shaped into rhyme or simple dialogue. His World War I poems are taken from the revised *Complete Poems* (1992). He was born in Oak Park, Illinois. While never a soldier himself, Hemingway drove a Red Cross ambulance in World War I, where he was severely wounded by a mortar shell in Italy during an Austrian bombardment; his legs badly hit, he still managed to carry an Italian soldier to safety. Through 1937 and 1938, he served as a war correspondent in the Spanish Civil War, reporting on the siege of Madrid and the campaign on the Ebro; he also witnessed the fall of Barcelona. In World War II, he observed the troop landings on D-Day as a correspondent. For most of that war he remained in Havana, where he outfitted his fishing boat with submachine guns, with the idea that he was patrolling Cuban waters looking for German U-boats.

WILLIAM HEYEN (B. 1940)

Born in Brooklyn and raised on Long Island, William Heyen has for many years been a distinguished professor at the State University of New York at Brockport. Taking political and historical events as the substance of several of his collections of poetry, Heyen, in the National Book Award–winning *Crazy Horse in Stillness* (1996), wrote more than 400 poems centering on the catastrophic cultural collision of the warrior-mystic Chief Crazy Horse and General George Armstrong Custer. In addition to this book of opposing messianic visions, in 1984 Heyen published *Erika: The Swastika Poems*; and in 2003, *Shoah Train*. A recent anthology he edited, *September 11, 2001: American Writers Respond*, continues the political preoccupations of the past few years.

ROLANDO HINJOSA (B. 1929)

Rolando Hinojosa was born in the Rio Grande Valley of Texas to a Mexican-American father and an Anglo-American mother. His Mexican forebears settled on the north bank of the Rio Grande in the 1740s; his Anglo grandfather settled in Texas in the 1880s. Much of Hinojosa's writing focuses on the fusions and conflicts of this split heritage. He served in the army for two years, breaking his first years of service with college; his second term of service began with his callback in 1949. He was sent to Korea in July, 1950, shortly after the North Korean invasion. Becoming a tank crewman with a reconnaissance unit, he was wounded twice. His best-known poems from this war are in *Korean Love Songs: From Klail City Death Trip* (1978). For many years, he taught at the University of Texas in Austin.

TONY HOAGLAND (B. 1953)

Born in 1953 in Fort Bragg, North Carolina, Tony Hoagland has published three collections of poetry, the most recent being *What Narcissism Means to Me* (2003). Hoagland teaches in the poetry program at the University of Houston.

OLIVER WENDELL HOLMES (1809–1894)

A famous conversationalist, Holmes regularly wrote a column in *The Atlantic Monthly*, later collected and published as *The Autocrat at the Breakfast Table*. "Old Ironsides," protesting the destruction of the frigate USS *Constitution*, appeared in the *Boston Daily Advertiser* in 1830. Holmes taught anatomy at the Harvard Medical School for many years, writing a landmark paper on puerperal fever in 1843. Holmes was born in Cambridge, Massachusetts. His son Oliver Wendell Holmes became a justice of the U.S. Supreme Court.

JULIA WARD HOWE (1819–1910)

Raised in New York City, Julia Ward Howe married the banker Samuel Howe, spending most of her early married life caring for her six children and supervising large-scale entertaining. Her most famous poem, "The Battle Hymn of the Republic," was written after a visit to a Union army camp. Of the composition of this poem, Howe writes: "I awoke in the gray of the early dawn, and to my astonishment found that the wished-for lines were arranging themselves in my brain. I lay quite still until the last verse had completed itself in my thoughts, then hastily arose, saying to myself, 'I shall lose this if I don't write it down immediately.'" Published in *The Atlantic Monthly* in February, 1862, and set to the music of "John Brown's Body," an earlier popular song, the poem quickly became the anthem of the Northern cause. Nearly a decade later, while the Franco-Prussian War was in progress, all of her antiwar feeling crystallized in her "Mother's Day Proclamation," a document radically different from the sturdy, embattled vision of her most famous poem. Translated into several languages, the "Mother's Day Proclamation" substituted an earnest pacifism for the high-flown grandeur and vivid imagery of Howe's earlier effort.

ANDREW HUDGINS (B. 1951)

Born in Killeen, Texas, Andrew Hudgins earned an M.F.A. at the University of Iowa in 1983. He has published six books of poetry, including *After the Lost War: A Narrative* (1988). These poems are spoken in the person of Sidney Lanier, the Southern poet noted for the nature imagery of his post–Civil War work. Hudgins's poems are drawn from Lanier's letters and fiction about the war. Currently, Hudgins teaches at Ohio State University.

DAVID HUDDLE (B. 1942)

Born in Ivanhoe, Virginia, David Huddle interrupted his undergraduate years at the University of Virginia to serve in the U.S. Army from 1964 to 1967. After reading William Faulkner's "Two Soldiers" in Germany, he requested a transfer to Vietnam, and served with the Twenty-fifth Military Intelligence in Cu Chi from 1966 to 1967, where "every GI I knew had to function in systematic craziness." His first publications were stories about Vietnam: "it was that experience that gave me my writing career." Huddle has published fifteen books of poetry, fiction, and essays. The sonnet sequence based on his year in Vietnam appears in *Stopping By Home* (1988). Huddle began teaching at the University of Vermont in 1971, where he remains.

LANGSTON HUGHES (1902–1967)

From Joplin, Missouri, Hughes graduated from Lincoln University in Pennsylvania. A busboy, an English teacher in Mexico, a seaman, and finally a journalist and war correspondent in Madrid during the Spanish Civil War, Hughes's poetry evolved as a free-flowing, jazz- and folk-inspired body of work "racial in theme and treatment, derived from the life I know." Drawing the many strands of American black vernacular into modernist montage, Hughes's poems were infused with the radical Romantic vision of American inclusiveness, celebrating the worker. But by the onset of World War II, a deep resistance to fascism had joined his own bitter knowledge of American racism.

RICHARD HUGO (1923–1982)

A Seattle native, Hugo attended the University of Washington, and during World War II, served in the U.S. Army Air Forces. As he recounts in 1969's *Good Luck in Cracked Italian,* he was stationed in Italy. After many bombing campaigns over the Balkans, he received both the Distinguished Flying Cross and the Air Medal. Returning to Europe after the war, he wrote several moving poems, some in letter form, about war's aftermath.

LAWSON FUSAO INADA (B. 1938)

Born to third-generation Japanese-American parents, Lawson Fusao Inada absorbed from his mother a semiurban culture; from his father, he learned deep ties to rural Japan: "Inada" means *rice field.* This background, important to Inada's sense of his particular kind of Americanness, feeds his poetry richly. His childhood in the Amache internment camp for Japanese-Americans during World War II provides another kind of history about which he writes in *Legends from Camp* (1993). Inada has provided texts for the composer Andrew Hill; his own musical interests lie in jazz and bebop. He has been a multicultural consultant for schools and agencies nationally, and has taught at Southern Oregon State College since 1966.

DALE JACOBSON (B. 1950)

Dale Jacobson is the author of several books of poetry, the most recent being *Voices from the Communal Dark* (2000). His literary criticism appears in various journals, and he has written extensively on Thomas McGrath's poetry. He is from Minnesota, where he lives.

RANDALL JARRELL (1914–1965)

Randall Jarrell enlisted in the U.S. Army in 1942, with his career as a poet and critic already underway. After washing out of flight school, Jarrell remained stateside at airfields in Texas, Illinois, and Arizona throughout the war. Developing his own fresh, inimitable balance of colloquial and literary language, Jarrell wrote more than fifty war poems, reflecting his distrust of the garrison state as well as his sense of the soldier in the modern army as a cog in a machine or an infantilized prisoner. The poems adopt the perspective of wartime pilots, infantry, civilians, prisoners of war, and refugees. The five lines of "The Death of the Ball Turret Gunner" no doubt comprise the best-known American poem about any war.

ROBINSON JEFFERS (1887–1962)

Born in Pittsburgh, Pennsylvania, Robinson Jeffers was a maverick in American poetry, and his first lyric poems were privately printed. He built a rambling stone house overlooking the Pacific Ocean in Carmel, California, and much of the narrative poetry he wrote is associated with that coast and with Western history, embodying themes of the necessary triumph of the natural world over the corrupt human. During World War II, he attacked American political leaders and involvement in that war to such an extent that Random House, his publishers, in a "Publisher's Note," felt obligated to record their disagreements with *The Double Axe* (1948). *The Collected Poems of Robinson Jeffers* appeared in 2000.

FRANCIS SCOTT KEY (1779–1843)

A lawyer of pacifistic inclinations, Key was tapped for negotiations with the British over a noncombatant American hostage. Arriving on board a British ship at the mouth of the Potomac, Key obtained the release of his prisoner, but both men were detained during the bombardment of Fort McHenry. The elderly hostage could not see the Fort's giant American flag, a piece of woolen bunting twenty-nine feet wide and thirty-six feet long, and asked Key repeatedly, "Is the flag still there?" Key, struck by the phrase, replied in the affirmative, and jotted down additional phrases of his own on an envelope. After the bombardment, forming a poem based on the meter of a British drinking song, Key published his text in the Baltimore *Patriot* on September 20, 1814. In 1931, an Act of Congress established "The Defence of Fort McHenry" as the national anthem.

MYUNG MI KIM (B. 1957)
Born in Seoul, Korea, Kim's parents emigrated to the United States when she was nine. Her meditative, experimental poetry uses her mixed Korean and American background as a point of departure. She says of her work in relation to avant garde traditions, "the poem is what is in fact emerging at the very moment of encounter, with your ear, with your psyche, with your body, with your historical conditions." Austerely theoretical, her work nonetheless remains enmeshed in narrative.

SUJI KWOCK KIM (B. 1968)
Educated at Yale and the Iowa Writers' Workshop, Suji Kwock Kim was a Fulbright Scholar at Seoul National University and a Stegner Fellow at Stanford. Her first collection of poems, *Notes from a Divided Country* (2003) received the Walt Whitman Award. She has cowritten a multimedia play, *Private Property*, produced at the Edinburgh Fringe Festival and featured on BBC-TV. She is "bicoastal," dividing her life between San Francisco and New York.

GALWAY KINNELL (B. 1927)
Galway Kinnell was raised and schooled in Rhode Island. He enrolled at Princeton University, and from 1944 to 1946, participated in the Princeton officer training program. He graduated *summa cum laude* in 1948. Fulbright scholarships took Kinnell to France and Iran; he has also lived in Spain and Australia, and in Chicago, New York, and Hawaii. During the 1960s, Kinnell took odd jobs and worked as a member of the Congress of Racial Equality to register Southern black voters, then becoming active in demonstrations and readings against the Vietnam War. He is the Erich Maria Remarque Professor at New York University.

LINCOLN KIRSTEIN (1907–1996)
A native of Rochester, New York, Lincoln Kirstein was educated at Harvard. His first poetry collection, *Low Ceiling*, appeared in 1935. He served in northwestern Europe with Third Army Headquarters as a courier, driver, and interpreter, and assisted in the recovery of looted artwork after the Nazi surrender. *Rhymes of a PFC* (1964) details his wartime experiences in rough satiric rhymes, whose comic effects cannot obscure the range of serious observations, delivered with succinctness and pungency. The effect of his visionary energy on the dance

world was enormous. He cofounded and directed several ballet schools, including American Ballet and Ballet Caravan, and founded the New York City Ballet, establishing George Balanchine as its creative center and serving as the company's director from 1948 to 1989.

YUSEF KOMUNYAKAA (B. 1947)

At his birth in Bogalusa, Louisiana, Yusef Komunyakaa was officially James Willie Brown, Jr. Komunyakaa took his present name from a grandfather that the family claimed had been smuggled in to the United States on a banana boat from Trinidad. *Dien Cai Dau*, the Vietnamese for "crazy," is the phrase used for the title of Komunyakaa's second book, in which he retrieved the half-buried war experience of his year in Vietnam, where he had served in 1969 and 1970 as a reporter and editor for the military newspaper *The Southern Cross*. Komunyakaa had returned from Vietnam, earned a university degree in Colorado and an M.F.A. from the University of California at Irvine, and begun writing and publishing poetry before he could begin to access, as an artist, the memory of his service. Quite like no one else, Komunyakaa filters Vietnam through the complicated race relations of black and white soldiers in action against their Asian counterparts, all engaged in a brutal war not of their instigation, and for the Americans, only questionably in their interest.

GREG KUZMA (B. 1944)

Greg Kuzma has published collections of poetry over several decades, the most recent being 1993's *Wind Rain and Stars and the Grass Growing: Poems*. His darkly funny, deeply personal voice has never been simply confessional; always the poems reach and project a wider notion of the poetic self, living its vocal life in the human community. Kuzma now teaches at the University of Nebraska in Lincoln. He is the editor of Best Cellar Press.

SIDNEY LANIER (1842–1881)

Born in Georgia, Sidney Lanier was trained as a flutist, and after graduating from Oglethorpe College, joined the Confederate Army. After hard campaigning at Chancellorsville and the Battle of the Wilderness, he and his brother Clifford were captured and brought to a Union prison camp, where both men suffered starvation and illness, Sidney contracting tuberculosis. Lanier never recovered his health after the four years of his military service and imprisonment. After establishing himself as a writer, he died aged thirty-nine.

PHILIP LEVINE (B. 1928)

Philip Levine's working-class origins have very much been part of a poetry that is both fiercely and tenderly autobiographical, as well as politically oriented to liberal causes. He was born in Detroit to Russian immigrant parents, and educated at Wayne State University, after which he received an M.F.A. from the Writers' Workshop at the University of Iowa in 1957. Levine has written many poems about living in Spain and has translated Spanish poets. He taught for many years in the writing program at the University of California in Fresno.

DENISE LEVERTOV (1923–1997)
Denise Levertov was born in Ilford, Essex, England, and became an American citizen in 1956. Schooled at home, Levertov began writing the poems of her first book, *The Double Image* (1946), when she was seventeen. During World War II, Levertov served as a civilian nurse throughout the London bombings. In 1947, she moved to the United States. Openly influenced by William Carlos Williams's free verse, her American poems nevertheless carried their own independently lyrical and feminist stamp. During the Vietnam War, she helped to organize and to participate with other writers in poetry readings, rallies, and demonstrations against the war, eventually becoming a member of the War Resisters League. Some of her most notable antiwar poetry appeared in *The Sorrow Dance* (1967), although poems through the first Gulf War continue to display her consistent political convictions.

HENRY WADSWORTH LONGFELLOW (1807–1882)
Born into a prominent family in Portland, Maine, Henry Wadsworth Longfellow was admitted to Bowdoin at fourteen, where he shone as a prodigy, and was invited to occupy a professorship in modern languages, contingent upon his finishing a suitable stint of education in Europe. Longfellow complied with these terms, becoming the genuinely urbane cosmopolitan, in contrast to Emily Dickinson's isolation or Walt Whitman's barbaric yawp. "Paul Revere's Ride," part of *Tales of a Wayside Inn* (1862), became instantly canonical, although in the twentieth century, Longfellow's lucid narratives took a back seat to modernist irony and ambiguity, image fragmentation, and narrative disjunction. Longfellow was an early abolitionist, liberal and progressive in his politics. In his personal life, he remained both literally and metaphorically scarred by the death of his first wife, fatally injured in an accidental domestic fire; yet his son Charley escaped a severe bullet wound in the Civil War and came home safe and sound.

AMY LOWELL (1874–1925)
The big woman with the big cigar, Lowell in her energetic lifetime published six volumes of poetry, becoming the powerful editor of *Poetry* magazine and the touring lecturer who promoted what she perceived as the principles of Imagism. T. S. Eliot called her "a demon saleswoman"; Ezra Pound mocked her ideas as "Amygism." Although her work received a posthumous Pulitzer in 1926, in the

years after her death her star gradually sank, to be pulled up again in the 1970s and 1980s by contemporary feminists who defended her love lyrics. She was also a translator and biographer. While the setting of her most famous poem, "Patterns," makes reference to the Lowland wars of another century, most readers take the poem as a veiled pacifist response to the opening years of World War I.

JAMES RUSSELL LOWELL (1819–1891)

James Russell Lowell published the first series of *Biglow Papers* in 1848, a series of satiric comic letters written in New England dialect. His protagonist, Birdofredum Sawin, becomes a volunteer in the Mexican War, and a mouthpiece for Lowell's anti-imperialist and increasingly abolitionist views, decrying the extension of proslavery territory. Lowell concludes these adventures with a second series, revived in 1867, following his protagonist into the Civil War, with an energetic defense of the Northern cause. A good Latinist and a gifted philologist with a mastery of American dialect, Lowell preceded Mark Twain in his creative use of the vernacular.

ROBERT LOWELL (1917–1977)

Born a New England blueblood, Robert Lowell converted to Catholicism. Registering for the draft in 1942, Lowell contemplated joining as an officer, but by September 7, 1943, he had written to President Roosevelt refusing induction. Citing Allied aggressive action against civilians, Lowell saw military service as a betrayal of American political traditions. Arraigned in New York for draft dereliction, he spent ten days in the West Street Jail, and was transferred from there to Danbury, Connecticut, where his felony sentence of "a year and a day" was reduced to four months, after which he was paroled to perform hospital duties. While his religious convictions altered, Lowell continued his pacifist stance during the Vietnam War, refusing an invitation to a White House Arts Festival to protest the war. Many Lowell poems reflect the antiwar stance of these periods, although his Civil War elegy "For the Union Dead" acquires a broader historical significance.

ARCHIBALD MACLEISH (1892–1982)

Born in Glencoe, Illinois, to a privileged family with a sense of social conscience, MacLeish trained as a lawyer at Harvard, and practiced several years in Boston. In World War I, he wangled his way into the 146th Field Artillery, a regiment of the National Guard; in April, 1918, he was briefly stationed near the front lines at the Second Battle of the Marne. The death of MacLeish's beloved brother Kenneth figured prominently in many poems: Kenneth, a pilot, was shot down by the Germans over Belgium. His corpse was located months later by a Belgian; eventually his plane was found intact. The speculation ran that Kenneth had died in a poison gas attack laid down by the British in the area where he had managed to land his plane. During World War II, MacLeish held many official posts; through 1944 and 1945, he joined Franklin Roosevelt's cabinet as an Assistant Secretary of State. In the course of being a fearless opponent of Senator Joseph McCarthy's communist witch hunts, 600 pages were amassed in MacLeish's FBI file. Winning many major awards for broad public service as well as for the arts, in 1977, he received the Presidential Medal for Freedom, and in 1978, the National Medal for Literature.

EDGAR LEE MASTERS (1868–1950)

Spoon River Anthology was a huge critical and popular success when it appeared in 1915. The idea of the cemetery full of talking headstones sprang from Masters's reading of W. Mackail's collection *Selected Epigrams from the Greek Anthology.* Blunt, pithy, and direct, the poems establish a model for many later free-verse dramatic monologues. Masters regarded the American war against the Philippines as the advent of American imperialism, driving the last nail in the coffin of Jeffersonian democracy. Born in Kansas and brought up in Illinois, he served with distinction as a lawyer in Chicago for most of his life.

JOHN MATHIAS (B. 1941)

John Mathias teaches English at the University of Notre Dame. A native of Ohio, he lived for much of the 1970s in the East Anglia region of Great Britain. Poet, translator, and editor, his most recent publication is *New Selected Poems* (2004).

GERALD MCCARTHY (B. 1947)

Technically and thematically, Gerald McCarthy's sequence of poems in *War Story* reflects the jarring fit with civilian life to which the Vietnam War veteran returned. In the U.S. Marine Corps from 1965 to 1968, McCarthy writes: "I served with the First Combat Engineer Battalion in Chu Lai and then Da Nang, but my last four months in country were spent . . . hitching rides on C-140s and scavenging wheel cylinders (and other parts) for our heavy equipment. After only a few months back in the U.S., I deserted and spent time in The Brooklyn Brig/Brooklyn Naval Yard, and later in Norfolk/Portsmouth Brig in Virginia. I was discharged in April, the day they buried Martin Luther King. I got my first civilian jobs as a stonecutter and then a shoe factory maker before going to college." McCarthy is a professor of English at Thomas Aquinas College in New York.

J.D. MCCLATCHY (B. 1945)

Editor, critic, scholar, and poet, J. D. McClatchy has published five books of poetry, the most recent, *Hazmat* (2003), taking its title from the familiar abbreviation for "Hazardous Materials," seen on trucks and containers. The title reflects McClatchy's style: its all-embracing diction, diverse subject matter, and utter sophistication of form. He teaches at Yale and is the editor of *The Yale Review*.

WALTER MCDONALD (B. 1934)

Walt McDonald has published twenty-two collections of poetry, on subjects from Saigon to the Southwest. His latest book is *Faith is a Radical Master* (2005). In May, 2002, he retired from Texas Tech University. From 1957 to 1971, he was a stateside pilot and instructor in the U.S. Air Force. From 1969 to 1970, he served in Vietnam.

THOMAS MCGRATH (1916–1990)

Describing his politics as "unaffiliated far left," Thomas McGrath's views began forming when he worked as a labor organizer on the West Side docks of New York City. McGrath was born near Sheldon, North Dakota, publishing his first poems in 1940. During World War II, he served with the Army Air Force in the Aleutian Islands. After he appeared as an unfriendly witness before the House Un-American Activities Committee, McGrath was dismissed from his job at Los Angeles State University. Later, teaching at North Dakota State University and Moorehead State University, he founded the journal *Crazy Horse*.

HERMAN MELVILLE (1819–1891)

Next to Walt Whitman's sensual elegiac lyricism or Emily Dickinson's swift memorable compression, Herman Melville's poems are apt to seem rough, his rhyme forced and often clumsily mechanical. Yet nothing quite equals the restrained but deeply felt grief of "Balls Bluff" or "Shiloh: a Requiem." Melville was a keen observer of the politics of the Civil War, and one who understood that the advances in technology that the ironclad ships represented would undermine traditional heroic codes. During the war, the doughty seaman who had written of whaling in *Moby Dick* and of naval life in *White Jacket* was not too far into middle age to visit a camp of soldiers, sleep on the ground, and join a scouting party of younger friends and relatives going after Mosby's Rangers. After the war, he was a generous advocate of reconciliation with the South.

WILLIAM MEREDITH (B. 1919)

Graduating from Princeton in 1940, William Meredith spent the next five years in the armed services, most of it as a naval aviator in the Pacific theater. After a Woodrow Wilson Fellowship and resident fellowship in creative writing—both at Princeton—Meredith took up active service again, reenlisting to fly missions in the Korean War in 1952. A prolific writer, he was born in New York City.

W. S. MERWIN (B. 1927)

A contemporary of Galway Kinnell's at Princeton, William Stanley Merwin graduated in 1947, initiating his writing career as a poet and translator in the 1950s. Living intermittently in France and England in the 1950s and 1960s, Merwin continued the translations of French and Spanish classic and modern poetry that have gained him as much recognition as his own poems. Because of their technical variety, Merwin's poems have been associated with aesthetic movements as widely different as neoformalism and ecopoetry. During the Vietnam War, he was active in protests. Currently, he teaches at the University of Hawaii, where he lives on an old pineapple plantation he is restoring to rainforest. A native of New Jersey, Merwin's first writing began with hymns for his father, a Protestant minister.

EDNA ST. VINCENT MILLAY (1892–1950)

Millay was recognized at once as a star of her generation; her poem "Renascence" was published in 1912, when she was nineteen. In 1923, Millay was the first woman to win a Pulitzer Prize. By the 1950s, however, what had initially been perceived as dazzling became, for a later generation, a shallow facility: recently, critics have begun to reverse this judgment, and the tight, witty sonnets, the defiant feminism, the radical political passion, and the raw energy and generosity of spirit of her writing have won Millay fresh admirers. She was born in Rockland, Maine, graduated from Vassar College in 1917, and as a playwright was associated with the Provincetown Playhouse during its peak years.

JOAQUIN [CINCINNATUS HINER] MILLER (1837–1913)

Joaquin Miller liked to boast that he was born in a covered wagon "pointed west"; he and his family left Indiana to arrive in the Oregon Territory in 1852. In his youth, Miller lived with Indians, was wounded in an Indian massacre, and briefly jailed for horse theft in Shasta, California. He became a partner in a pony express service, practiced law and journalism, and was elected to a judgeship in Oregon. His florid, declamatory poems were first published in 1868; from 1870, he sought and won literary success in New York and London, drawing his pen name from the Mexican bandit Joaquin Murietta. During the Civil War, his sympathies lay with the Confederate side.

WILLIAM VAUGHAN MOODY (1869–1910)

William Vaughan Moody entered the national arena to protest the conversion of the Spanish-American War into a war of imperial acquisition; he followed this position with a further objection to the quelling of Philippine independence. Moody was raised in Indiana, and wrote both plays and poems. He died of cancer at the age of forty-one.

MARIANNE MOORE (1887–1972)

A poet of the High Modernist generation, Moore was born in Kirkwood, Missouri, and educated at Bryn Mawr, but she spent most of her adult life in New York, her Brooklyn apartment visited as a shrine of poetry by many leading writers. She was an influential editor at *The Dial*. Moore expressed her feelings about World War II with diffidence, saying to one correspondent in 1942: "I feel almost numbed by the irretrievable deaths the war is causing, am uncertain of permission to assert feelings in any direction." Yet Moore's poem "In Distrust of Merits" sturdily insists on the cause of war as within ourselves, naming all resistance to a reliance on force as personal duty.

JOHN NEAL (1793–1876)

The son of a Quaker schoolmaster, John Neal was born in what is now Portland, Maine. The partner of John Pierpont in a dry goods business, Neal was a member of a literary circle publishing *The Portico* until 1818; his friendship with Pierpont dissolved after an amatory quarrel. Active as a journalist, poet, and fiction writer, Neal found his connection terminated with the Friends Society because of a street brawl. He campaigned for women's rights, and defended the reputation of Edgar Allan Poe.

HOWARD NEMEROV (1920–1991)

Howard Nemerov's coolly ironic, frequently satiric poems resist conventional thinking or predictable mental patterning. He was born in New York City, educated at Fieldston, and graduated from Harvard in 1941. After a summer vacation, he enlisted in the Royal Canadian Air Force, becoming a pilot and flying combat missions from 1942 to 1944 against German shipping vessels in the North Sea. He joined the U.S. Army Air Corps for the last two years of the war. *War Stories: Poems About Long Ago and Now* (1987) contains much of Nemerov's caustic insight into war and politics. *The Collected Poems* (1977) contains even more of worth on these subjects.

DUANE NIATUM (B. 1938)

A Klallam Indian, Duane Niatum was born in Seattle, Washington, under the name McGinniss; after his parents' divorce, he assumed the name of his Klallam grandfather. At the age of seventeen, he enlisted in the Navy and served two years in Japan. Niatum edited *Carriers of the Dream Wheel: Contemporary Native American Poetry* in 1974, an early and influential collection of Indian poetry. The author of many books of poetry and fiction, he has written copiously about Indian artists and Indian culture.

JIM NYE (B. 1939)

Aftershock: Poems and Prose from the Vietnam War (1991) was written after Jim Nye returned from two twelve-month tours of duty in Vietnam. He was first a platoon leader with the 2/502D of the 101st Airborne, and then served with Command and Control South, Fifth Group, Special Forces. He writes of his book: "Some of these things happened. Some did not. But that does not matter, because all were true."

ADRIAN OKTENBERG (B. 1947)

Adrian Oktenberg's most recent book, *Swimming with Dolphins*, was published in 2002; *The Bosnia Elegies* appeared in 1997. She is currently involved in a non-fiction book about lesbian communities and has produced radio shows, taught law courses and creative writing, owned a bookstore, and lectured on women's studies.

SHARON OLDS (B. 1942)

Brought up in Berkeley, California as, in her words, "a hell-fire Calvinist," Sharon Olds translated that early ardor and drive into the sexually explicit, emotionally candid, and lyrical poems that have come to stand for the first-person orientation of her generation of poets. What this ignores is how Olds's poetry embodies the idea that the rigors of a bold, honest, and thorough exploration of the body's life cannot help but reflect the mind. The poem then becomes a vehicle for the pursuit of truths beyond the merely personal, often mirroring the politics and history of the larger society in which all bodies are planted.

GEORGE OPPEN (1908–1984)

Born in New Rochelle, New York, George Oppen and his wife moved to France and established To, Publishers, a press that published writers of the Objectivist movement. Returning to New York in the 1930s, Oppen joined the Communist Party and became an organizer in the Worker's Alliance. From 1940 to 1942, he was a factory worker in Detroit, Michigan, and then served in the U.S. Army from 1942 to 1945, where he was wounded just before V-E Day. After working as a carpenter in Los Angeles, because of harassment by the FBI, in 1950, Oppen and his family fled to Mexico City, where they stayed until 1958, refusing to inform on friends and colleagues. These were dry years: Oppen returned to writing late in the 1950s, after political witch hunting had died down. Oppen's book *Of Being Numerous* won a Pulitzer Prize in 1969; this poetry contains the distillate of Oppen's thinking about poetry and politics, and includes the evocative writing on his experience in World War II, which the agitation against the Vietnam War had dislodged.

THOMAS PAINE (1737–1809)

Thomas Paine was the son of a Quaker corset maker; he began in that trade and then collected excise taxes before immigrating to Philadelphia in 1774. There he published *Common Sense*, issued in 1776, a clear and powerful argument for American independence, republicanism over monarchy, and equal rights for men. His influence on the writing of the Declaration of Independence was considerable. Returning to Europe in 1787, he wrote *Rights of Man* in response to Edmund Burke's *Reflections on the Revolution in France*. A fervent abolitionist, Paine continued his opposition to the monarchy, and pressed such policies as progressive taxation, retirement benefits, and public employment. Charged with seditious libel, he fled to revolutionary France, ultimately being imprisoned for resisting the Reign of Terror. Returning to America in 1802, he came under attack by evangelical Christians for his deism, eventually dying in miserable circumstances.

BASIL PAQUET (B. 1944)

Along with Larry Rottman and Jan Barry, Basil Paquet was the first to collect soldier poems from the Vietnam War, and was among the first to note that these poems, unlike previous war poems, openly acknowledged the complicity of American soldiers in war's atrocities. Their anthology, *Winning Hearts and Minds: War Poems by Vietnam Veterans*, refused to present the soldier wholly as a victim of bad policy, as earlier protest poems had done. This anthology, which Paquet helped edit and that contained his poems, appeared in 1972. Basil Paquet served in the U.S. Army from 1966 to 1968; he was a medic in Vietnam from 1967 to 1968.

JOHN PIERPONT (1785–1866)

Preacher, lawyer, and candidate for political office in Massachusetts, John Pierpont wrote the sort of elevated verbiage considered essential for a man of culture in his time. As a young man, he was admitted to the Massachusetts bar, subsequently floundering in both law and business. In 1819, he was ordained as a minister at the Hollis Street Unitarian Church in Boston. His health declining, he traveled in Europe and the biblical lands; in 1848, he became the minister of the Unitarian Church in Medford. At the age of seventy, he served as a chaplain for the U.S. Army.

EZRA POUND (1885–1972)

One of the half dozen modernist poets who reshaped poetry in the English language, Ezra Pound was born in Hailey, Idaho, to an old American family proud to boast at least one horse thief, as well as a grandfather who built a railway. The family moved to Philadelphia, where during his college and university years Pound began his lifelong friendship with H. D. and William Carlos Williams. In England,

Pound edited, translated, lectured, and published poetry and cultural and literary criticism, energetically promoting the careers of T. S. Eliot, James Joyce, and Robert Frost, among others. Sections of Pound's "Hugh Selwyn Mauberley," published in 1920, epitomized his sense of the waste of human life that was World War I trench warfare. By World War II, Pound had moved to Rapallo, Italy, where he became an ardent supporter of Mussolini. During that war, he broadcast a series of talks full of hysterical anti-Semitism and Roosevelt-baiting. In 1943, he was indicted for treason by a federal grand jury, and in 1944 imprisoned in a stockade camp in Pisa. *The Pisan Cantos*, begun in imprisonment and continuing earlier *Cantos*, are collage-like, fragmented in syntax, disjunctive in narrative, occasionally ranting, and very beautiful in isolated passages. Declared mentally unfit to stand trial for treason, Pound was institutionalized at St. Elizabeth's Hospital in Washington, D.C. In 1958, poets including Archibald MacLeish and Robert Frost interceded, and his indictment was quashed. Pound died in Italy.

LUCY TERRY PRINCE (1730–1821)

The first black American poet, Lucy Terry came to Rhode Island as an enslaved child, and was eventually bought by Ebenezer Wells of Deerfield, a community in which she became well known as a storyteller. When she married Abijah Prince, a freedman who purchased his wife's freedom, Lucy Terry moved with him to Vermont. "Bars Fight" (1746) is her only surviving poem, and was handed down for generations in Deerfield until it was published by Josiah Holland in his *History of Western Massachusetts* in 1885.

INNES RANDOLPH (1837–1887)

A lawyer and poet born in Winchester, Virginia, Innes Randolph served in the Confederate Army as a topographical engineer, with a rank of major. After the Civil War, he published sketches and poems in newspapers, eventually becoming the editorial writer at *The Baltimore American*. Randolph's *Poems* appeared in 1898, compiled by his son.

LIZETTE WOODWORTH REESE (1856–1935)

A poet of small, tight, vivid rhymes, into which a great deal of restrained feeling is poured, Lizette Woodworth Reese taught school for forty-five years, half of them in Baltimore, Maryland. *Spicewood*, from which "A War Memory: 1865" is taken, appeared in 1920. Her autobiographical novel *Victorian Village* appeared in 1929.

CARTER REVARD (B. 1931)

Born in Pawhuska, Oklahoma, part Osage on his father's side, Carter Revard grew up in the Buck Creek Valley, working in the hay and harvest fields and graduating from a one-room schoolhouse in Buck Creek. Winning a radio quiz scholarship to the University of Tulsa, he achieved a B.A. in 1952, and then a second B.A. at Oxford University, where he was a Rhodes Scholar. His scholarly work has been in medieval English and American Indian literature. He has published many collections of poems, including *Winning the Dust Bowl* and *Family Matters, Tribal Affairs.*

ADRIENNE RICH (B. 1929)

The daughter of a Jewish doctor in the segregated South, Adrienne Rich was groomed early for intellectual and creative achievement, later using this experience of male authoritarianism as the ground for feminist rebellion, as well as for an early experience of privilege. Her first book, *A Change of World*, was selected for the Yale Younger Poets Award by W. H. Auden, who commended the book for its poetic good manners. Since that time, Rich has moved fiercely and steadily toward a strongly individual voice full of respect for ambivalence and complexity. All of her writing has been marked by a search for an ethical stance as both a public and a private citizen. Readers have come to admire the large, bold ambitions of Rich's poetry, as well as its sensual richness and self-questioning morality. Her latest collection is titled *The School Among the Ruins* (2005). Rich lives in northern California.

DALE RITTERBUSCH (B. 1946)

Dale Ritterbusch served in the U.S. Army as a medic from 1969 to 1971; during 1970, he was stationed in Vietnam and elsewhere in southeastern Asia. He currently teaches English at Colorado State University. His books include *Laotian Fragments*, a work of fiction. Ritterbusch compiled and edited *Vietnam Voices*, and has also written critical and scholarly books about both English and American literature.

EDWIN ROLFE (1909–1954)

Known as the Poet of the Lincoln Brigade, Edwin Rolfe was born Solomon Fishman, to leftist Russian Jewish emigrants, who moved with their son to Coney Island in New York. Rolfe joined the Communist Party when he was fifteen and published his first poem in *The Daily Worker* in 1927. Living in New York as a left-wing journalist, Fishman adopted the pen name Edwin Rolfe. In 1937, after hiking from France into Spain through the Pyrenees, Rolfe trained for a fighting unit, but instead was tapped as an editor for *Volunteer for Liberty*. Until August 1938, Rolfe stayed in Madrid, two kilometers away from the front, under fascist siege and frequent bombardment. Rolfe then joined the brigadistas in the field for the Ebro campaign, and soon took over as Spanish correspondent for *The Daily Worker* and *New Masses*, leaving Spain in 1939. Rolfe entered the U.S. Army briefly in 1943, until illness caused his withdrawal. He lived most of the rest of his life in California, and during the postwar era wrote against the harassment and blacklisting of the left.

LEE ANN RORIPAUGH (B. 1965)

Of mixed Japanese and Anglo parentage, Lee Ann Roripaugh was born and raised in Laramie, Wyoming. Her degrees include an M.F.A. in creative writing. Selected as a winner in the National Poetry Series of 1998, *Beyond Heart Mountain* was Roripaugh's first book. The sequence "Heart Mountain, 1943" consists of dramatic monologues told by Japanese-American detainees. She lives in Columbus, Ohio.

WENDY ROSE (B. 1948)

Wendy Rose was born Bronwen Elizabeth Edwards in Oakland, California, to a mixed-blood family: her father was Hopi; her mother descended from both Miwok and European stock. Attending several colleges in California, Rose went on to complete a Ph.D. in anthropology at the University of California at Berkeley. She has published a dozen books of poetry dealing with Native American life, legend, and culture. *Bone Dance: New and Selected Poems, 1965–1992* appeared in 1993.

JEROME ROTHENBERG (B. 1931)

Perhaps best known as the editor of *Technicians of the Sacred* (1968), Rothenberg promoted the idea that "primitive" or archaic poetries had their own links to later avant-garde experimentalism through a universal, mythic consciousness. Rothenberg embraced exuberantly ambient sounds, opening reception to all styles of oral poetry, leading to his own coinages, like *ethnopoetics*, and toward the technique of the *deep image*. His own fusion of the irreverent and the sacred is evident in his poems, even in those that give a full range of language and sensation in response to the Shoah; this work is collected in *Poland/1931* (1969, 1974) and in *Khurbn, and Other Poems* (1989). He was born in New York City, and served in the U.S. Army in 1954 and 1955.

MURIEL RUKEYSER (1913–1980)

Interested in all aspects of modernism, Muriel Rukeyser never underrated the powers of poetry to alter consciousness, and by altering consciousness, to alter the world. In the 1930s, *The Book of the Dead* both celebrated and protested the death by silicosis of West Virginia coal miners; she later traveled to Spain, supporting the loyalist cause. During World War II, she worked for the Office of War Information; in 1972, she traveled to Hanoi with Denise Levertov to protest

American participation in the Vietnam War. Later she was an activist for human rights, flying to Korea as the president of P.E.N., the writers' organization, to denounce Korean treatment of poet Kim Cha.

MARY JO SALTER (B. 1954)

At Harvard, Mary Jo Salter worked with Elizabeth Bishop and Anthony Hecht. While engaging largely with domestic and familiar subjects, Salter's poems, widely published, also examine the history and politics of her time. She is an editor and essayist, and teaches at Mount Holyoke College.

CARL SANDBURG (1878–1967)

Of his *Chicago Poems*, published in 1916, Carl Sandburg said that he wanted "to sing, blab, chortle, yodel, like people, and people in the sense of being subtracted from formal doctrines." The open lyricism and journalistic accessibility of his poems was part of his advocacy for a working-class America. Born in Galesburg, Illinois, of Swedish parents, at twenty, Sandburg enlisted in the Spanish-American War, writing letters back to his hometown newspaper about being a private in Puerto Rico. Initially at loose ends before cobbling together a career in journalism, he rode the rails and served ten days in a Pittsburgh jail. A popular poet and public figure, Sandburg supported himself through his writing, combining a hatred of injustice with an old-fashioned egalitarian faith in America.

REG SANER (B. 1929)

"I have not really tried to write about Korea," Reg Saner has said. "I wanted to forget." Coming from Jacksonville, Illinois, Saner entered the army as an officer, serving in Korea in 1952 and 1953, where he was an infantry platoon leader for six months and was awarded a Bronze Star. Much of his post–Korean War poetry deals with outdoor life and the American West. *The Ontario Review* published "Flag Memoir" in 1991. Those war poems that Saner has allowed to surface are savagely satiric accounts of military glory.

ALAN SEEGER (1888–1916)

Graduating from Harvard in 1910, Alan Seeger went to Paris, and at the start of World War I, had enlisted in the French Foreign Legion. Of death in battle, he wrote: "Why flinch? It is by far the noblest form in which death can come. It is in a sense almost a privilege." He was killed at the Battle of the Somme at Belloy-en-Santerre, on July 4, 1916. Seeger echoes the sentiments of noble death expressed by British poets like Rupert Brooke or Julian Grenfell; the bitter, angry poems of Wilfred Owen and Siegfried Sassoon were the mark of a later attitude to World War I and its battles of attrition.

KARL SHAPIRO (1913–2000)

Poet and critic Karl Shapiro was born in Baltimore, and published his first book, *Poems*, in 1935. In World War II, he served as a medical corps clerk in the South Pacific, largely in New Guinea. *V-Letter*, written during wartime, shared the largely conventional poetic manners of the time. The book, published in 1944, won the Pulitzer Prize. A stinging and articulate critic of contemporary poetry, Shapiro was an influential editor at *Poetry* and *Prairie Schooner*.

CHARLES SIMIC (B. 1938)

Charles Simic was born in Belgrade, Yugoslavia at the onset of World War II. Caught between opposing partisan factions at the close of World War II, Simic's family emigrated first to France, then eventually arrived as refugees in the United States. Simic is a prolific translator, essayist, and cultural commentator, having published over a dozen collections of poetry. *A Fly in the Soup* (2002) contains his wartime memoirs. Charles Simic teaches at the University of New Hampshire.

WILLIAM GILMORE SIMMS (1806–1870)

William Gilmore Simms was born in Charleston, South Carolina. Simms studied law, and then devoted himself to writing in poetry, fiction, biography, political treatises, and essays on literature. The novel *Yemassee* (1835) is his most widely known work. An ardent defender of slavery who drew hostile crowds in New York, he returned to settle at his wife's estate in Charleston. During the Civil War, he saw this home destroyed by stragglers from Sherman's army. He fled to Columbia, South Carolina, and witnessed the burning of that city. After the war, he struggled to earn a living as a journalist and editor.

LOUIS SIMPSON (B. 1923)

Born in Kingston, Jamaica, Simpson's sense of identity was split between his Jamaican father and his Russian Jewish mother. His subsequent attendance at Columbia University in New York City was interrupted in 1943 by World War II. He served as a company runner in the 101st Airborne Division during the Battle of the Bulge in 1944. In autobiographical essays, Simpson describes the effect of the war on his life and his poetry: after returning to Columbia, he had blocked his memories of the war; when those memories broke through, he was hospitalized for war trauma. Thereafter, he wrote some of the sharpest and most moving American poems about surviving battle.

GEORGE STARBUCK (1931–1996)

For many years, George Starbuck directed the writing program at Boston University; before that he was the director of the Writer's Workshop at the University of Iowa, and before that, an editor. "Of Late," from *White Paper*, remains one of the most striking poems of the Vietnam War era.

WALLACE STEVENS (1879–1955)

A fragment of a Wallace Stevens poem is instantly recognizable as his. A master of playful, colorful, and evocative language and of brilliant, exotic imagery, Stevens also wrote poems distinguished for their philosophic weight. Born in Reading, Pennsylvania, he attended Harvard and was admitted to the bar in 1904. He spent most of his life as a lawyer and administrator for the Hartford Accident and Indemnity Company. "The Death of A Soldier," written with World War I in mind, is decorous and respectful of conventional pieties. The last section of "Notes Toward a Supreme Fiction," published first in the dark year of 1942, is in stark contrast, affirming the prior importance not of the man of war but of the poet who gives the soldier the "proper words" and "the bread of faithful speech." Here the sundering between the poet's and the soldier's duties is quite differently rendered than for a poet like Edwin Rolfe, who saw the necessity of linking ideas and action.

FRANK STEWART (B. 1946)

Frank Stewart left the United States during the Vietnam War. He has published two collections of poetry, *The Open Water* and *Flying the Red Eye*, as well as edited several collections of poetry and fiction that center on Hawaiian writing. He is a professor of English at the University of Hawaii.

LUCIEN STRYK (B. 1924)

Born in Chicago, Lucien Stryk served in the U.S. Army during World War II. A translator of Japanese, Stryk has published many books of his own poetry and teaches at Northern Illinois University at Dekalb.

GENEVIEVE TAGGARD (1894–1948)

Raised by Christian missionary parents, Genevieve Taggard published her first poem as a student at Berkeley. From this early beginning, she wrote a poetry guided by her principles as an activist dedicated to social change. In New York, she played a vigorous role in radical journals like *The Masses*, *The Freeman*, and *The Liberator*. "To the Veterans of the Abraham Lincoln Brigade" was written in defiance of the House Un-American Activities Committee, who were investigating these veterans and looking for possible indictments.

ALLEN TATE (1899–1979)

For Allen Tate, his identity as a Southerner was a major component of his identity. Born in Winchester, Kentucky, to a family that on his mother's side had been slaveowning planters, Tate was associated with the Fugitive and Agrarian movements. Southerners all, they viewed modern industrialization with repugnance. In Tate's ornate and densely allusive "Ode to the Confederate Dead," the Confederates represented "not merely moral heroism but heroism in the grand style, elevating even death from mere physical dissolution into a formal ritual."

JAMES TATE (B. 1943)

James Tate was born in Kansas City, Missouri, during the year that his pilot father was reported missing in Germany. He received an M.F.A. in creative writing from the University of Iowa. At twenty-three, he won the Yale Younger Poets Award with his collection *The Lost Pilot*. The title poem of the collection is dedicated to his father. Other collections of poems, like *The Oblivion Ha-Ha* (1972), have relied increasingly on a tricky negotiation between levels of diction and on wry surrealist manipulation.

ELEANOR ROSS TAYLOR (B. 1920)

A native of North Carolina, Eleanor Ross Taylor now lives in Charlottesville, Virginia. Married to the writer Peter Taylor, she was part of a circle that included Randall Jarrell and Robert Lowell. While Taylor's Southern background is essential to the quality of voice she projects in her tightly woven, sparsely lyrical poems, it is not the august South of spacious and entitled tradition, but something much grittier. History is an active and formidable presence, informing the lives of her struggling protagonists. *Days Going/Days Coming Back* (1992) collects her early and later work.

SARA TEASDALE (1884–1933)

First published in 1907, Sara Teasdale became immensely popular for her romantic themes and pleasing poetic manners. *Flame and Shadow* (1920) is the book regarded by most critics as containing her best work, showing to best advantage her metrical deftness. Although she had married and divorced a businessman, the poet Vachel Lindsay had been a suitor. His suicide in 1931 affected her deeply, and two years later she ended her own life with an overdose of pills. *The Collected Poems of Sara Teasdale* appeared in 1937.

DIANE THIEL (B. 1967)

Born in Coral Gables, Florida, Diane Thiel grew up in Miami Beach. She has traveled extensively throughout Europe and South America, and was a Fulbright scholar recently in Odessa. Besides teaching creative writing in many schools, she has been a longtime participant in the National Science Foundation's interdisciplinary program, Ecology for Urban Students. Her first collection of poems, *Echo-locations*, appeared in 2000.

HENRY DAVID THOREAU (1817–1862)

Famous mostly as the author of *Walden*, one of the primary documents of the New England transcendental embrace of nature above a materialist striving, Henry David Thoreau also wrote poems. "When with Pale Cheek and Sunken Eye I Sang" is curiously aligned with other, more traditional laments, however, which mourn the passing of the heroic. Thoreau himself was jailed for refusing to pay a tax he believed would support the Mexican-American War. His 1849 essay on this subject, "Civil Disobedience," became the classic argument in favor of dissent from militarism, and its ethical positions were frequently cited by conscientious objectors in later wars.

HENRY TIMROD (1826–1867)

Henry Timrod, born in Charleston, South Carolina, was one of the better-known Confederate poets. After studying at what became the University of Georgia, he began publishing love poems and poems idealizing Southern life. During the Civil War, he enlisted in the Confederate army, but was discharged because of ill health. In his last years he married, lost his only son in infancy, and suffered poverty and illness, dying of tuberculosis two years after the war ended.

BARBARA TRAN (B. 1965?)

Barbara Tran earned an M.F.A. at Columbia University. Along with Monique T. D. Truong and Luu Truong, she edited *Watermark*, a collection of Vietnamese poetry and prose written in America. Tran's first poetry collection, *In the Mynah Bird's Own Words*, was a winner of the Tupelo Press chapbook competition. Most of her life has been spent in New York City.

BRIAN TURNER (B. 1967)

For seven years, Brian Turner served with the U.S. Army. In the second Iraq War, he led the Third Stryker Brigade Combat Team, Second Infantry Division; prior to that, in 1999 and 2000, he deployed to Bosnia-Herzegovina with the Tenth Mountain Division. Before his military service, Turner earned an MFA at the University of Oregon. His work is featured in the documentary film *Voices in Wartime*. Turner was born in Visalia, California.

ROBERT PENN WARREN (1905–1989)

A poet, fiction writer, and influential critic, Robert Penn Warren was born in Guthrie, Kentucky, and graduated *summa cum laude* from Vanderbilt University in 1925. Arguably his best novel, *All the King's Men* (1946) is a fictionalized account of Louisiana politician Huey Long. Starting out as a colleague of Allen Tate and John Crowe Ransom, Warren was associated with the Agrarian movement; yet eventually Warren pulled away from Southern conservatism and came openly to support the growing civil rights movement. Generations of college students cut their critical teeth on Cleanth Brooks and Robert Penn Warren's *Understanding Poetry*, a leading text in the New Critical school of reading.

BRUCE WEIGL (B. 1949)

In the U.S. Army from 1967 to 1970, Weigl was trained in communications. He served in Vietnam in 1967 and 1968, with the First Air Cavalry. Weigl collaborated with Thanh T. Nguyen to produce *Poems from Captured Documents*, or Vietnamese soldier poems, in 1994. He has published nine books of poetry, written critical books, and edited anthologies. He writes: "The paradox of my life as a writer is that the war ruined my life and in return gave me my voice." In 1996, Weigl returned to Vietnam with the purpose of adopting a Vietnamese child; *The Circle of Hanh* is the story of that journey. *The Monkey Wars* (1985) and *Song of Napalm* (1988) were the principal books in which Weigl wrote powerfully about his war.

PHILLIS WHEATLEY (1753–1784)

Purchased for the Wheatley family of Boston directly from a West African slave ship, Phillis Wheatley was not emancipated until the age of fourteen, when she was already a writer. Her first poem appeared in *The Newport Mercury* of Rhode Island in 1767. Because of the difficulty raised in America for publishing a black woman, Wheatley's first book, *Poems on Various Subjects, Religious and Moral*, appeared first in England. After the death of the Wheatleys, Phillis was left destitute. She married another free African, John Peters; poverty forced the family to a boarding house, where all three of their children died. Subsequently, Phillis became very ill and died, and was buried in an unmarked grave with her third child. To the last, she refused to sell for food the copy of Milton's *Paradise Lost* that Benjamin Franklin had given her. Written in splendid formal meters, Wheatley's poems manage to suggest her equality as a Christian woman; her address to Washington makes clear that it is his virtue and his dedication to freedom that make him great.

WALT WHITMAN (1819–1892)

Walt Whitman was born in Brooklyn, one of nine children. At twelve he began in the printer's trade, and fell in love with language. Self-taught, he read Homer, Dante, Shakespeare, and the Bible. At seventeen a teacher, then a carpenter, in 1836, he turned to journalism. In 1848, he left the *Brooklyn Eagle* for New Orleans, where for the first time he experienced slavery. Back in Brooklyn, he founded a Free Soil paper, *The Brooklyn Freeman*. By 1855, he sold his house to pay to have *Leaves of Grass* published, eventually winning the stamp of approval from Ralph Waldo Emerson. While it took decades for Whitman to establish a reputation, after him, American poetry was never the same: the ardent, original energy, the comprehensive, egalitarian outlook, and the bursting exuberant detail have never been matched. While Whitman published most of his best work before the outbreak of the Civil War, at least a dozen poems drawn from his experience as a nurse, comforter, and companion of wounded soldiers stand out. In 1861, Whitman moved to Washington, D.C., and through a series of small government posts and with the help of various benefactors, he continued his daily visits to local hospitals. After the war, his health broken by the unending intensity of his vigils, he received a small government pension in recognition of his services.

JOHN GREENLEAF WHITTIER (1807–1892)

Author of the much-beloved poem "Snowbound," Whittier was born in Haverhill, Massachusetts, to a Quaker family, and paid for his early education by making slippers. A schoolteacher, bookkeeper, and dedicated abolitionist in early life, in addition to a long and distinguished career as a man of letters, he later served as a newspaper editor and state legislator. As a presidential elector, Whittier voted for Lincoln four times.

RICHARD WILBUR (B. 1921)

The elegance of Wilbur's fine ear and fine eye for detail are always in fertile and creative disagreement with his nose for chaos and disorder in the world. Of war and how it shaped his attitude toward his craft, he writes: "It was not until World War II took me to Cassino, Anzio, and the Siegfried Line that I began to versify in earnest." Wilbur served in the signal company of the Thirty-sixth Infantry Division in Italy, France, and Germany. He was born in New York City and attended Amherst College. His verse translations of Moliere and Racine have been frequently produced; he wrote the book for the musical *Candide*, based on the classic by Voltaire, collaborating with Leonard Bernstein. In 1987 he was the poet laureate of the United States.

C. K. WILLIAMS (B. 1936)

The wide, discursive lines that C. K. Williams has used for much of his poetry challenge our sense of lyric compression, urging a greater role for a different music, a different rhythm. He has published numerous books of poetry, the latest, *The Singing*, in 2003, as well as five works of translation. C. K. Williams was born in Newark, New Jersey. He teaches in the creative writing program at Princeton University, and until recently has lived a part of every year in Paris.

ELEANOR WILNER (B. 1937)

A native of Ohio, Eleanor Wilner's *Reversing the Spell: New and Selected Poems* appeared in 1998. She is a former editor of *The American Poetry Review* and a contributing editor of *Calyx.* She earned a B.A. from Goucher College and an M.A. and Ph.D. from Johns Hopkins University; she has held a MacArthur Foundation Fellowship. Wilner is currently a faculty member for the M.F.A. Program in Writing at Warren Wilson College.

KEITH WILSON (B. 1927)

A native of Clovis, New Mexico, Keith Wilson had initially intended a career in the Navy. As an ensign fresh out of the Naval Academy, he went to Korea for his first tour of duty, returning from two more periods of service in Korean waters in 1953. He writes: "I expected nothing from war . . . I was a professional. I didn't, however, expect to be lied to and betrayed. I was very proud of the U.N. flag at our mast head when we went in to launch attacks. When I found out that Korea was all a very dirty and murderous joke, I was silenced for many years." His book of poems, *Graves Registry,* from which the poems in this anthology were taken, was written in 1966, provoked by anger at American involvement in Vietnam. Wilson is an emeritus professor at New Mexico State University, with an interest in the culture and history of the Southwest.

JAMES WRIGHT (1927–1980)

Writing early poems of great delicacy and formal elegance, James Wright shifted his style to something looser, far more personal, and wildly distinctive in his book *The Branch Will Not Break* (1963). *Above the River: The Complete Poems* appeared in 1990. Writing within the emotional parameters of his working-class background, Wright's later poems show a potent lyric tenderness in a leveling American diction, and his free verse remains a tonal and technical model for many. His love of American culture, however, did not preclude a wide and sophisticated reading, evident in his work. Wright was born in Martins Ferry, Ohio, and he graduated *cum laude* in 1952 from Kenyon College. He served in the U.S. Occupation Forces in Japan in 1946 and 1947.

RAY A. YOUNG BEAR (B. 1950)

A member of the Mesquakiehe tribe, Young Bear is the author of several collections of poetry, and the editor of *Stories from the Woodland Region,* a collection of stories, memoirs, translations, and traditional tribal tales. His last collection, *The Invisible Musician* (1990), mediates between the collective and the individual modern voice.

FURTHER ACKNOWLEDGMENTS
AND PERMISSIONS

Thomas Bailey Aldrich, "Accomplices" and Fredericksburg," from *Aldrich's Complete Poems* (Boston: Houghton Mifflin, 1907).

American Indian Poetry, "Song for A Fallen Warrior," 680; from *American Poetry: The Nineteenth Century*, vol. 2, ed. John Hollander (New York: The Library of America, 1993).

"Cherokee War Song," Versions 1, 2, from Henry Rowe Schoolcraft, *Archives of Original Knowledge*, 1860.

Doug Anderson, "Infantry Assault," "Purification," "Papasan," from *The Moon Reflected Fire* (Farmington, Maine: Alice James Books, 1994).

Philip Appleman, "Peace with Honor," from *New and Selected Poems 1956–1996* (Fayetteville, Ark.: The University of Arkansas Press, 1996).

John Balaban, "April 30, 1975," from *Blue Mountain* (Greensboro, N.C.: Unicorn Press, 1974, 1982); "Thoughts Before Dawn," from *Locusts at the Edge of Summer: New and Selected Poems* (Port Townsend, Wash.: Copper Canyon Press, 1997).

Joel Barlow, from *The Columbiad* (Philadelphia: C. & A. Conrad and Co.; Baltimore: Conrad, Lucas & Company, 1809); "Advice to a Raven in Russia," *Huntington Library Quarterly*, October 1938.

Wendy Battin, "Mondrian's Forest," from *Little Apocalypse* (Ashland, Ohio: Ashland Poetry Press, 1997).

Ambrose Bierce, "The Confederate Flags," from *Phantoms of a Blood-Stained Period: The Complete Civil War Writings of Ambrose Bierce*, ed. Russell Duncan, David J. Klooster (Amherst: University of Massachusetts Press, 2002).

Elizabeth Bishop, "From Trollope's Journal," from *The Complete Poems 1927–1979* (New York: Farrar, Straus & Giroux, 1983).

Alexander Bergman, "To Eugene J. Loveman," from *They Look Like Men* (New York: Bernard Ackerman, 1944).

Robert Bly, "Counting Small Boned Bodies," from *Eating the Honey of Words: New and Selected Poems* (New York: Harper Collins, 1999).

Louise Bogan, "To My Brother Killed: Haumont Wood: October, 1918," from *The Blue Estuaries: Poems, 1923–1968* (New York: Farrar, Straus & Giroux, 1975).

Joseph Brodsky, "Bosnia Tune," from *Collected Poems in English* (New York: Farrar, Straus & Giroux, 2000).

Gwendolyn Brooks, "Negro Hero," from *Blacks* (Chicago: Third World Press, 1945, 1987). By permission of Brooks Permissions.

D. F. Brown, "When I Am 19 I Was a Medic," from *Returning Fire* (San Francisco: San Francisco State University Poetry Chapbook, 1984).

William Cullen Bryant, "The Disinterred Warrior," from *The Prairies: Poems* (New York: Harper & Bros, 1836).

Hayden Carruth, "On a Certain Engagement South of Seoul" and "On Being Asked to Write a War Poem," from *Collected Shorter Poems 1946–1991* (Port Townsend, Wash.: Copper Canyon Press, 1992).

William Childress, "Trying to Remember People I Never Really Knew," from *Burning the Years and Lobo: Poems, 1962–1975* (East St. Louis, Ill.: Essai Seay Publications, 1986).

Bao Long Chu, "My Mother's Pearls," from *From Both Sides Now: The Poetry of the Vietnam War and Its Aftermath*, ed. Phillip Mahony (New York: Scribner Poetry, 1998).

John Ciardi, "Elegy Just in Case" and "A Box Comes Home," from *The Collected Poems of John Ciardi* (Fayetteville, Ark.: The University of Arkansas Press, 1997.)

Horace Coleman, "OK Corral East," from *In the Grass* (Woodbridge, Conn.: Vietnam Generation, Inc., and Burning Cities Press, 1995). By permission of the author.

David Connolly, "The Little Man," from *Lost in America* (Woodbridge, Conn: Vietnam Generation, Inc., and Burning Cities Press, 1994). By permission of the author.

Jane Cooper, "The Faithful," from *The Flashboat* (New York: W. W. Norton, 2000).

Malcolm Cowley, "Chateau de soupir: 1917," from *Blue Juniata: A Life* (New York: Penguin, 1985).

Stephen Crane, "War Is Kind" and "The Battle Hymn," from *Poems and Literary Remains*, ed. Fredson Bowers (Charlottesville: University of Virginia Press).

Edward Estlin Cummings, "i sing of Olaf," from *Poems: 1923–1954* (New York: Harcourt, Brace & Company, 1954).

William DeForest, "In Louisiana," from *American War Ballads and Lyrics: A Collection of the Songs and Ballads of the Colonial Wars, the Revolution, the War of 1812–15, the War with Mexico, and the Civil War*, ed. George Cary Eggleston (New York: G. P. Putnam & Sons, 1889).

James Dickey, "Hunting Civil War Relics at Nimblewell Creek" and "The Fire-bombing," from *The Whole Motion: Collected Poems, 1945–1992* (Hanover, N.H.: Wesleyan University Press, 1992).

Emily Dickinson, "It feels a shame to be Alive—." From *The Poems of Emily Dickinson*, ed. Thomas H. Johnson (Cambridge, Mass.: Harvard University Press, 1958).

H.D. (Hilda Doolittle), "The Walls Do Not Fall," from *Trilogy* (New York: New Diections, 1973).

Norman Dubie, "Aubade of the Singer and Saboteur, Marie Triste: 1941," from *Selected and New Poems* (New York: W. W. Norton, 1983).

Alan Dugan, "Portrait from the Infantry" and "Fabrication of Ancestors," from *New and Collected Poems, 1961–1983* (New York: Ecco Press, 1983).

Paul Laurence Dunbar, "Black Samson of Brandywine," "The Unsung Heroes," and "The Conquerors: The Black Troops in Cuba," from *Collected Poetry*, ed. Joanne M. Braxton (Charlottesville: University of Virginia Press, 1993).

Richard Eberhart, "The Fury of Aerial Bombardment," from *Selected Poems, 1930–1965* (New York: New Directions, 1965).

W. D. Ehrhart, "Beautiful Wreckage," "How It All Comes Back," and "Finding My Old Battalion Command Post," from *Beautiful Wreckage: New and Selected Poems* (Easthampton, Mass.: Adastra Press, 1999)

T. S. Eliot, "Coriolan: Part I: Triumphal March," from *Collected Poems, 1909–1962* (New York: Harcourt Brace, 1964) Reprinted with the permission of Harcourt, Inc., and Faber and Faber.

Ralph Waldo Emerson, "Concord Hymn" and "Ode, Inscribed to W. H. Channing," from *The Collected Poems and Translations of Ralph Waldo Emerson*, ed. Harold Bloom and Paul Kane (New York: Library of America, 1994).

Louise Erdrich, "Dear John Wayne" and "Captivity," from *Original Fire: Selected and New Poems* (New York: Harper Collins, 2003).

Martin Espada, "The Other Alamo," from *City of Coughing and Dead Radiators* (New York: W. W. Norton, 1993).

Carolyn Forché, "The Colonel," from *The Country Between Us* (New York: Harper Collins, 1981).

Philip Freneau, "The American Soldier," "Jeffery, or, The Soldier's Progress," "A New York Tory, to His Friend in Philadelphia," from *Poems Written and Published During the American Revolutionary War*, 3rd ed., vol. 2 (Philadelphia: Lydia R. Bailey, 1809).

Robert Frost, "Not to Keep," from *The Poetry of Robert Frost*, ed. Edward Connery Lathem (New York: Henry Holt, 1969).

Kristi Garboushian, from "The Ribbons on Hell's Tree." By permission of author.

Allen Ginsberg, from "Iron Horse," from *Collected Poems, 1947–1980* (New York: Harper Collins, 1984).

Rayna Green, "Coosaponakeesa." By permission of author.

Charlotte Forten Grimke, "The Gathering of the Grand Army," from *African-American Poetry of the Nineteenth Century*, ed. Joan R. Sherman (Urbana: University of Illinois Press, 1992).

Joy Harjo, "I Give You Back," from *She Had Some Horses* (New York: Thunder's Mouth Press, 1983).

Anthony Hecht, "Still Life," from *Collected Earlier Poems* (New York: Alfred A. Knopf, 1983).

Ernest Hemingway, "Champs d'Honneur" and "Riparto d'Assalto," from *Complete Poems* (Lincoln: University of Nebraska Press, 1992).

William Heyen, "The Steadying," from *Crazy Horse in Stillness* (Rochester, N.Y.: BOA Editions, 1996).

Rolando Hinojosa, "The January–May 1951 Slaughter" and "Jacob Mosqueda Wrestles with the Angels," from *Korean Love Songs: From Klail City Death Trip* (Berkeley, Calif.: Justa Publications, 1978).

Tony Hoagland, "The Kind of Shadow That Calls out Fate."

Oliver Wendell Holmes, "Old Ironsides," from *Poems* (Boston: Otis, Broaders, 1836).

Julia Ward Howe, "The Battle Hymn of the Republic," from *The Atlantic Monthly* (February 1862).

Andrew Hudgins, "The Road Home," from *After the Lost War* (New York: Houghton Mifflin, 1988).

David Huddle, "Work," "Haircut," and "Vermont," from *Summer Lake: New and Selected Poems* (Baton Rouge: Louisiana State University Press, 1999).

Langston Hughes, "Beaumont to Detroit, 1943," from *The Collected Poems of Langston Hughes*, ed. Arnold Rampersad (New York: Random House, 1995).

Richard Hugo, "On Hearing a New Escalation," from *Making Certain It Goes On: The Collected Poems of Richard Hugo* (New York: W. W. Norton, 1984).

Lawson Fusao Inada, "The Legend of the Great Escape," "The Legend of the Magic Marbles," "The Legend of the Full Moon Over Amache," from *Legends from Camp* (Minneapolis: Coffee House Press, 1993).

Dale Jacobson, "Night Vision of the Gulf War," from *After the Storm: Poems on the Persian Gulf War*, ed. Jay Meek and F. D. Reeve (Washington, D.C.: Maisonneuve Press, 1992).

Randall Jarrell, "Losses," "Prisoners," "The Death of the Ball Turret Gunner," "Protocols," and "The Truth," from *The Complete Poems* (New York: Farrar, Straus & Giroux, 1969, 1997). By permission of Mary von Schrader Jarrell.

Robinson Jeffers, "Sinverguenza," from *The Collected Poetry of Robinson Jeffers, 1928–1938*, vol. 2, ed. Tim Hunt (Palo Alto, Calif.: Stanford University Press).

Francis Scott Key, "The Defence of Fort McHenry," from *Analectic Magazine*, 1814.

Myung Mi Kim, "Under Flag," from *Under Flag* (Berkeley, Calif.: Kelsey Street Press, 1991).

Suji Kwock Kim, "The Chasm," from *Notes from the Divided Country* (Baton Rouge: Louisiana State University, 2003). Corrected text for "Fragments of a Forgotten War" provided by the author.

Galway Kinnell, "When the Twin Towers Fell," from *The New Yorker* (2002). By permission of author.

Lincoln Kirstein, "Snatch" and "DPs," from *Rhymes and More Rhymes of a PFC* (New York: New Directions, 1964).

Yusef Komunyakaa, "Starlight Scope Myopia," "Tu Do Street," "*Bui Doi*, Dust of Life," and "Facing It," from *Dien Cai Dao* (Hanover, N.H.: Wesleyan University Press/University Press of New England, 1988).

Greg Kuzma, "Peace, So That," from *Poetry* 120 (September 1972).

Sidney Lanier, "Laughter in the Senate," from *Sidney Lanier: Poems and Poem Outlines*, vol. 1, ed. Charles Anderson (Baltimore, Md.: The Johns Hopkins Press, 1945).

Denise Levertov, "Weeping Woman" and "At the Justice Department," from *Poems, 1968–1972* (New York: New Directions, 1972).

Philip Levine, "On the Murder of Lieutenant Jose Castillo by the Falangist Bravo Martinez, July 12, 1936," from *They Feed They Lion and The Names of the Lost* (New York: Alfred A. Knopf, 1999).

Henry Wadsworth Longfellow, "Paul Revere's Ride," from *Poems and other Writings*, ed. J. D. McClatchy (New York: Library of America, 2000).

James Russell Lowell, *The Poetical Works of James Russell Lowell*, from vol. 2, *The Biglow Papers* (Boston: Houghton Mifflin and Company 1848).

Amy Lowell, "Patterns," from *Men, Women, and Ghosts*, 1916.

Robert Lowell, "For the Union Dead," "Memories of West Street and Lepke," and "The March," from *Collected Poems*, ed. Frank Bidart and David Gewanter (New York: Farrar, Straus & Giroux, 2003).

Archibald MacLeish, "Wildwest," "Memorial Rain," from *The Collected Poems of Archibald MacLeish* (Boston: Houghton Mifflin, 1962).

Edgar Lee Masters, "Harry Wilmans," from *Spoon River Anthology* (New York: The MacMillan Company, 1915).

John Mathias, "Bogomil in Languedoc," from *Swimming at Midnight: Selected Shorter Poems* (Athens: Ohio University Press, 1995).

Gerald McCarthy, "The Hooded Legion," from *War Story* (Trumansburg, N.Y.: Crossing Press, 1977).

J. D. McClatchy, "Jihad," from *Hazmat: Poems* (New York: Alfred A. Knopf, 2002).

Walter McDonald, "Hauling Over Wolf Creek Pass in Winter," from *The Flying Dutchman* (Columbus: Ohio State University Press, 1987). By permission of the author.

Thomas McGrath, "Ode for the American Dead in Asia" and "Remembering That Island," from *The Movie at the End of the World: Collected Poems* (Chicago: Swallow Press, 1980).

Herman Melville, "The March Into Virginia, Ending in the First Manasses," "Ball's Bluff," "A Utilitarian View of the Monitor's Fight," "Shiloh," and "The College Colonel," from *Battle Pieces: The Civil War Poems of Herman Melville* (Edison, N.J.: Castle Books, 2000).

William Meredith, "A Korean Woman Seated by a Wall," from *Effort at Speech: New and Selected Poems* (Evanston, Ill.: Triquarterly Books, Northwestern University Press, 1997).

W. S. Merwin, "The Asians Dying," from *The Second Four Books of Poems* (Port Townsend, Wash.: Copper Canyon Press, 1993); "The Dachau Shoe," from *The Miner's Pale Children* (New York: Atheneum Press, 1970).

Edna St. Vincent Millay, "Say That We Saw Spain Die," from *Collected Poems* (New York: Harper & Row, 1956). By permission of Elizabeth Barnett, literary executor.

Joaquin Miller, "The Defense of the Alamo," from *Complete Poetical Works* (London: 1897).

William Vaughn Moody, "On a Soldier Fallen in the Philippines," *Modern American Poetry: An Introduction*, ed. Louis Untermeyer (New York: Harcourt Brace Howe, 1919); "Ode in a Time of Hesitation," from *Yale Book of Modern Verse* (New Haven, Conn.: Yale University Press, 1912).

Marianne Moore, "In Distrust of Merits," from *The Complete Poems of Marianne Moore* (New York: MacMillan, 1970).

John Neal, from *Battle of Niagara, a Poem, without Notes; and Goldau, the Maniac Harper* (1818).

Howard Nemerov, "Grand Central with Soldiers, Early Morning," "A Fable of the War," and "Redeployment," from *The Collected Poems of Howard Nemerov* (Chicago: University of Chicago Press, 1977). By permission of Margaret Nemerov.

Duane Niatum, "A Tribute to Chief Joseph," from *Drawings of the Song Animals: New and Selected Poems* (Duluth, Minn.: Holy Cow! Press, 1991).

Jim Nye, "Dead Weight," from *Aftershock* (El Paso, Tex.: Cincos Puntos Press, 1991).

Adrian Oktenberg, "it was an open-air market . . . ," from *The Bosnia Elegies* (Ashfield, Mass.: Paris Press, 1997).

Sharon Olds, "May 1968," from *Strike Sparks: Selected Poems, 1980–2002* (New York: Alfred A. Knopf, 2004).

George Oppen, "Survival: Infantry," from "Of Being Numerous," from *The Collected Poems of George Oppen* (New York: New Directions, 1975).

Thomas Paine, "Liberty Tree," from *American War Ballads and Lyrics: A Collection of the Songs and Ballads of the Colonial Wars, the Revolution, the War of*

1812–1815, the War with Mexico, and the Civil War, ed. George Cary Eggleston (New York: G. P. Putnam & Sons, 1889).

Basil T. Paquet, "Basket Case" and "It Is Monsoon at Last," from *Carrying the Darkness*, ed. W. D. Ehrhart (Lubbock: Texas Tech University Press, 1989).

John Pierpont, "Warren's Address to the American Soldiers," from *Airs of Palestine, and Other Poems* (Boston: James Munroe & Company, 1840).

Ezra Pound, from "Hugh Selwyn Mauberley," from *Personae: Collected Shorter Poems of Ezra Pound* (New York: New Directions, 1926).

Lucy Terry Prince, "Bars Fight," from *History of Western Massachusetts*, by Josiah Holland (Springfield, Mass.: n.p., 1855).

Innes Randolph, "The Rebel," from *Poems* (Baltimore, Md.: Willins & Wilkins Company, 1898).

Lisette Woodworth Reese, "A War Memory," from *A Quiet Road* (n.p.: 1896).

Carter Revard, "Parading with the V.F.W.," from *How the Songs Come Down: New and Selected Poems* (Cambridge: Salt Publishing, 2005).

Adrienne Rich, "The School Among the Ruins," from *The School Among the Ruins: Poems, 2000–2004* (New York: W. W. Norton, 2004).

Dale Ritterbusch, "Choppers," from *Lessons Learned* (Woodbridge, Conn.: Vietnam Generation, Inc., Burning Cities Press, 1995); "A Thousand Cranes." By permission of the author.

Edwin Rolfe [Solomon Fishman], "City in Anguish," "First Love," from *Collected Poems*, ed. Cary Nelson and Jefferson Hendricks (Urbana: University of Illinois Press, 1993).

Lee Ann Roripaugh, "Hiroshima Maiden" and "Heart Mountain, 1943," from *Beyond Heart Mountain* (New York: Penguin, 1999).

Wendy Rose, "The Day They Cleaned up the Border, El Salvador, February 1981" and "Three Thousand Dollar Death Song," from *Lost Copper* (Morongo Indian Reservation, Banning, Calif.: Malki Museum Press).

Jerome Rothenberg, "Dos Oysleydikhn (The Emptying)," from *Khurbhn and Other Poems* (New York, New Directions, 1989).

Muriel Rukeyser, "Poem out of Childhood" and "Sestina," from *The Collected Poems of Muriel Rukeyser* (New York: McGraw Hill, 1979).

Mary Jo Salter, "Welcome to Hiroshima," from *Henry Purcell in Japan* (New York: Alfred A. Knopf, 1984).

Carl Sandburg, "Buttons" and "Grass," from *The Complete Poems of Carl Sandburg* (New York: Harcourt Brace, Jovanovich, 1969).

Reg Saner, "They Said," "Flag Memoir," from *Retrieving Bones: Stories and Poems of the Korean War*, ed. W. D. Ehrhart, Philip K. Jason (New Brunswick, N.J.: Rutgers University Press, 1999).

Alan Seeger, "I Have a Rendez-vous" and "The Aisne," from *Poems* (New York: Scribners, 1926).

Karl Shapiro, "Troop Train," from *V-Letter and Other Poems* (New York: Reynal & Hitchcock, 1944).

Charles Simic, "The Prodigy," from *Classic Ballroom Dances* (New York: George Braziller, Inc., 1980).

William Gilmore Simms, "The Voice of Memory in Exile, from a Home in Ashes," from *Selected Poems of William Gilmore Simms* (Athen: University of Georgia Press, 1958).

Louis Simpson, "Carentan, O Carentan," "Memories of a Lost War," and "The Battle," from *Collected Poems* (New York: Paragon House, 1990).

George Starbuck, "Of Late," from *White Paper* (Boston: Little, Brown & Company, 1966).

Wallace Stevens, "The Death of a Soldier" and from "Notes Toward a Supreme Fiction," from *The Collected Poems of Wallace Stevens* (New York: Alfred A. Knopf, 1957).

Frank Stewart, "Black Winter." By permission of the author.

Lucien Stryk, "The Pit," from *And Still Birds Sing: New and Collected Poems* (Athens, Ohio: Swallow Press, 1998).

Genevieve Taggard, "To the Veterans of the Abraham Lincoln Brigade," from *Collected Poems, 1918–1938* (New York: Harper & Row, 1966) By permission of Judith Benet Richardson.

Allen Tate, "Ode to the Confederate Dead," from *Collected Poems, 1919–1976* (New York: Farrar, Straus & Giroux).

James Tate, "The Lost Pilot," from *The Lost Pilot* (New Haven, Conn.: Yale University Press, 1967).

Eleanor Ross Taylor, "After Twenty Years," from *Days Going, Days Coming Back* (Salt Lake City: University of Utah Press, 1991).

Sara Teasdale, "There Will Come Soft Rains," from *Collected Poems*, rev. ed. (New York: MacMillan, 1937).

Diane Thiel, "The Minefield," from *Echolocations* (Ashland, Ore.: Story Line Press).

Henry David Thoreau, "When with pale cheek and sunken eye I sang," from *Collected Poems of Henry Thoreau*, ed. Carl Bode (Baltimore, Md.: Johns Hopkins University Press, 1943).

Henry Timrod, "Charleston" and "The Unknown Dead," from *Poems of Henry Timrod* (Richmond, Va.: B.F. Johnson Publishing, 1901).

Barbara Tran, "The Women Next Door," from *Viet Nam Forum* 16 (Spring 1997). By permission of author.

Brian Turner, "Here, Bullet," from *Here, Bullet* (Farmington, Maine: Alice James Books, 2005).

Robert Penn Warren, "A Confederate Veteran Tries to Explain," from *The Collected Poems of Robert Penn Warren*, ed. John Burt (Baton Rouge: Louisiana State University Press, 1998).

Bruce Weigl, "What Saves Us," from *What Saves Us* (Evanston, Ill.: Triquarterly Books, Northwestern University Press, 1992); "Burning Shit at An Khe," "The Last Lie," from *The Monkey Wars* (Athens: University of Georgia Press, 1985).

Phyllis Wheatley, "To His Excellency General Washington," from *Cavalcade: Negro American Writing from 1760 to the Present*, ed. Arthur P. Davis and Saunders Redding (Boston: Houghton Mifflin, 1951).

Walt Whitman, "Cavalry Crossing a Ford," "By the Bivouac's Fitful Flame," "Come up, from the Fields, Father," "A March in the Ranks Hard-Prest," "The Wound-Dresser," "Reconciliation," and "O Captain! My Captain!" from *Walt Whitman: Complete Poetry and Selected Prose*, ed. James E. Miller Jr. (Boston: Houghton Mifflin, 1959).

John Greenleaf Whittier, "The Angels of Buena Vista," "Metacom," "Barbara Frietchie," "The Battle Autumn of 1862," from *The Complete Poetical Works of John Greenleaf Whittier*, ed. Horace Scudder (Boston: Houghton Mifflin, 1894).

Richard Wilbur, "First Snow in Alsace," from *New and Collected Poems* (New York, London: Harcourt Brace Jovanovich, 1988).

C. K. Williams, "Shrapnel," from *The Threepenny Review* 102 (Summer 2005). By permission of the author.

Eleanor Wilner, "Found in the Free Library." By permission of the author.

Keith Wilson, "The Circle," "Waterfront Bars," "Memory of a Victory," from *Graves Registry* (New York: Grove Press, 1969). By permission of the author.

James Wright, "Centenary Ode: Inscribed to Little Crow, Leader of the Sioux Rebellion in Minnesota, 1862," from *Above the River: The Complete Poems* (Middletown, Conn.: Wesleyan University Press, 1990).

Ray Young Bear, "*Wa ta se Na ka mo ni*, Viet Nam Memorial," from *The Invisible Musician* (Duluth, Minn.: Holy Cow! Press).

Every effort has been made to make due acknowledgments and to secure appropriate permissions from the writers and publishers of the poems used in this anthology.